Broadcast News:
Writing, Reporting, and Producing
5th Edition

Broadcast News:
Writing, Reporting, and Producing
5th Edition

Ted White, Frank Barnas

AMSTERDAM • BOSTON • HEIDELBERG • LONDON
NEW YORK • OXFORD • PARIS • SAN DIEGO
SAN FRANCISCO • SINGAPORE • SYDNEY • TOKYO

Focal Press is an imprint of Elsevier

ELSEVIER

Focal Press is an imprint of Elsevier
30 Corporate Drive, Suite 400, Burlington, MA 01803, USA
The Boulevard, Langford Lane, Kidlington, Oxford, OX5 1GB, UK

All photo courtesy of iStockphoto unless otherwise specified.

Library of Congress Cataloging-in-Publication Data
Application submitted

British Library Cataloguing-in-Publication Data
A catalogue record for this book is available from the British Library.

ISBN: 978-0-240-81183-3

For information on all Focal Press publications
visit our website at www.elsevierdirect.com

10 11   5 4 3 2 1

Printed in the United States of America

Contents

Part 2   **Writing the News**

Acknowledgments

As this is the fifth edition of this text, it is important to recognize that this is a continuation of Ted White's previous four editions. Ted authored the first four editions on his own, while I was honored to update this text after his passing. It is my hope that the flavor of his original writings lives on through this edition.

My deep appreciation goes out to those who supported this work, including my colleagues and students at Valdosta State University. It is only through practicing broadcast journalism that we can better learn the craft and I thank VSU for allowing me that opportunity. I'm also indebted to VSU's John Gaston, Carl Cates, Mike Savoie, Walter Rollenhagen, and Janet Wade for their support.

A special thanks goes to those who allowed their images and words to be inserted into this edition, including Mike Linn of Black Crow Media, Mark Bauer and Kate Gelsthorpe of WSB–TV, the Freedom Forum, the Poynter Institute, and the Radio and Television News Directors Association (RTNDA). I am also indebted to the town of Wheatland, Missouri, which is referenced in writing examples throughout this text.

Further, I am grateful to those broadcast professionals and researchers who contributed to this text, including Mary Berger, Jim Boyer, Barbara Cochran, Morton Dean, Christine Devine, Diane Doctor, Bob Dotson, Bob Engleman, Marc Fisher, Karen Frankola, Pauline Frederick, Luke Funk, Jim Geisler, Lisa Goddard, Ed Godfrey, Lisa Greene, Marty Haag, Jeff Hoffman, Norman Karlin, Ted Kavanau, Bruce Kirk, Jane Kirtley, Michelle Kosinski, Charles Kuralt, Jack La Duke, Peter Landis, Craig Le May, Robert Logan, Robert McKeown, Judy Muller, Charles Osgood, Bob Papper, Chuck Peters, Jim Polk, Jeff Puffer, Rick Ragola, Carol Dearing Rommel, James Rosen, Michael Rosenblum, Elizabeth Semel, Barry Serafin, Bernard Shaw, Ben Silver, John Spain, Bill Small, Lesley Stahl, Steve Sweitzer, Lennie Tierney, Al Tompkins, and Cliff Williams.

A special acknowledgment is also due to Sherlyn Freeman, a former Fox News producer in New York who co-authored Chapter 18, *Convergence and the Media*.

Thanks to those journalism faculty members across the country who served as reviewers for this edition of the text, including Robert Ferraro of Purchase College, Robert Heinrich of Middle Tennessee State University, Elena Jarvis of Daytona Beach College, Tom McDonald of Fairfield University, Glenn Mosley of the University of Idaho, and Larry Stuelpnagel of Northwestern University.

Other professionals who had a significant impact on this book include the late Nick Cominos from the University of Texas, KOMU's Stacey Woelfel, and KETK's John Jenkins. The combined knowledge of these three men could easily fill several academic bookshelves. Special thanks also go to V. Damon Furnier, Eddie Jackson, and Hansi Kursch.

Of course, a great deal of gratitude is owed to Michele Cronin of Focal Press for her expert direction and motivation for this edition. Finally, I am indebted to Edison Church and Aloura Jayne for their tireless work as motivators and cheerleaders. This is for them.

Frank Barnas
Valdosta State University

Introduction

This fifth edition of *Broadcast News Writing, Reporting, and Producing* is structured to guide broadcast journalism students through every facet of their chosen field. Each chapter begins with *Key Words*, a list that notes the important terms and definitions that will appear in the following pages. The text of each chapter contains practical advice and tips from industry professionals about that chapter's subject matter. Finally, each chapter concludes with three segments: a *Summary*, which reviews the chapter's main points; a *Test Your Knowledge* section, which offers questions relevant to the chapter; and *Exercises*, which allows students to apply the chapter's themes with practical experience.

The text begins with an introductory chapter of *Ethical Considerations*, providing an overview of some of the challenges facing news reporters today. The book is then divided into the natural progression of how a newscast is assembled. Part 1, *Acquiring the News*, contains chapters that cover how to find the news, develop sources, and collect information from both real and virtual documents. The section concludes with a chapter on the different types of stories and assignments that broadcast journalists will encounter.

Part 2 concentrates on *Writing the News*, the most fundamental skill a reporter must possess. In addition to detailing the mechanics of newswriting, there is in-depth analysis on both the style of newswriting and how a broadcast journalist can write effective leads.

Part 3, *Reporting the News*, expands from writing into merging video and audio into a news report. Topics in this part of the book include fieldwork, interviewing, covering planned events, and live reporting. The section ends with an in-depth look at the different types of story formats that appear on a typical newscast.

The final part of this text, *Producing the News*, examines how to assemble the day's stories into a comprehensive newscast. Chapters deal with producing for both television and radio. For those who would like to deliver the news as reporters or anchors, a chapter on delivering the news provides on-air talent with professional advice on how to communicate with the audience effectively. Chapters on Global/Network News and Convergence address how globalization and Internet technology are reshaping how news is delivered.

Although the text is designed to be used linearly, journalism instructors and students may use the chapters in whatever order works best for their individual programs. Finally, a sample syllabus and instructors' notes are available through the Focal Press textbook Web site.

PART 1

Acquiring the News

Ethical Considerations

KEY WORDS

Ambush Interview

Conflict of Interest

Fair Comment

False Light

File Footage

Gratuities

Jump Cut

Libel

Privilege

Reenactment

Reverse Question

Reversal

Truth

INTRODUCTION

This chapter focuses on the important and complex issue of ethics, one of the cornerstones of good journalism. The pillars of journalism (accuracy, fairness, and objectivity) are among the major ethical considerations for those who work in the news industry. Additionally, there are ongoing debates over bias, objectivity, favoritism, and a number of other ethical issues.

A grounding in ethics is essential to those in news, as journalists are confronted with choices about stories, interviews, sound bytes, rundowns, shot angles, editing, and a host of other potential hazards on a daily basis. This chapter does not provide individual case studies. The daily newscast is rife with ethical challenges; thus there is never a shortage of exemplars. Instead, this chapter details the ethical dilemmas that appear frequently among broadcast journalists. We begin with the basic need to get the story right.

ACCURACY

Accuracy means writing and reporting in a manner that is as objective and fair as possible, despite any personal feeling, belief, or attitude on the subject. Taking responsibility means the following: (1) looking at all the issues, not just the easy or popular ones; (2) examining controversies and producing special reports throughout the year, not just during the sweeps rating periods;

(continued) **3**

(3) covering important stories that don't always offer good pictures; (4) writing and reporting with care, understanding, and compassion; and (5) dealing with people in a professional and civil manner.

As detailed in further chapters, many news directors require reporters to double-source and even triple-source stories before they air. This means every piece of information must be confirmed by at least two or three independent sources.

Some inaccuracy will always creep into newswriting and reporting because people write and report news. People make mistakes. If errors occur, the reaction is to correct the mistakes immediately.

Accuracy is an ethical journalistic concern, but when information in a story is inaccurate because of bias or carelessness, it can also become a legal issue—libel.

FIGURE 1.1

LIBEL

Although it should not be the motivating factor for insisting on accuracy, there is always the threat of libel facing those journalists who through carelessness, ignorance, or malice make inaccurate statements in their reports that reflect on the character or reputation of an individual or group. Libel laws differ from state to state, but essentially writers or reporters can be sued for libel if anything they write or report (1) exposes an individual or group to public scorn, hatred, ridicule, or contempt; (2) causes harm to someone in their occupation or profession; or (3) causes someone to be shunned or avoided.

Reporters must also remember that it is not necessary to have actually used a person's name to be sued for libel. If the audience knows to whom a reporter is referring, even without the name, the reporter could be sued for libel if the comments harm the person's reputation.

Although libel traditionally refers to printed material and slander to spoken words, the distinction between the two terms has little meaning for broadcast reporters. Recognizing that broadcast material is usually scripted, many state laws regard any defamatory statements on radio and television as subject to libel laws. Remember also that using the word *alleged* before a potentially libelous word does not make it any less libelous.

DEFENSES

Courts usually recognize only three defenses against libel: truth, privilege, and fair comment.

The *truth* is the best defense, but in some states the courts have ruled that truth is only a defense if the comments were not malicious.

Privilege covers areas such as legislative and judicial hearings and debates and documents that are in the public domain. If a reporter quotes a potentially libelous comment made by a senator during a debate, the reporter could not be sued for libel.

Fair comment also is used as a defense against libel. Public officials, performers, sports figures, and others who attract public attention must expect to be criticized and scrutinized more than most people. If a sports commentator, for example, says that college football coach Joe Brown is a "lousy coach and the team would be better off if this inept, incompetent jerk moved on to a high-school coaching job, which he might just possibly be able to handle," he might get a punch on the nose if he ran into the coach, but he would not end up in court for libel.

There are limits, however, to what reporters can say even about public figures—the facts must be true. If the sports commentator had included the comment that "Brown's real problem is that he is smoking too many joints at night," then Brown would have a libel case unless the sports commentator could prove that Coach Brown actually spends his nights smoking marijuana.

FALSE LIGHT

A complaint similar to libel, called *false light*, involves the improper juxtaposition of video and audio that creates a false impression of someone. This invasion-of-privacy issue has actually caused more suits against TV news organizations than libel has, and it is more difficult to defend.

Professor Karen Frankola described a case involving a reporter's story about genital herpes. The reporter was having difficulty figuring out how to cover the story, so she relied on some walking-down-the-street file video. Frankola said that in the package used on the 6 o'clock news, none of the passersby was identifiable. The story was edited differently for the 11 o'clock news, though, and the audience saw a close-up of a young woman while the anchor was saying, "For the 21 million Americans who have herpes, it's not a cure." The woman in the close-up won damages from the TV station.

Frankola said that false light "may get past a journalist more easily because it's not as obvious that false information is being given." She noted that the reporter in the herpes story did not say "the woman has herpes," which would

FIGURE 1.2

have been a red flag to the editor. But, Frankola said, "the combination of words and pictures implied that the woman had the disease."

The Reporters' Committee for Freedom of the Press issued a report showing that 47 percent of subpoenas issued to TV stations deal with such invasion-of-privacy actions. The group's executive director, Jane Kirtley, believes the number of suits is growing because "people are developing a much greater sense of privacy, a desire to be let alone."

BOUNDARIES

How far should reporters go to get a story? If reporters have a strong suspicion that someone in government is a crook, don't they have the right to do whatever it takes to report the story to the public? Some journalists say they do. Other news people believe that if they bend the rules too much, they become suspect and may be viewed no differently from the people they are investigating. Each reporter must decide the ethical merits involved in certain investigative practices.

Some of the controversial information-gathering techniques employed by investigative reporters include impersonation, misrepresentation, and infiltration. Should journalists use such techniques to get a story? Consider the following scenarios:

- Is it right for a reporter to pretend to be a nurse so that she can get inside a nursing home to investigate charges that residents are being mistreated?

- Is it proper for a journalist to tell a college football coach that he wants to do a story about training when he's really checking on reports of drug abuse and gambling?

- Is it permissible for a reporter to pose as a pregnant woman thinking about having an abortion in order to find out what kind of material a right-to-life organization is providing at its information center?

- Is it ethical for journalists to take jobs in a supermarket and then spy on the operations to try to show improper food handling?

All of these incidents actually occurred, and they represent only a few examples of the controversial methods used on a routine basis. Are they ethical?

HIDDEN CAMERAS AND MICROPHONES

Reporters sometimes use hidden cameras and microphones when they're doing an investigative story in an effort to record incriminating material. They also use wireless microphones to eavesdrop on conversations. Such devices are used routinely by teams working for *60 Minutes, 20/20,* and other investigative TV news programs.

There seem to be no laws against using a hidden camera to videotape something that is going on in public. Reporters must know state and federal laws, however, if they plan to use hidden microphones. Federal law forbids their use unless one person involved in the conversation knows of the recording. If a reporter places a hidden microphone in a hotel room to record a conversation between two or more people, that would be a violation of federal law. If a reporter is carrying a hidden microphone, there is no federal violation, but some states do forbid the practice. It's also a violation of some state laws to use so-called wires—microphones that transmit a conversation to another location.

FIGURE 1.3

CNN's Jim Polk admits that he has used hidden cameras from the back of a truck with one-way glass, but he says it is really "espionage, spying—a dirty little technique." But, he says, "We have used it on the mob." Polk says that as long as the video that's shot with a hidden camera is of people doing illegal things in public view, he has no problem using the technique. He says, however, that using hidden microphones is "playing with fire. It's a dangerous technique that is easily mishandled, and it should be used with caution and only under certain circumstances."

AMBUSH INTERVIEWS

One interview technique used by broadcast journalists is the *ambush interview,* where the reporter surprises the interviewee on camera. As the name implies, reporters who are unable to schedule an interview with an

FIGURE 1.4

individual often stake out the person's home or office until they can ambush the person as he or she enters or exits the building. The reporter and cameraperson force themselves on the individual, trying to shoot video and ask questions as the person tries to escape. Is this reporting technique appropriate?

ABC News correspondent Barry Serafin says an ambush interview is justified only when there's "a genuine public accountability involved. Sometimes you cannot allow a person in public office to refuse to talk to you; you really have to get to the person and make him accountable."

John Spain, the former general manager of WBRZ–TV in Baton Rouge who has received a number of awards for investigative reporting, says he does not like the ambush interview unless, as Serafin notes, it involves the public interest. "If we have made every effort to interview an individual and have been denied access," said Spain, "we would do an ambush. If you raise your hand and take an oath," he added, "you have an obligation to answer to the public."

GRATUITIES

Reporters are often tempted with *gratuities*, or gifts. It is impossible for reporters to maintain their credibility if they accept any kind of gift from people or organizations they cover. Many offers come from public-relations people. Some gifts may come at Christmas, whereas others may arrive at the door of a reporter or producer after the broadcast of a story about a product or service. The gifts should be returned.

Some news directors pass out such gifts to nonnews staff, but doing so sends the wrong message to the donor. If the gifts are not returned, the senders have no way of knowing that they were not appreciated and might assume that they can expect some favor the next time they're promoting something.

One news director says that when Christmas gifts arrive, he gives them to the people in the mailroom but does not say who sent them. He says he also calls the donor and lets him or her know that he can't accept gifts and has passed them along to the mailroom staff. "That's easier than packing the stuff up and sending it back," he says. "It also lets the PR people know that I can't be bought, and it makes the people in the mailroom a little bit happier."

CONFLICT OF INTEREST

Sometimes the issue of what is an acceptable practice is not so clearly defined. Is it wrong for a theater or film reviewer to receive free tickets from the show's producers? Some newspapers pay for their reviewers' tickets, but most review-ers do accept free tickets, and there is no reason to believe that this practice influences what they write about a film or play.

Some news organizations fear a *conflict of interest*. For example, hotel owners sometimes offer news people a free plane ride and accommodations to promote a new hotel. Is it possible for the reporter to maintain objectivity when the host has provided him or her with a thousand dollars or more for travel and entertainment? Some journalists claim it would take more than that to corrupt them. Some of them may even write negative stories about the trip, but the temptation to be favorable toward the host is great. To avoid such potential conflicts of interest, many news directors forbid such trips.

REENACTMENTS AND STAGING

Considerable debate has been generated over the use of reenactments of events to tell a news story. Most news directors frown on the technique, but some see nothing wrong with them as long as they are clearly designated as such with a supertitle plainly stating "This is a reenactment."

The most important ethical consideration in the use of reenactments is that they should not confuse the audience about what they are looking at. Viewers should be able to determine quickly which scenes are actual and which are reenactments. Some news directors believe reenactments have no place in news. As one news director puts it, "Let the tabloid newspeople do the reenactment."

Another serious ethical concern is staging, the faking of video or sound or any other aspect of a story. Staging can and should be a cause for dismissal. Ironi-cally, some reporters see little harm in staging if the staging is accurate. "What's wrong," one reporter asks, "if you round up protesters at an abortion clinic who may be out to lunch and get them shouting again? That's what they would be doing after lunch, anyway."

It is not the same, and reporters who think that way pose a serious threat to their news organizations. Many other kinds of staging go on all too often. All of them are unethical. Here are a few examples:

- A reporter misses a news conference, so he asks the newsmaker to repeat a few of the remarks he made and pretends the sound bytes actually came from the news conference.

- A news crew goes to a park to film some children playing on swings and seesaws, but there are none there. A cameraperson is sent to find some children.

- A reporter doing a story about drugs on campus needs some video to support the story so he asks a student he knows to "set up" a group smoking marijuana in a dorm room.

- A documentary unit doing a story on crime asks police officers in a patrol car to make a few passes by the camera with the sirens blasting. Harmless deceptions? Perhaps. But where does staging end?

If reporters are willing to set up a marijuana party, is there anything that they would feel uncomfortable about staging?

"UNNATURAL" SOUND

Natural sound is one of the most effective tools used by broadcast journalists. No one wants to see children riding down a hill on sleds without hearing their shouts, and video of a marching band would not be interesting without the music. What does a reporter do, however, when the audio recorder or camera does not pick up the sound? Should the reporter add "unnatural sound," that is, sound effects? Sound-effects tapes and records are available to match just about any activity. Certainly, the sound of laughing children is available. The reporter might not be able to match exactly the music the band in the parade was playing, but how many people would know the difference?

The answer to these questions is that such use of sound effects would be unethical. The same goes for dubbing in any natural sound that the recorder might have missed at the scene of a story. If the sound of fire engines was lost at the scene, that's unfortunate; the answer is not to substitute sound effects. It would be better for the reporter or anchor to admit to the audience that there were sound problems on the story.

VIDEO DECEPTION

Most TV stations maintain a videotape library that includes footage of events going back several years. Most stations pull some of that video, known as *generic footage* or *file footage,* when they need shots of a general nature to cover portions of the script. Some stations routinely superimpose the words "File Footage" over such video, but other stations run the video without any such admission unless it's obvious that the video is dated.

Most journalists have no problem using file footage of people walking down the street or shots of cars and trucks rolling down the highway if it works with the script. However, pulling old video about disturbances in Miami for a story about a new outbreak of violence in that neighborhood would be deceptive unless the audience knew the difference between the old and new footage they were watching. Instead of the words "File Footage," many news directors insist that the file footage have the original date superimposed over the old video.

TV stations usually do not plan to deceive the audience when they use old footage; oftentimes they are just careless. Yet there have been examples of deliberate deception over the years, such as when old war footage is used to cover new fighting. In some cases, stations have used footage of a completely different war to go along with a story on fighting in another country. Such deception, if discovered (and it often is), can cause the station to lose its license.

FIGURE 1.5

IMPROPER EDITING

Video and audio recordings are rarely accepted in court cases because they can easily be doctored. As one audio engineer puts it: "With enough time, I can make people say anything I want." Most of the time, the distortion of people's comments on radio and television is not intentional; the tape is just poorly edited. There have been many cases in which people who have been interviewed by radio and TV reporters complained that the editing changed the meaning of their comments. By clipping or editing a statement, they charged, the editing distorted the point they were trying to make. A reporter or producer intent on showing someone in a certain light can accomplish that goal rather easily. The error of omission is a serious concern. The individual's remarks could certainly be distorted by picking up one part of a person's statement and ignoring an equally important part of it.

When tape must be edited for time purposes (which is almost always the case), the reporter or producer must ensure that the sound byte is representative of what the person said. If it is not, it is essential that in narration following the byte, the reporter accurately sum up the part of the sound byte that was eliminated.

JUMP CUTS

Some of the tricks employed in the editing process also raise ethical questions. In order to avoid *jump cuts*—the jerking of the head that occurs when video cuts are juxtaposed—film editors (it started long before the advent of video) came up with cutaways, reversals, and reverse questions.

These techniques are designed to cover up video edits. Editors, producers, and everyone else in the newsroom defend the use of most of these techniques because they make the finished product much smoother to watch. "Who wants to watch a head jumping across the screen?" is the answer editors give for using a cutaway, or a reverse shot. It is hard to argue with that response. Such techniques are not completely honest because the audience usually does not realize what the editors are doing. In an effort to avoid jump cuts, editors also distract the audience's attention from what the editors are doing by inserting other video between the edited material.

In a *cutaway,* it appears that the cameraperson just decided in the middle of an interview or speech to show the TV audience that the room was crowded with spectators and reporters. This cutaway shot may show another camera-person shooting the scene, a reporter scribbling in a notepad, or just a row of the audience. That shot makes it possible for the editor to take part of the video comment and marry it to any other video comment made by an individual while he or she was speaking. The first part might have been at the beginning of the speech, while the second comment might have been made 10 or 21 minutes later.

"So what? There's nothing dishonest about that," is the response from many editors. In general there probably isn't anything dishonest about this technique if one accepts that it is not necessary for the audience to know that the tape was edited. The real harm comes when the video is badly edited and does not accurately represent what the individual said during the interview or speech and the audience has no way of knowing this.

Another editing technique used to avoid jump cuts is the *reversal,* also referred to as a *reverse shot* or *listening shot.* After completing an interview, the reporter pretends to be listening to the interviewee while the cameraperson takes some shots of the reporter. The worst examples show the reporters smiling and nodding their heads in agreement. These shots then are sandwiched between two bytes of the interview and, again, the audience usually believes that the cameraperson simply decided to take a picture of the reporter at that point in the interview or believes there were two cameras in the room.

One key scene in the movie *Broadcast News* pointed out the unethical use of the reverse shot. In the film, an ethically minded TV news producer breaks off a relationship with an anchor–reporter because he used a reverse shot of himself crying in the middle of an interview when he actually had not cried during the interview itself. A cameraperson took the crying shot later—that was outright deception.

Fortunately, such examples are not typical of the reverse shots that appear in TV news stories. Most objections to the reverse shot are not about deception but about concern over the audience's inability to discern that the video has been edited.

The most dangerous technique, which is not as popular as it once was, is the *reverse question*. A reverse question is one the reporter asks a second time after the interview has been completed. The camera is facing the reporter this time. The technique allows the editor to avoid a jump cut by inserting video and audio of the reporter asking the question. The problem occurs when the reporter does not ask the question exactly the same way the second time.

Newsmakers themselves have sometimes complained about reverse questions when they realized that the questions they heard on their televisions were not exactly the same as those they were asked when they were in front of the camera. If any change at all is made in the second version of the question, it could be a serious ethical issue. Most newsrooms have stopped using reverse questions.

Producers and news directors who routinely allow the use of such techniques sometimes draw the line when the president or some other top official is making an important policy statement. In such cases, many producers allow the jump cut, particularly if it is not jarring, so that the audience knows that the remarks by the chief executive or other official have been edited. Instead of using a jump cut, some producers prefer to use a wipe between bytes.

INFLATING THE NEWS

Reporters must attempt to keep a news story in perspective. Otherwise, it is easy to give the audience the wrong impression about what is actually happening. As mentioned earlier, a reporter should never stage video by rounding up demonstrators who were on a lunch break; however, let's assume that when the reporter showed up, the protest was in full swing. Did the presence of the camera have an effect on the demonstration? Did the shouting suddenly get louder? If the camera did have an effect on the crowd, which would not be unusual, the audience might get the wrong impression. In such a case, it might be appropriate for the reporter to make a statement like the following:

> Actually, the turnout for the demonstration was smaller than was predicted … and our camera seemed to encourage some in the crowd to whip it up just a bit more than when we first arrived.

It is also important for the cameraperson to show accurately what was going on at the scene. If there were only a half-dozen demonstrators, the audience might, again, get the wrong impression if the camera shot used was a close-up, when a wide shot would have revealed that the group was small.

WILL THE REAL REPORTER PLEASE STAND UP?

There always has been a certain amount of glorification of anchors in broadcasting, and there's a growing tendency to give more credit to anchors and less to those who actually do the work. It's common practice for producers and writers to write copy for anchors. Everyone knows about this practice, and there's no ethical issue involved, even though a portion of the audience probably thinks anchors write their own copy. Many do write part of it; however, some journalists are concerned about the growing practice of using writers and producers to prepare packages that make use of the anchor's voice; packages that, some would argue, would best be prepared by reporters. Part of the problem, of course, is that some stations are cutting back on their reporting staffs and are compensating for the loss by having writers and producers handle some of the work reporters once did, without leaving the newsroom. Is this deception?

Bill Small, former senior vice president of *CBS News*, said it's "always improper if you leave the impression that you covered a story when you didn't." Small noted, however, that at CBS and other networks it isn't "uncommon" for producers to do most of the work on some stories. It's routine for producers to conduct an interview in advance of a correspondent's arrival on the scene to "tie it all together."

Small is also concerned about the proliferation of material available to broadcast stations via satellite and the increasing use of the same syndication video by all the networks. "I'm a firm believer that there shouldn't be one story for all the networks," he said. "Each one should do its own." Small is even more annoyed by video news releases, which he calls "handout journalism." He said that if any of this material is picked up, its source should be properly identified.

CAMERAS IN THE COURTROOM

The use of cameras in courtrooms has raised serious questions about journalistic ethics and the responsibility of broadcast media, particularly television. The issue of whether to allow camera coverage of trials has been a continuing debate. TV news representatives generally argue that cameras should be allowed in courtrooms. Those opposed to the idea argue that the cameras compromise the rights and privacy of everyone involved in a trial and could have an impact on the outcome of the trial itself. Even in states where cameras are allowed to record the proceedings, the cameras are operated on a pool basis to minimize the intrusion. The jury is not shown.

There also are a variety of restrictions in most of the states where cameras are allowed. In some states, the judge decides; in others, everyone involved in the case must agree to allow the cameras; in still other states, the decision depends on the nature of the case. And in some states, cameras are permitted only in certain courts. Sound confusing? It is.

What are the advantages and disadvantages of allowing cameras in court? The most obvious reason for cameras, in the opinion of most of the media, is the "public's right to know," which is guaranteed by the First Amendment. Others argue that camera coverage would educate the American people on how the jurisprudence system works. The most important argument against allowing cameras in the courtroom is that the coverage may impact the trial itself and the defendant's right to a fair trial.

Elizabeth Semel, a prominent San Diego defense attorney, said she believes cameras change the performances of witnesses. "Who is the audience for the witness?" asked Semel. She said, "*Audience* is a troubling word, but if there is an audience, it should be the jury and not the camera."

That view is shared by professor Norman Karlin of Southwest Law School. "Lawyers," he said, "tend to 'play' to a camera"; however, a 3-year experiment regarding television coverage in selected cities completed by the federal court system showed that cameras had little effect on trial participants, courtroom decorum, or any other aspects of the trials. Regardless of that survey, the federal court system decided to resume its total ban on TV cameras in federal courts. A spokesperson said federal judges remain concerned about the impact that cameras would have on trials.

FIGURE 1.6

THE FAIRNESS DOCTRINE

Fairness is both a legal and an ethical consideration. Until now we have concentrated on the ethical importance of fairness. Now let's consider the legal aspects. Do broadcast stations have a legal responsibility to be fair? Broadcast managers, the Federal Communications Commission (FCC), Congress, and numerous special interest groups have been fighting over that issue for decades.

In 1949, the FCC established the Fairness Doctrine, which said, in part, that broadcasters had an obligation to serve the public interest by "not refusing to broadcast opposing views where a demand is made of the station for broadcast time." It also said that licensees have a duty "to encourage and implement the broadcast of all sides of controversial issues."

Over the following years, the broadcast industry and the Radio–Television News Directors Association applied extreme pressure on the FCC to eliminate the doctrine, arguing that because newspapers are not forced to present all sides of an issue, broadcasters should not be required to do so either. According to supporters of the Fairness Doctrine, the major distinction between newspapers and broadcasters is that the government, in selecting only one licensee for a frequency, is in effect limiting access to the airwaves, which have traditionally been considered the property of the public.

The Fairness Doctrine was challenged on occasion but was upheld in the courts. In 1964, the Supreme Court upheld the doctrine. But over the intervening years, even the FCC itself questioned the Fairness Doctrine. In 1984 it acknowledged that the doctrine was not serving the public and was probably unconstitutional. It ceased trying to enforce the doctrine. But there has always been strong support in Congress for the doctrine and, in 1987, it passed a bill making the Fairness Doctrine law. But the bill was vetoed by President Reagan.

The Fairness Doctrine got a new look in Congress and elsewhere, in 1995, because of the bombing of the federal building in Oklahoma City. President Clinton started a controversy when he accused certain broadcasters (not by name) of spreading hate on the airwaves. He appeared to be speaking of Oliver North, J. Gordon Liddy, Rush Limbaugh, and other right-wing commentators and talk-show hosts who criticize the government, often suggesting that strong action by President Clinton could increase antigovernment violence and spread hate that divides Americans.

Should these commentators go unchallenged? Should they be allowed to use the airwaves, which supposedly belong to all Americans, to urge radical and often violent behavior? The ultraconservative broadcasters claim their First Amendment rights, and they have a legitimate point. But some people ask: Shouldn't those who oppose such views have a right to use the airwaves to express their opinions as well?

Pollsters tell us that about 20 percent of Americans strongly oppose any sort of government. How many of those people are capable of violence is, of course, unknown. But should those who feed that hatred of the government be allowed to espouse their views on radio and TV without allowing equal time for opposing views? The Constitution and the First Amendment do *not* refer to fairness in speech, just to its protection.

Many people believe the Fairness Doctrine, when it was in force, was unconstitutional, and it may very well have been; however, one cannot help but wonder if our founding fathers were sitting around the table in Philadelphia today, would they add a line or two to the First Amendment after watching the coverage of the bomb attack on the federal building in Oklahoma City and listening to convicted criminal J. Gordon Liddy speaking about "shooting federal agents in the head or groin" if they invaded one's domain.

INVASION OF PRIVACY

Privacy is defined generally as "the right to be let alone." That concept has become increasingly more difficult with the development of a variety of electronic devices, particularly the computer. For broadcast journalists, microphones, tape recorders, cameras, and telephoto lenses have been wonderful additions to the practice of collecting news. But they also have caused their share of troubles when it comes to privacy.

The Constitution does not say anything about the right of privacy, at least by name; however, several amendments to the Constitution and the Declaration of Independence's demand for the right to "life, liberty, and the pursuit of happiness" make it clear that the founding fathers were concerned with privacy. Also, the Supreme Court for more than 40 years has recognized privacy as a constitutional right.

From a media perspective, the right to privacy often conflicts with the First Amendment, freedom of the press, or the people's right to know. For example, the courts have found that it is not an invasion of privacy in most cases to take photographs or to use film and video cameras in a public place; however, the use of these same devices to get pictures in private places can, and often does, get broadcast journalists in trouble.

Videotaping in a public place also can be a problem for broadcast journalists. A CBS-owned station, WCBS–TV in New York, was sued after a camera crew and reporter entered a famous restaurant, Le Mistral, unannounced and began filming the interior of the restaurant and its customers. The film was for a series the reporter was doing on restaurant health code violations. The restaurant won its suit against CBS for invasion of privacy and trespass.

The end result? Broadcast journalists can photograph in public places, but if their behavior becomes overly intrusive, they also can find themselves in court.

SUMMARY

Accusations of improprieties when covering the news are ongoing. It is not uncommon for the motives of journalists to be questioned, their political leanings to come under scrutiny, and even the phrasing of their questions to be dissected. For reporters, the best response is to maintain a code of ethics by politely declining gifts and favors, evaluating their own work with a critical eye, and accepting criticism professionally.

FIGURE 1.7

FIGURE 1.8

Likewise, the use of certain undercover devices by reporters, such as hidden microphones and cameras, raises ethical questions that must be resolved by each news person or news manager. Their use also has legal implications because, in some states, it is forbidden. Certainly, the argument used by many journalists that you "do what you have to do" to catch someone breaking the law or deceiving the public seems reasonable on the surface. However, many reporters believe that they must stay within the law or they stoop to the level of those they are investigating.

The most critical guidelines for ethics are the simplest: strive for accuracy, be fair, and produce the story as neutrally as possible. By following these basic guidelines, the day-to-day process of reporting the news will have a solid ethical foundation.

Test Your Knowledge

1. Should reporters ever accept gifts? Discuss this issue.
2. When does accuracy become an ethical issue?
3. What are the defenses against libel? Do they always work?
4. Explain the term *false light*.
5. Name some of the controversial techniques employed by investigative reporters.
6. For what purpose are reversals used by most TV stations? Is there anything unethical about them?
7. Are cameras still banned in some courtrooms?
8. What types of restrictions do some states have on cameras?
9. What is the media's argument for using cameras in courtrooms?
10. What was the Fairness Doctrine? How do you feel about the issue?

EXERCISES

1. Ask two or more reporters from radio and TV stations to take part in a discussion of controversial techniques used by some investigative reporters. It might be a good idea to record the session so that it can be played for other classes to get their reactions.
2. Suppose you are a TV reporter assigned to a demonstration. When the assignment editor sent you out, the demonstrators were shouting and waving fists. When you arrived, however, they had stopped for lunch, except for one person who continued to picket. How would you and your cameraperson handle the situation?
3. Attend a trial where cameras are being used and discuss whether you believe they were beneficial for the public or detrimental to those involved in the trial. If a judge bans cameras in a trial in your city for some reason, interview the judge about the issue.
4. Watch each of the TV stations in your market and report on their selection of stories and if you believe they presented those stories fairly.

Locating the News

KEY WORDS

Advancing Stories
Assignment Board
Assignment Desk
Beat Checks
Direct Competition
Enterprised Stories
Incident Report
Indirect Competition
Motor Vehicle Accident Report
Objectivity
Planned Stories
Public Information Officer
Rundown
Spontaneous Stories
Stacking
Subjectivity
Time Code
Wires

INTRODUCTION

One of the simple truths about news coverage is that whenever you aim a camera at one person, you aim it away from all others. When you write one crime story, you effectively ignore the rest. And when a precious 20 seconds of air time is allocated for a single city council item, you negate everything else farther down the agenda.

The personality traits needed to effectively acquire news are straightforward: be informed, be curious, and have a consistent desire to know what happens next. Nor is there a mystery to the mechanics of tracking down stories—Web sites may be bookmarked, sources and their phone numbers may be placed on speed-dial, and a tally of upcoming events may be logged on the calendar.

But one theme that must underlie all others is the essence of news judgment, or the *why* of covering stories. News stations set the agenda of the community, promote certain events over others, spotlight one crisis instead of another, and play one news sound byte more frequently than the rest. These judgment calls are understandable, as news producers must cover a full day's news in a finite amount of time. Still, as stories are acquired during the day, judgment calls are made in the field, on the phone, at the production meeting, in the editing bay, and during the newscast itself.

FIGURE 2.1

FIGURE 2.2

Many of these judgment calls are based on the characteristics of what makes a strong local story. Is the story in the nearby area so it has physical proximity to the audience? Is a prominent person involved? Is there a disaster or controversy to the story? Is it novel or unusual?

Before we investigate the *why* of pursuing certain stories, we'll cover the *how* of locating news stories. It is the actual acquisition of news stories that faces a news team as it begins its day.

SPONTANEOUS, PLANNED, AND ENTERPRISED STORIES

In the purest sense, ideas for news stories evolve in one of three patterns. The first source is *spontaneous* news. These spot news stories cover events that happen without prior knowledge during the news cycle. Traffic accidents, fatalities, burning buildings, and criminal acts fall into this category. As these are breaking stories, the newsroom must respond quickly; a building won't burn forever nor will a hostage standoff necessarily last all day. If the news team doesn't cover it, it's a loss for them and a victory for the competing station. Ironically, days without fatalities and crime are disdained as "slow news" days.

The second source of news ideas are *planned* stories. While the overriding concept of news is "new," the bulk of stories on a daily newscast are known well in advance of the actual program. City council meetings, political rallies, school board functions, and any events scheduled in advance are essentially planned news events. If a reporter knows the time, location, and the principal players and agenda items, the story can be scheduled into a news day. The biggest variable is the actual outcome of the meeting.

The third category of stories is the *enterprised* report. These are the stories that a reporter generates independently of preplanned meetings or sudden house fires. Instead, the news reporter begins an investigation of documents, asks questions in a neighborhood, and constructs a story from the ground up. Reporters who deliver enterprised stories are highly valued by both the news team and the viewer, simply because they find news that other stations miss. The best mark of an enterprised story is when a competing station follows it with a similar story a day later.

Juggling the planned, spontaneous, and enterprised stories is a team of reporters, anchors, producers, and assignment editors. The planned events are needed for several reasons: to ensure that the competition does not nab an easy scoop, to keep viewers attuned with the day's events, and to maintain a profile in the community. If a news team misses a simple city council meeting, there are immediate ramifications. The competition beats the station to the story, the viewer is not informed of an important event, and the newscast's advertisers see their newscast as either uncaring or incompetent. Further, the absence of a reporting crew is noticeable to those in attendance, including the mayor, the city councilmen, the city's public information officer, and everyone else at the meeting. And if one were to survey those in the audience what station they would watch that evening, the likely consensus would be for the news outfit that bothered to show up.

Clearly, covering planned events is crucial. But if news were comprised solely of such planned events, then developing newscasts would be a simple affair. However, spontaneous news events burst forth at irregular intervals with alarming speed. In these situations, the newsroom must be able to dispatch a camera crew immediately. This invariably means pulling a news crew from another story at the last minute.

Still, if all stations in a city covered the same planned and spontaneous events, there would be little difference among the newscasts. Enterprised stories, such as investigative reports, personality profiles, and spotlight series on certain topics (such as health or education), set newscasts apart from one another.

Blending all stories into a cohesive newscast is a challenge to confront later in this text. For now, let's concentrate on the mechanics of finding the stories that build the newscast. The entryway for most stories into a newscast is through the assignment desk.

ASSIGNMENT DESK

Assignment editors run the assignment desk, which is the central hub of the newsroom. While reporters track individual stories and producers focus on newscasts, the assignment editors are responsible for collecting and organizing most of the source material that comes into a newsroom.

Sometimes the assignment desk is small. There may be one person in charge of assignments, and then only during the daytime. At some small TV stations, the news director or perhaps an assistant news director functions as an assignment editor but does not have that title. Large-market TV stations normally have at least two assignment editors—one for the morning and one for the evening. In the largest newsrooms, the assignment desk operates around the clock.

FIGURE 2.3

Assignment desk at
WBZ-CBS 4, Boston.

Almost everything starts at the assignment desk because that is where all the information enters the system. Assignment editors are the "keepers" of the news wires. They monitor the wires and scanners constantly, looking for stories that will be of interest to the producers who put the newscasts on the air. Some stories are assigned to reporters, others are given to writers to put into the newscast, and still others need follow-up by the assignment editor. In a breaking story, that follow-up is immediate.

In addition to the written assignment outlooks, the assignment desk maintains an *assignment board* that lists all of the stories that have been assigned for that day. The board shows the names of the reporter and crew, the location of the story, the time it is scheduled, and, usually, the time the crew is expected back. There also should be room for additional notes on the progress of the story.

A chalkboard or a white plastic board with dry erase markers is used so that changes can be made throughout the day. Because the board is located behind or next to the assignment desk, it should be big enough so that producers, reporters, and others do not have to crowd around it to read the information. Keeping the board up-to-date is the responsibility of the assignment editor or desk assistants.

FIGURE 2.4

www.assignmenteditor.com is a resource for news stories.

FOLLOW-UPS ON PREVIOUS NEWSCASTS

The first source for stories is the most recent newscasts on the station. During a typical news day, most of the news crew arrives for work between 8 and 10 a.m. Some arrive earlier to prepare for the noon newscast, some arrive later to cover evening news. News anchors who cover the 6 and 11 p.m. newscast do not arrive until the afternoon.

As the morning evolves, the assignment editor is often the first one in, followed closely by the producers and reporters. An immediate task is to scan the *news rundowns* from the 11 p.m. and early morning newscasts.

The following news rundown is from an 11 p.m. newscast. Think of it as a map of the newscast, showing what stories are presented, what anchor reads them, and how much time is given to each story. The column headings across the top are as follows:

■ Number—Where a story appears in the newscast

FIGURE 2.5

(Foreground) Photographer Rick Portier and (background) photography editor Patrick Perry checking video at WBRZ, Baton Rouge, Louisiana.

- Slug—A two- or three-word description or title of the story

- Type—Whether a story is simply read by the anchor, has video, or is a field package from a reporter

- Cam Source—Tells the director what studio camera or tape machine must be used

- Talent—Which anchor reads the story

- Total Running Time (TRT)—In minutes and seconds

- Time Code—If a story has video, these numbers find it quickly on the videotape

- Gphx—Tells the director what graphics are needed, if any

For now, find the A40 story on "Governor's Luncheon." The slug does not detail if it was a luncheon the governor sponsored, attended, or shunned. For the whole story, read the script. If it shows that the governor proposed a new highway at the luncheon, then you have an easy lead to advance a new story. If the governor simply ate and left, you can move on.

Number	Slug	Type	Cam Source	Talent	TRT	Time Code	Gphx
A10	Hello On Camera	Onset	2	Jayne, Ed	:15		
A20	Holly Tease	Tease	VTR 2	Tape	:09	52;30;00	
A30	Open	Open	NTW 1	Tape	:30		
A40	Governor's Luncheon	RDR	1	Ed	:30		Ed Lower
A50	Local School Construction	Lead	3	Jayne	:15		OTS
A60	Local School Construction	PKG	VTR 2	Tape	1:51	52;41;12	4 Lowers
A70	District 1 Debate	RDR	1	Ed	:30		
A80	Folic Acid	VO	3, VTR 2	Jayne	:30	57;20;00	Jayne Low
A90	Disability Awareness Day	VO	1	Ed	:30	54;38;00	OTS
A100	Health News Wrap	VO	3, VTR 2	Jayne	:30	1;30;10	OTS
A110	Bump to Break	Onset	2	Ed, Jayne	:15		
	First Commercial Break	Tape	NTW 1		2:00		
B10	Sunday Alcohol Ordinance	Lead	3	Jayne	:15		
B20	Sunday Alcohol Ordinance	PKG	VTR 2	Tape	2:23	58;55;00	2 Lowers
B30	Drug/Alcohol Safety	RDR	1	Ed	:30		Ed Lower
B40	Alcohol Awareness Fair	RDR	3	Jayne	:30		
B50	Library Archives Week	Lead	1	Ed	:15		OTS
B60	Library Archives Week	PKG	VTR 2	Tape	2:01	1;01;23;00	2 Lowers
B70	State News Wrap	RDR	3	Jayne	:30		Jayne Low
B80	Bump to Break	Onset	2	Jayne, Ed	:15		
	Second Commercial Break	Tape	NTW 1		2:00		

Continued

Number	Slug	Type	Cam Source	Talent	TRT	Time Code	Gphx
C10	Toss to Weather	Onset	2	Jayne, Tim	:20		Tim Low
C20	Weather	RDR	1	Tim	2:30		WX Graphics
C30	Toss to News, Tease Sports	Onset	2	Jayne, Tim	:20		
	Third Commercial Break	Tape	NTW 1		2:00		
D10	Football Preview	RDR	3	Tim	:30		Lower/OTS
D20	Football Player of Week	RDR	3	Tim	:30		OTS
D30	Volleyball Player of Week	RDR	3	Tim	:30		OTS
D40	Cross Country Team	RDR	3	Tim	:30		OTS
D50	Baseball Playoffs	VO	3, VTR 2	Tim	:30	12;10;09	OTS
D60	New Team Scoreboard	RDR	3	Tim	:30		OTS
D70	Baseball Catcher Profile	Lead	3	Tim	:30		OTS
D80	Baseball Catcher Profile	PKG	VTR 2	Tape	1:30	13;44;17	3 Lowers
D90	Bump to Break	Onset	3	All	:10		
	Fourth Commercial Break	Tape	NTW 1		2:00		
E10	Sunbelt Agricultural Fair	RDR	3	Jayne	:30		Jayne Low
E20	Veteran's Job Fair	RDR	1	Ed	:30		Ed Lower
E30	Cheerleading Clinic	RDR	3	Jayne	:30		OTS
E40	Hot Dog Stand	Lead	1	Ed	:15		
E50	Hot Dog Stand	PKG	VTR 2	Tape	1:31	1;03;29;00	2 Lowers
E60	Bye	Onset	2	Jayne, Ed	:15		
E70	Closing Shot	Onset	3	All	:15		Lower

As a rule, local stories that ran in the A and B blocks of the newscast should be reviewed for possible follow-up. Thus, the governor's luncheon, local school construction, and district 1 debate should be checked from A block, whereas the Sunday alcohol ordinance should be read from B block. The remaining stories, such as the Disability Awareness Day and Alcohol Awareness Fair, can be ignored as they were dated events that don't require further information.

THE WIRES

Most national and international news comes into a newsroom from the Associated Press (AP). The term *wires* is still used to describe the services offered by news-gathering organizations such as the Associated Press or the British firm Reuters. The word *wires* refers to the telegraph cables that were originally used to transmit the news to newspaper clients. Today, the wires feed news to some 5000 radio and TV customers, as well as newspapers. Writers, producers, and anchors can print out stories that interest them or simply insert them into the teleprompter's news script with a click of the mouse.

FIGURE 2.6
The homepage for the Associated Press (www.associatedpress.com).

Most small-market radio stations use the AP broadcast wire that transmits hourly summaries of the news. The broadcast wire is designed for those stations with little or no news operation. The broadcast wire is popularly referred to as the "rip-and-read" wire because that is the way these summaries are most often used at stations lacking staff to rewrite news copy. The stories are designed to be read without any rewriting.

In addition to the various wires, the AP provides a variety of audio feeds via satellite, including news on the hour and the half-hour, special reports on the hour's major stories, and an hourly feed of actualities and natural sound. The AP also provides scripted national and international news, agricultural reports, business news, sports, entertainment news, special features, and a headline service designed for what the AP describes as stations with "a limited news appetite."

The AP also provides several photo and graphics services, including an interactive database that supplies thousands of head shots, maps, and images of breaking news and a high-speed, digital photo network that delivers color photos to TV stations.

Further, there are also satellite services available, such as CNN Newsource. With this service, subscribers can download video feeds, live footage, and other resources needed for their news programs. Because these feeds are available to individual computers, the sports reporter can watch hockey highlights while a news editor reviews political footage from Washington, DC.

LOCAL EXPERTS

While discussing the use of national video, reporters are keenly aware of how to *localize* a story. Localizing a story means taking information from a national event, pulling video footage off of the satellite feed, and then interviewing a local expert to provide a fresh perspective to the story. This technique allows the news team to make a national (or even international) story more relevant to the viewer.

For example, let's assume the Federal Reserve has increased interest rates by a full percentage point. A story can be made by tracking down satellite video footage of either the Federal Reserve or perhaps brokers on the Wall Street Stock Exchange. To effectively localize the story, the reporter then calls up a local expert for a quick interview.

Local experts are easily found. A nearby university, for example, will house a faculty that teaches economics. These faculty members will likely have insight on the interest rate change, thus becoming local experts to a national story. A national study about a flu outbreak will prompt a call to a local health clinic, while a farm subsidies story could use the input of a local farmer. A good assignment editor or reporter will know of local experts who can deliver a quality interview on a number of subjects. Local experts should be used sparingly so viewers aren't subjected to the same people too frequently. If they're used in moderation, these interviews are a powerful addition to the newscast.

FIGURE 2.7

MONITORING THE COMPETITION

The competition to a station's news program comes from multiple formats, especially in large media markets. *Direct competition* is the most obvious, as it refers to other television stations that offer a competing television news program. Markets with networks affiliates from ABC, CBS, FOX, and NBC can readily identify their competition, although there may also be an independent station, a campus news station, or a foreign-language channel eager to break stories.

Indirect competition consists of news providers in different media, such as radio and newspaper. Because of media consolidation and increased costs of maintaining radio newsrooms, few cities have more than one dedicated radio news station. A more likely scenario for local news radio is an affiliation with National Public Radio or a syndicated news-talk format (Rush Limbaugh, Sean Hannity, and the like) while offering local news updates or a morning news/talk show.

Many broadcast news managers do not like to admit it, but they often rely on newspapers as a source of news. Because they have much larger news staffs and more room for news, newspapers often have stories that broadcast newsrooms miss or do not bother to cover.

Some stations rely on newspapers more than others. Stations with enough reporters to do a good job covering the local scene are less dependent on newspapers than stations with small news staffs. Other stations are constantly playing "catch-up" because they cannot compete with the newspaper's beat system.

Broadcast newsrooms often find themselves trying to figure out ways to take a good newspaper story and *advance* it. Advancing the story—finding some new development to make it appear new or at least fresh—is often considered a justification for "borrowing" the information developed by the newspaper. It's important to remember that if a newspaper is the *only* source for a story, it is ethically proper—and a necessary protection in case the information is not accurate—to attribute the story to the newspaper. Remember also that most newspapers copyright their material. Few papers object when their stories are broadcast, as long as credit is given. Some news directors take the position that once the accuracy of information first disclosed in a newspaper has been independently verified by the station, it is no longer necessary to credit the paper.

Regardless of the level of competition, it must be monitored. Newsrooms have banks of televisions tuned to competing stations to watch their newscasts. When covering a story in the field, reporters note what other camera crews are there. To keep an eye on the indirect competition, newsroom assignment desks are littered with newspapers and community magazines, local radio newscasts are heard, and members of the news team scour the Internet for the latest leads.

BEAT CHECKS, COP SHOPS, AND POLICE SCANNERS

Morning in the newsroom begins at the assignment desk. The overnight news is checked, the newspaper is combed, and the competing radio and television newscasts are monitored.

As that is done, the assignment desk slides into the predictable pattern of making *beat checks*. These are phone calls made to law enforcement officials in the area, starting with the city's police department and the county sheriff's office. These calls tend to be informal as the newsperson and the police officer talk daily and develop a rudimentary working relationship. A basic conversation takes only 20 to 30 seconds and falls along these lines:

> Dispatch Officer: "Dispatch."
> Newsroom: "Good morning, this is Channel 11 checking in on you."
> Dispatch Officer: "Morning, Jeff. Pretty quiet last night."
> Newsroom: "Nothing on the activity report?"
> Dispatch Officer: "Two drug arrests and one minor fender bender, that's about it."
> Newsroom: "Thanks, we'll get someone by to check the press pad."
> Dispatch Officer: "No problem."

The dispatch officer is relaying information gleaned from a *patrol activity report.* At the end of a work shift, all field reports are funneled to the desk sergeant to compile this report. The form is fairly broad and lacks the detail necessary for a newscast. What it provides is an overview of the shift's events.

If the only items noted are minor accidents or barking dogs, the news reporter might feel free to move on. But what if it were the mayor in the accident or if the dog was in a homeowners' association that has a strict no-pet policy? While beat checks are an easy way to keep in touch with the police stations, the dispatcher may only provide you with information on "big stories," such as murders or arsons. Remember, even the most mundane stories may be worth a closer look.

Should something be of interest (in this case, the drug arrests are worth a follow-up) the dispatch officer on the phone is usually not authorized to provide more than broad information. To pursue the story, contact must be made with the *public information officer* (PIO) or someone must visit the police station or sheriff's department.

PATROL ACTIVITY REPORT

1 Date: _____

TYPE OF INCIDENTS	DAY SHIFT		EVENING SHIFT		MIDNIGHT SHIFT	
	Totals	Case #s:	Totals	Case #s:	Totals	Case #s:
Drug Arrests						
Assaults:						
Aggravated						
Battery						
Sexual Assaults: *(Rape, Sexual Assault, Sexual Battery, Sodomy, Aggravated Sodomy, Child Molestation)*						
Traffic Accident w/Fatalities						
Burglary:						
Residential						
Commercial						
Robbery:						
Armed						
Sudden Snatching						
Intimidation						
Homicide						
Deaths:						
Suicide						
Other						
Misc. Incidents:						
Arson						

The PIO is the police's source of information to the media. Police departments usually train a sergeant or lieutenant in media relations, thus instructing other officers to defer to the PIO at all times. During their training, PIOs learn what information can be released to the press without endangering an investigation, putting additional stress on a victim, or revealing confidential information. Except for the police chief or the sheriff, the PIO is the only contact a newsroom will have at the station. A good working relationship with a PIO is invaluable, as they sort through confusing details at a crime scene and provide reliable interviews. Further, most PIOs will alert the news teams to a crime scene during overnight or weekend hours.

If the PIO isn't available to field the assignment desk's call (and they likely aren't at this hour), a trip should be made to the police station or sheriff's office, often referred to as *cop shops*. Once there, the reporter reviews the incident log from the previous night. The incident log may be called a press pad or crime log, but the idea is consistent—it contains a stack of the police incident reports that have been filed during the past several work shifts.

The press pad should be open for review upon request, provided one presents a valid news station identification. If not, an immediate appeal should be filed with the commanding officer. Most police logs are available to the press, although records concerning minors or sexual assault victims are off-limits.

A standard practice is for law enforcement to have two types of reports available on the press pad. The first is an *incident report*. These may be referred to as crime reports, as they provide details of criminal activity. Theft, murder, and other criminal acts are filed on these, along with pertinent information including:

- The criminal act that occurred

- Time and location of the incident

- Suspect's description (if any) and information about the person if apprehended

There are other details, but the three crucial points just given are enough to determine the merit of the story. Consider a burglary (criminal act) at the East Elm Warehouse at 3 a.m. (time and location), where witnesses saw a 60-year-old white male (suspect description) flee on foot. It may be simply a minor theft, but if police are actively searching and warning residents to be aware, it could become a serious item. Either way, the newsroom has the basics of a story.

The second report is a *motor vehicle accident report*. Everything from minor fender-benders to multiple car collisions will be filed, but few are of interest unless the accident was fatal, involved a local celebrity, or tied up traffic for several hours. The reason that even minor accidents are recorded is that insurance companies and lawyers use these official documents to investigate automobile claims. Thus, there will be quite a bit of information that, while important to the victims of the accident, isn't newsworthy to the general public.

Finally, *scanners* are desktop or handheld units that monitor radio communications among those using two-way radios. Once used heavily by police and fire departments, scanners are being gradually replaced by cell phones and computers. But because some agencies have not yet upgraded beyond two-way radios to communicate, scanners are still used in newsrooms.

Scanners cycle through open frequencies, but they may be programmed to listen to specific channels. These scanner frequencies are readily available on Internet sites such as www.radioreference.com. In addition to police and state trooper channels, other radio frequencies can be found, programmed, and monitored with ease. Some groups that still use two-way radios include emergency medical services, a city's water division, city towing, street maintenance, city jail, city courthouse, the National Weather Service, the Civil Air Patrol, fire departments, oil spill cleanup crews, railroads, aircraft, highway maintenance, and other radio frequencies depending on their availability. Listening to these conversations can prove vital in times of emergencies; thus their frequencies are kept available.

No information obtained from these radio scanners is ever used alone in writing a story for broadcast; the incidents must be checked out by phone. The police and fire reports often turn out to be unfounded or less serious than one might expect from the code. It is also a violation of FCC regulations to rebroadcast any material heard on police, fire, or ham radio broadcasts.

NEWS RELEASES AND FUTURES FILES

A symbiotic relationship exists between reporters and public relations experts. Reporters are responsible for generating stories on a continual basis. Public relations experts, spokespeople, and advocates need their information distributed to a broad audience.

This interaction shows the clash of objectivity and subjectivity. Simply put, the reporter's credo is *objectivity*, which is absolute neutrality to an issue. But the public relations expert struggles for *subjectivity*, which advocates one point of view over another. This includes political assistants (who support their candidate over another), advocacy group spokesmen (who desire change to suit their mindset), and even salespeople (who crave exposure of their product over a competing brand).

With the enticement of a broad audience, free publicity, or a good old-fashioned soapbox, subjective groups consistently offer stories to newsrooms. These come in the form of e-mails, phone calls, press releases, faxes, and letters. As a rule, these public relations pieces are not trashed upon arrival regardless of their source. Instead, they are filed into a newsrooms' futures files.

Despite the computerization of newsrooms, futures files are often still nothing more than a regular filing cabinet. When a press release comes in for an event to be held on the 19th of the month, it is filed on the 17th or 18th. This allows a day or two of advance notice for the news crew. Additionally, the information is input into a computer calendar such as Microsoft Access or a news-specific scheduling system.

During a typical day, there may be a booster club meeting for the local football team, a guest speaker for the Kiwanis, a tree planting at an elementary school, a blood drive, a car wash to raise funds for a worthy cause, a hospital outreach program, and a mayoral luncheon. Are these necessarily stories? The answer is yes, particularly on a slow news day. On an active day, most of these will be dropped quickly.

The end result is that these story leads serve reporters well; thus they are still a cornerstone of news production. However, all news personnel must remain keenly aware of the source of the story. Some of the aforementioned stories are harmless enough (the tree planting, for example) but the mayoral luncheon could have overtones in a campaign season or if a controversial issue is in the public forum.

INFO CALLS

There is a danger in interviewing the same people over and over. Aside from triggering viewer burnout, it begs the question of whether the reporter will bother finding other points of view. Thus, even though info calls should be done frequently, they are meant to be a source of story ideas, not an on-air soapbox for the same person.

For example, most cities have a public information officer who performs in a similar capacity to the police department's PIO. The difference is that the city PIO provides information on upcoming meetings, recognitions, and events (instead of criminal activities from the police PIO).

The newsroom should contact the city PIO at least twice a week, if not daily, to check for story ideas. An excellent PIO will not only be willing to go on-air for an interview, but will also help arrange interviews with the mayor, city manager, or others with in-depth knowledge of an issue. Here, the PIO should be used as a frequent source but an infrequent interview subject. After all, the voters elected the mayor and want to hear him or her speak.

Other info calls should be to local leaders, including the chamber of commerce, the industrial authority, the airport manager, the county extension agent, and possibly the spokesperson for a prominent local business or organization. These calls need not occur every day, but it's important to maintain contact so that if a new business tells the chamber of commerce it's coming to town, the chamber will remember to phone the newsroom.

THE CALENDAR

This is often the simplest (yet most overlooked) source for a story idea. First, what holidays are approaching? Valentine's Day, Halloween, Thanksgiving,

FIGURE 2.8

FIGURE 2.9

and Christmas are all excellent visual holidays, whereas others such as MLK Day or Memorial Day will have their own specific rallies or events.

Second, is the end of a quarter or fiscal year coming up? Institutions such as schools may operate on three calendars (fiscal, academic, and annual), whereas governments use fiscal and annual. Changes at the start or end of any of these will generate reports, analysis, and budget outcomes.

Third, who is meeting? Councils, boards, and governing bodies meet on a regular, recurring basis. Additionally, there can always be previews of upcoming meetings or reactions to recent meetings.

Fourth, is there a seasonal angle? Farmers depend on crop cycles, thus reporters should be keenly aware of their region's major crops. An early cold snap may only be a surprise to early morning commuters, but it can mean devastation to a citrus farmer.

Finally, the calendar is an excellent resource to list "evergreen" stories. An evergreen story is one that does not need to air on a specific date. A profile of a local civic leader, for example, can air either today or later this week. But there are two important considerations for these stories: first, evergreen stories will eventually age, so reporters don't want to hold stories indefinitely. Second, because most of these stories are features, it's important that the subjects don't wait for their stories to air. It is poor practice to promise an interview subject that the story will air soon when it will actually sit for a few days.

INTERNET BOOKMARKS

The Internet provides a wealth of news ideas to reporters, but it takes some discretion in deciding where to focus attention. A daily check of the competitions' Web sites is mandatory. Beyond that, a reporter should create bookmarks and preferences of Web sites. Beat reporters, who cover specialized topics such as business or health, will create lists that are more suited to their areas. Conversely, general assignment reporters will maintain a broad array of contacts. In the next chapter, *Developing Sources*, we will create a list of Internet bookmarks that reporters may use as a starting point for finding stories. But in the broad sense, it's important to know that the Internet is a constant stream of updated news. Not only is it a cornerstone of developing stories, it's fundamental in working in newsrooms.

FIGURE 2.10

PRODUCTION MEETINGS

Once the story ideas have been gathered from the various sources, the producers, assignment editor, and reporters meet for their morning production meeting. This is a highly interactive meeting in which all parties are encouraged to speak up. The meetings last approximately 20 minutes, and during this time, stories are advanced, questioned, assigned to news crews, or discarded. Quite often, if a reporter or producer is not passionate about a story idea, it is dropped in favor of another.

Newsrooms have a major production meeting around 9 a.m. to assign the day's activities, although other meetings can be scheduled as needed for the late newscast. At the production meetings, many variables are considered, including:

FIGURE 2.11

- What are the follow-up stories to the previous newscasts?
- What stories are being covered by the direct and indirect competition?
- Were any crimes or notable accidents obtained during beat checks?
- Have the scanners yielded any stories?
- What news releases are in the futures files?

- Are there any ongoing series (health, business, etc.) that should continue?

- Are there significant events on the calendar?

- Have the info calls yielded any news ideas?

- Are there national events that could be localized with interviews?

- Does anyone have an enterprised story?

Once these basic questions are satisfied, news crews are assigned and the producers begin the job of *stacking* the newscast. Stacking involves taking the available stories and placing them in a logical flow in a newscast. This is the essence of producing, which is covered later in this text.

SUMMARY

The assignment desk is where most information enters the newsroom. The assignment desk staff monitors the news wire, the police and fire radios, and the telephones and receives an endless assortment of news releases by mail and e-mail. Assignment editors also look for story ideas from reporters. The assignment editor, who may be the news director as well in some markets, makes the initial decisions about which material should be considered for coverage. He or she also assigns reporters and photographers to stories.

Assignment editors and news directors rely heavily on the rest of the news team, especially producers. The producers select material and decide what goes on the air; they are responsible for the look of the news. Most newsrooms hold daily meetings to plan the newscast and maintain assignment boards to keep staff members apprised of their duties for the day.

Test Your Knowledge

1. What are the differences among spontaneous, planned, and enterprised stories?
2. What does it mean to localize a story?
3. What is a public information officer?
4. How can a reporter's objectivity be at odds with a public relations person's subjectivity?
5. What are futures files?
6. Why are there special radios in broadcast newsrooms? How are they used? Are they important?
7. It is routine for many broadcast news staffs to make certain telephone calls each morning. What kinds of calls? Why are they important?
8. Explain why the assignment desk is an integral part of a news operation.

EXERCISES

1. Part of the assignment editor's job is to look for updates on stories. Look at the wire or your newspaper and pick stories that have potential to be updated. Explain how you would update them.
2. The assignment editor is always looking for local reaction-type stories to national and international developments. Look at the wire and newspapers for stories that might provide local reaction. Tape a reaction from someone.
3. Review the calendar and identify the main holidays and events occurring for the next two weeks. Then list the stories that one could produce along those themes.
4. Search the Internet for radioreference.com or a similar source of radio frequencies. List 10 frequencies you could monitor in your area.

Developing Stories

KEY WORDS

Accuracy

Advancing Stories

Background Briefings

Confidentiality

Double Sourcing

Leaks

Localization

Pack Reporting

Trial Balloons

Triple Sourcing

INTRODUCTION

As reporters and anchors become known and respected by their audience, they receive telephone calls, e-mails, and letters about a variety of subjects. Some are letters of praise, some are complaints. Also included among those calls and letters are news tips. A number of the most important stories aired on radio and TV stations come from tipsters. Others come from sources cultivated at public agencies and insiders at corporations and other institutions. This chapter discusses how to develop relationships with such sources.

As reporters craft stories, they need to be concerned with two aspects of broadcast reporting: advancing the story and avoiding the pack. This chapter discusses both of these techniques before illustrating how to create ongoing sources for news stories.

ADVANCING THE STORY

If news were a commodity, it would be a bad investment because it doesn't last long—it's perishable. As a result, reporters must keep looking for new angles to update, or *advance*, the news. In previous decades, news had a shelf life that lasted as long as the time until the next newscast. If a major network only had one evening newscast, then producers knew they had a full 24-hour cycle to update a story.

Obviously, this is not the case today. Around-the-clock news channels, ongoing Internet updates, and constant "news ticker" headlines have made the art of

FIGURE 3.1

advancing stories a never-ending fight for the latest morsel of information.

Updating a story—putting a new lead on it—is only part of what is involved in advancing a story. A new lead reporting, for example, that the death toll in an airplane disaster climbs from 100 to 115 does advance the story, but it is a rather routine update. In the more traditional sense, this story could be advanced if, for example, the cause of the crash was determined or it was suddenly discovered that a famous person was on the plane. The story also could be advanced if a reporter learned that this particular type of aircraft had been involved in a series of similar crashes in recent months or if a reporter discovered that the Federal Aviation Administration was about to ground all planes of the same make.

By expanding on the example of the airplane disaster, a reporter could broaden the net of possible interviewees, thus bringing new insight into the story. Is there a local representative of the Civil Air Patrol or a pilot who has logged thousands of flying hours? Such perspective could advance the story by adding information beyond a grim update of those who died.

AVOIDING THE PACK

Good reporters are always looking for an unusual angle for their stories. Sometimes it is difficult to report a story differently from other reporters because the lead seems so obvious. It is that finding of a new twist to a story that distinguishes some reporters from the rest of the pack.

Former *ABC News* correspondent Morton Dean says he tries to get "an edge" on his colleagues by doing research before he goes out on a story. "I try to get as much background and history as I can," says Dean. "I try to find my own sources. I try to make an extra phone call. One way or another I try to find a nugget of information that might give me an edge."

NBC's Robert McKeown notes that "good reporters aren't to be found" in the pack. They are out seeking people other than officials. He also says it's important to "know the beat and become familiar with it so that you sound like you know what you are talking about when a story develops. You should have a sense of what is really happening."

As you can see, *pack reporting* is the mentality of only speaking to officials and basically transcribing the same information that every other reporter also receives. Instead, developing stories requires that reporters talk to the extra witness, interview another bystander, and stay for just a few more sound bytes. Developing solid news sources is the best way to produce exceptional stories; the following pages address how to do just that.

INTERNET

Although the next chapter on *Collecting Information from Real and Virtual Documents* deals extensively with researching stories on the Internet, we must acknowledge the Internet's power in developing sources here. Many everyday sources are developed through casual conversations, ongoing relationships with newsmakers, and via tips, trial balloons, leaks, and the like.

A quick online search can reveal a number of potential interviewees. As an example, let's assume you need to find a local contact for a food safety story. By using a search engine such as Google or Yahoo, you may type in "food safety" and receive an astronomical number of matches; this example yielded no fewer than 1,130,000,000.

To narrow the search, enter more specific terms. If the food is asparagus, search for "asparagus food safety"—your search is now down to a mere 179,000. But remember, you want to find a local expert on this subject. If your market is Sacramento, California, search for "asparagus food safety Sacramento." The search results are still far too many to track down individually (8520), yet better connections are being made. A quick scan of the results shows that a nearby university has some data, plus there is a county extension agent with information as well.

Additionally, there are several Internet Web sites that connect journalists to experts, authorities, and spokespersons in a wide variety of topics. One excellent Web site is www.expertclick.com, which allows journalists to search for experts on subjects ranging from abortion to zoos. Of course, you should always enter these interviews with the knowledge that the person may strenuously advocate one point of view; there is no harm in tracking down interviews through such portals.

LOCALIZATION

In an ideal news world for local producers, there would always be several dominant stories in the region jockeying for position in the rundown. News from outside the area, such as Washington politics or an Asian civil war, might be bundled into a tidy 40-second wrap-up at the end of A block. But local news, at least in theory, would always lead the news.

FIGURE 3.2

Search for experts for news stories with www.expertclick.com.

Yet that isn't necessarily the case in daily news coverage. There are many days when the local news simply isn't that strong—these are "slow news" days when

FIGURE 3.3

there are no meetings, traffic is smooth, the temperature is mild, and the crime rate is unbelievably low. On these days, what if Washington issues a new tax code that hurts small businesses, a spike in the number of homeless people is noticed in a nearby metropolitan area, or an Eastern European nation suddenly announces war on a neighboring country? These are A block stories, but short of sending your local reporters scurrying for their passports, how can they be incorporated into your local newscast?

The solution is *localization*, which involves developing distant news ideas into stories with local impact. For the tax code story listed earlier, a call to the Chamber of Commerce is in order. The homeless story can mean a trip to the local shelter or social services provider, while a political science professor at the nearby university can provide some insight into an overseas conflict.

Let's expand briefly on the asparagus food safety story from our Sacramento newsroom. For starters, we can contact the previously mentioned county extension agent or the university professor who has knowledge of the subject. Beyond that, we think of who may be impacted by the story. If there are asparagus farmers in the viewing area, that's an immediate contact. Those who transport and sell the food are also impacted so a local grocer or farmer's market can discuss what they're doing with the product. To develop the story, simply trace the food trail. Is there a local vegan's group or store that may have an asparagus lover? Could you advance the story with "The safety issues regarding the asparagus crop may make you think twice about eating it, but one local vegan support group says there's no problem at all"?

TIPS

Stations that establish reputations for doing investigative stories are more likely to get tips than others. Astute news directors encourage tipsters, often setting up private telephone lines just for that purpose. Most calls involve breaking news—fires, accidents, crime— but sometimes the caller has information that leads to an investigative story.

FIGURE 3.4
Reporters must find a way to localize national news stories.

Tips are usually the result of stories that were reported earlier by the station. For example, a story about a politician using public funds for a personal trip to Las Vegas may attract calls from viewers who know about similar trips by other politicians. Who makes such calls and why? The calls and letters are often from people who have been working closely with the wrongdoers. They may be annoyed because of the misuse of public funds, because they lost their jobs, because of jealousy, or because of a long-standing grudge. The caller then becomes a source who might provide additional information on other stories or the names of additional sources. The way the phone conversation might go is: "I don't know all the details, but I can give you the name of someone who can, as long as you don't reveal my name." The phrase "don't reveal my name" is key to developing and keeping sources.

CONFIDENTIALITY

The fastest way to lose a source is to break a promise of confidentiality. Few

FIGURE 3.5
Reporters who break a promise of confidentiality risk losing their source.

sources give reporters sensitive information without a promise of secrecy. Once a reporter gives that promise, it must be respected, regardless of the consequences. A reporter's right to protect sources has often been tested in the courts, and reporters do not always win. On rare occasions, reporters have gone to jail or been fined for refusing to disclose a source.

Before entering into such an agreement with a source, reporters must analyze what they are agreeing to keep secret. Reporters disagree, for example, on whether it's a good idea to offer confidentiality to those who admit that they are actively involved in crime. Some reporters say they agree to such a pact if that's the only way to break the story. Other reporters say they would never enter into such an agreement and warn those sources that if they disclose any information about criminal behavior on their part, the reporters will not guarantee secrecy.

If a reporter promises to keep a source secret and that promise is broken, it can be costly. The U.S. Supreme Court ruled in 1991 that news organizations cannot break promises of confidentiality to news sources.

ACCURACY OF SOURCES

A reporter should never use a source as a basis for a story until the information is checked for accuracy. Verifying a story is not always easy, especially when a reporter is working under deadlines. One of the best ways to ensure that a story is accurate is to find several other sources who will disclose exactly the same information. This is known as *double sourcing* or *triple sourcing*. Dan Rather and *CBS News* discovered that the hard way when they based a widely criticized story about President Bush's alleged failure to fulfill his National Guard duties during the Vietnam War to a single source that turned out to be unreliable.

Most station managers have a policy that requires reporters to disclose their sources or documentation to at least one person in authority at the station before they are allowed to broadcast the investigative material; this allows someone who is more removed from the story to give a second, unbiased opinion about the story. Failure to provide such safeguards invites disaster.

GAINING CONFIDENCE

Reporters who find good, reliable sources and prove to them that they will protect their confidentiality usually find that those sources will continue to provide information, sometimes for many years. Self-esteem is often one motive for tipsters, and feeling good about being involved in the breaking of a story often encourages them to find new items. Smart reporters tell their sources that they are providing a service to the community. This allows sources to see themselves as part of a team, and they will actively look for new information to provide to their colleague at the radio or TV station.

Other good information comes from contacts that reporters cultivate in offices where records and documents are housed and, particularly for crime-beat reporters, at police desks.

Experienced reporters once suggested that "hanging out" at restaurants, coffeehouses, and bars where politicians and city and county employees gather was a good way to develop new sources. Unfortunately, this strategy is not as effective today. While occasionally bumping into a news contact at a social function is acceptable, too much contact smacks of cronyism, which can ultimately lead to the audience questioning the reporter's objectivity.

Further, much of the social networking today does not revolve around the neighborhood coffee shop. Instead, a number of reporters have Facebook or LinkedIn sites that provide them elementary access to potential news sources. While these may be good for an initial contact, reporters will only gain confidence after repeated contacts, most of which will happen face to face.

FIGURE 3.6

Social networks can be a good way to find sources, but face-to-face meetings build confidence.

LEAKS

Information from an unidentified source in the government, political, or corporate world is known as a *leak*. As with sources who provide tips, government insiders, for one reason or another, reveal information of a sensitive nature to the press with the promise of confidentiality. Such insiders could be White House staff members, assistants to members of a state assembly, or someone in a mayor's office who wants the media to know something about an individual or about an action that is being planned or debated behind closed doors.

As noted earlier, the information from a leak is not enough to warrant charging onto the air with the story. The information needs to be double sourced or triple sourced and then cleared with a superior in the newsroom before the story makes it into the evening news.

TRIAL BALLOONS

A different type of leak is the *trial balloon*. In this case, the leak has the endorsement of the White House, the mayor, or some other government official or agency. The trial balloon tips off one or more people in the media about some controversial action the department or official is thinking of taking. The purpose of the trial balloon is to measure reaction in advance not only from the people but also from the media, lobbying groups, and others. If the trial balloon is greeted with strong opposition, then the official or agency could quietly forget the action it had contemplated. However, if there is no loud protest, or the planned action is received with enthusiasm, the action probably would proceed as planned.

AUTHORITATIVE OR INFORMED SOURCES

When sources of information cannot be substantiated by ordinary means, reporters often attribute the information to a spokesperson, or authoritative or informed sources. There are times, for example, when correspondents at the White House, State Department, and Pentagon obtain information from government officials that may only be used with the understanding that the source is not to be named. So reporters who wish to use the information must say, "a spokesman at the Pentagon or a source at the State Department revealed today. ..."

Reporters who do not wish to use such vague attribution would be unable to use the information. Most people in the radio and TV audience take such attributions for granted, assuming that if the reporter is quoting a spokesperson the story is probably true. Often it is, but there's no guarantee.

FIGURE 3.7

BACKGROUND BRIEFINGS

Government officials often give information to reporters but insist that neither the officials nor the agencies they represent be identified. These meetings are called *background briefings*. If reporters wish to use the information revealed at such briefings, they must attribute it, again, by using phrases such as "official sources" or "well-informed sources."

It's important to note that such background briefings do not happen by accident. Instead, they are well planned so the government official can relay information without revealing too much to the reporter. Of course, if the reporter actually names the government official who provided the background briefing, that reporter would never receive another story. Background briefings are one occasion when the reporter and news source firmly agree on the breadth of the information and the anonymity of the government official.

FIGURE 3.8
White House press briefings are available online at www.whitehouse.gov/briefing_room/PressReleases/.

KEEPING IN TOUCH

Finally, as the field crews are advancing stories and tracking down their sources, it is imperative that they stay in touch with the newsroom. The news director and the assignment editor always must know what's going on "out there." If, for example, a demonstration is getting out of hand and is turning into a riot, the newsroom must be told. Any changes in stories, even routine ones, should be reported. Nothing irritates an assignment editor more than a crew and reporter who "disappear."

Reporters must keep the newsroom informed as much as possible about the status of a story. Is it running late? Is it falling apart? Is the video poor? All of these things and more must be shared so that those working on the newscast in the newsroom know what to expect. They also have the right to expect the reporter and crew to return early enough so that the story can be edited and aired on time. The team in the field should decide on a cutoff time—the time at which they must stop shooting and start packing up their gear and heading for home.

SUMMARY

Developing good sources and keeping them confidential constitute the backbone of effective reporting. This chapter focused on the importance of maintaining relationships with sources. Most reporters honor confidentiality agreements, and some have even gone to jail rather than disclose their sources. They knew if they had revealed their sources, they would have lost their credibility and effectiveness as journalists.

It is equally important to know whether your sources are reliable. It is essential to check and double-check the information they provide; never use information from only one source as the basis for a story. At the same time, don't dismiss information without thoroughly checking to see if it could be true.

If you agree to keep information off the record, make sure you do; otherwise it will be the last time that person gives you any information. Also, remember that when you do agree to keep something off the record, start looking for sources you can quote for the record.

Test Your Knowledge

1. What motivates people to give tips to a radio or TV station?
2. Explain why you would or would not broadcast information provided by a tipster.
3. What is localization?
4. What is a leak? Give an example.
5. What is a trial balloon?
6. What does "off the record" mean?

EXERCISES

1. Suppose that you are a TV assignment editor and you receive a call from an individual who claims she saw the mayor meeting with a well-known mobster. Describe how you would handle the situation.
2. Suppose you are a news director for a radio station. You get a call from a student at the local university who says he has been dealing in narcotics but wants to quit. He says he will tell you the whole story about drugs on campus, but you have to keep his identity secret. Do you agree and put a reporter on the story? Explain your decision.
3. An individual has been leaking information to you for several years and has always been reliable; however, she now tells you a story about corruption that could bring down the city administration if it is true. Do you tell anyone else at the station what you have been told? Do you disclose your source? Explain in detail.
4. Identify three national and international stories from a news Web site and then list three local contacts for each story that may enable you to localize the story for the evening news.

CHAPTER 4

Collecting Information from Real and Virtual Documents

INTRODUCTION

Although the interview is the most common method of gathering information, it is not always the most accessible or convenient. Most spot news stories—fires, accidents, natural disasters, crime—usually can be covered with a few quick sound bytes and video that support the reporter's story. But if the story is more complex or interviews fail to provide all the answers, reporters must look to other sources of background information.

The explosion of news sources available through the Internet has reshaped how many novice reporters research their stories. Google, Yahoo, and other one-stop sites provide countless links to queries on a daily basis. Checking the competition, which is traditionally performed by simply watching another station's newscast, can now be accomplished online. And newspaper files, long held on microfiche in rows of filing cabinets, are now readily available for background research with the click of a mouse.

While some reporters regard media convergence as a mere tool to send the news out via multiple formats, the digital age has ushered in new methods of searching for and retrieving documents. In addition to detailing what documents are available to reporters, this chapter also describes how to use the various government files maintained by police and the courts, tax and land offices, and bureaus that keep records on births, deaths, licenses, and numerous other activities. Finally, we demonstrate two online searches to illustrate what information can be found: the first tracks down sex offenders in a given zip code, whereas the second search shows how to uncover data on someone with nothing more than a given address.

(continued) **51**

FIGURE 4.1

Traditional newspaper files are now available online with the click of a mouse.

FIGURE 4.2

Open records

The phrase *open records* is associated most commonly with governmental documents, such as agenda for meetings or lists of official procurements. There are several notable exceptions to what may be accessed; the following section on the Freedom of Information Act (FOIA) lists some of them, such as those pertaining to national security. For local reporters, the most commonly restricted records deal with personnel, as many of those are still off-limits. This may seem counterintuitive, as many government employees' annual salaries are accessible online. Other forms (such as disciplinary actions or personnel reports) are generally closed to the press.

PUBLIC RECORDS AND "SUNSHINE LAWS"

One freedom people enjoy in a democracy is the openness of society. Very little goes on in public life that is not recorded in one way or another. At times, those in public office attempt to cover up some of their activities. They can, and often do, complicate the reporter's efforts to uncover information. Persistent journalists are often able to circumvent such attempts at secrecy by examining public records. Reporters also have another strong weapon—the Freedom of Information Act.

Congress passed the FOIA in 1966, allowing public access to records held by federal agencies of the executive branch. Since then, all 50 states have passed similar laws that permit the public to examine most records maintained by state and local governments. Freedom of information laws have been dubbed *sunshine laws* because they are designed to shed light on the workings of government. That light hasn't always shined brightly. Government agencies often refuse to disclose public records to private individuals or to journalists. The federal government, for example, has often claimed that revealing certain information would threaten national security. The issue was usually not the nation's security but information that would prove embarrassing to the agency or bureaucrat involved.

With that in mind, Congress amended the FOIA in 1974 and 1976, requiring federal agencies to release documents to the public unless the agencies could show some valid reason for not doing so. Nine exemptions were added to the FOIA, but the ones used most pertain to national security and foreign policy, advice and recommendations made within a federal agency, unwarranted invasion of privacy, files dealing with criminal cases that are current or pending, and trade secrets.

Because state sunshine laws vary, reporters seeking information from a state or local government office must examine that state's law before filing.

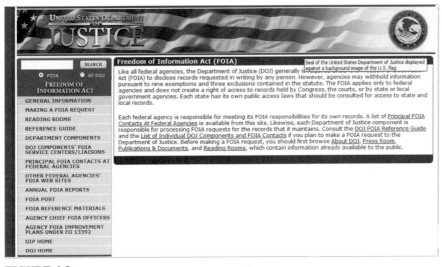

FIGURE 4.3

For more information on the Freedom of Information Act, visit the Department of Justice at www.usdoj .gov/oip/index.html.

FILING AN FOIA REQUEST

The first thing a reporter must do when seeking government information is to determine which federal agency has the information being sought. Sometimes, a telephone call to the agency is enough to produce the information. If not, the reporter must then file an FOIA request in writing. The request should be written on the news organization's letterhead and should include the following.

1. An opening sentence making it clear that the letter deals with a Freedom of Information Act request.

2. An offer to pay reasonable fees for reproduction of records. (Some news organizations prefer to list an amount they are willing to pay, say $50, rather than use the term "reasonable amount.")

3. A request that fees be waived because the information would benefit the public. (An optional statement indicating how the information would be beneficial increases the likelihood of the waiver being granted.)

4. A specific description of the documents being requested, including the actual titles of the documents, if they are known.

5. A reminder that, by law, the agency has 10 days to provide the information requested or to explain why it is denying the request.

6. Some reporters like to inquire whether any other government agencies have requested the same information. This "fishing expedition" sometimes provides some unexpected information that's helpful.

It is a good idea to send the letter by certified mail and to request a return receipt. The envelope should indicate "FOIA Request" or "To the Attention of the FOIA Officer." Although the FOIA states that the agency has 10 days to respond to the request, it also allows the agency to take more time as long as it informs the reporter. Many agencies assign a number to the request, which should be used in any future contacts with the agency. A telephone call to the agency sometimes speeds up responses. If the agency does not reply within a reasonable time—2 or 3 weeks—the reporter should send another letter, again reminding the agency of the time limits.

If an FOIA request is denied, the requester can file an appeal with the agency, which must be answered within 20 days. If that fails, the reporter can go to court to try to obtain the information—a costly and often lengthy endeavor. However, the threat of a lawsuit sometimes can convince an agency to release the information.

Because filing an FOIA request is so much trouble, few journalists use it to find information; indeed, only a small percentage of broadcast journalists have filed FOIA requests. Actually, prisoners and businesses have used the FOIA more than any other group. Although some information obtained through FOIA requests can be found in other places, there are times when there is no way to do the story without the FOIA.

THE PRIVACY ACT

Some members of Congress were concerned that the FOIA would impinge on one of Americans' most treasured freedoms—privacy. In 1974, Congress passed the Privacy Act in an attempt to protect individuals from unwarranted invasion of their privacy. The act forbids the government from disclosing information in its files pertaining to individuals. Many journalists argue that the government uses the act to keep important information from the public.

COLLECTING GOVERNMENTAL INFORMATION

Governmental records are best divided into two categories: records that contain information *about the government* and information that is collected by the government *about businesses and private citizens*. We'll address these topics separately, although some of the sources overlap and may be applicable to both.

GOVERNMENT

Ironically, while the government often fails to disclose certain information to the public, it publishes volumes of manuals and directories that are important sources of information for journalists. Sometimes, the information found in these government publications is as embarrassing as the material an agency does not disclose.

The government publications found at public and university libraries that are particularly useful to journalists are the reports issued by the General Accounting Office (GAO), which is a congressional agency. The GAO issues more than a thousand reports annually and its recommendations to Congress often provide interesting and sometimes provocative story ideas for journalists. The now-famous stories about the Pentagon paying 20 and 30 times what it should for hammers and other basic tools came from GAO reports.

Other government publications (and their respective Web sites) useful to reporters include the following.

- The *Code of Federal Regulations* (www.gpoaccess.gov/cfr/index.html) describes how laws and regulations are enforced.

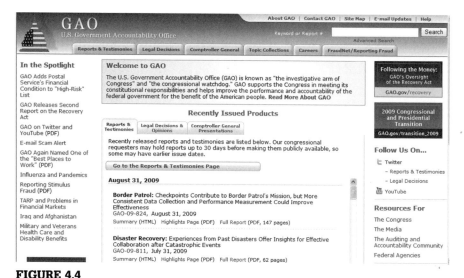

FIGURE 4.4

The Government Accountability Office investigates government spending (www.gao.gov).

- The *Congressional Record* (www.gpoaccess.gov/crecord/index.html) offers a daily report of congressional debate and other business. It also lists most agencies and high-ranking government officials, including members of Congress, its various committees, and members of the judicial and executive branches.

- The *Federal Register* (www.gpoaccess.gov/fr/) gives a daily account of federal-agency activities and executive orders from the White House.

- The U.S. Bureau of the Census (www.census.gov) provides statistical information on almost every aspect of life in America.

- The *U.S. Government Manual* (www.gpoaccess.gov/gmanual/) outlines the responsibilities and organization of the federal government. It includes all types of valuable information, including addresses, phone numbers, and names of officials at various government branches.

All of these publications—and a great many more—are also housed in government depository libraries located throughout the United States and on many university campuses.

BUSINESSES AND INDIVIDUALS

Reporters have another useful method of locating information, particularly information about individuals' government files. Governments at all levels maintain files on numerous activities that happen within their borders. When a baby is born, when someone dies, is married or divorced, registers a car, opens a liquor store, buys a piece of land, is arrested, sues somebody, or opens a restaurant, someone issues a document that is kept on permanent record. Anyone who wishes to do so may look at and copy such documents.

BUSINESS PUBLICATIONS AND INDEXES

Reporters working on complex or investigative stories about business can find a variety of useful publications in the library, including Dun & Bradstreet's directory of companies (www.dnb. com). *Standard & Poor's Register of Corporations* (www.standardandpoors. com) is also useful because it not only lists the corporations but also includes background information on major business leaders.

Reporters looking for information on specific products use the *Thomas Register of American Manufacturers* (www. thomasnet.com) series.

Magazines and newspapers also write about business and industry. The most respected of these sources are the *Wall Street Journal, Forbes, Fortune,* and *Business Week.*

FIGURE 4.5

TRADE PUBLICATIONS

The story of American industry is also told in hundreds of magazines and publications available in libraries. Many of these publications are biased because they speak for the industry they represent. Nevertheless, reporters often find useful information in such publications, which can provide leads for reporters seeking industry spokespeople. Trade publications are also an important source for information on what position various industries are taking on an issue.

FIGURE 4.6

POLICE RECORDS

The amount of information that reporters can obtain from police records varies from community to community. Reporters who establish a good rapport with a police public information officer often get the information they want with little trouble. Technically, any information on the police log or blotter should be available to reporters—a sample of these reports was available in Chapter 1. Without a good rapport, it sometimes takes the threat of court action to get the information. The records include the name of the individual, the date of the arrest, the charges, and the disposition of those charges. Once a person is behind bars, that information is normally available where the individual is being held.

COURT RECORDS

Information about the court cases most reporters deal with—criminal and civil cases—is available at a court clerk's office. In a civil case, anyone can obtain information about the complaint or petition brought by the plaintiff. The complaint usually describes what the defendant has allegedly done and why the plaintiff wants the court to award damages.

In criminal cases, reporters also have access to the charges brought against an individual. The records list the name of the complainant, most often a police officer, and the name of the defendant. The records cite the charge and describe what allegedly occurred that led to the arrest and court action. Reporters soon learn that it's a lot easier, and quicker, to find these records if they are on a first-name basis with the court clerks.

FIGURE 4.7

Reporters can find information on court cases at the court clerk's office.

LAW ENFORCEMENT DATABASES

One of the more visible outcomes of Internet research deals with locating crime statistics throughout a community. For this example, we examine the amount of data available on sex offenders who are either incarcerated or who have been released into traditional neighborhoods. Although the laws vary across the country, it is common for local law enforcement to compel sex offenders to register their home addresses when they are released from prison. Remember, just because a sex offender's photograph, address, and name are online is not justification to put the information on the air; there are privacy rights that must be acknowledged.

However, there is still statistical data that can be compiled from such databases. Because these records are generally searchable by either county or zip code, a reporter can easily compare two jurisdictions or identify trends.

Most of these databases are accessible to the public with little effort. To locate them, start with either the county sheriff's office or the state bureau of investigation. As a brief example of the information that can be found, let's conduct a quick search of the Georgia Bureau of Investigation's (GBI) Web site.

1. Enter the GBI homepage at http://gbi.georgia.gov.

2. In the search box, type "sex offender registry."

3. Click on the "sex offender search page" link.

4. Select a county. For this example, use "Cobb County" in the Atlanta metro region.

5. You'll see a number of registered sex offenders appear with mugshots, names, addresses, descriptions, crimes, and other information.

6. Then, go back and conduct a new search with "DeKalb County," also in the Atlanta metro region.

By comparing two nearby counties, one can enterprise a story using readily available crime statistics. The GBI (as well as most other jurisdictions) also provides similar databases on murder, rape, larceny, family violence, and other felonies. Data within these reports may be limited to broad statistics, such as how many murders were committed in a given county in a certain month. Knowing how to quickly locate accurate numbers can be invaluable when conducting background research or developing a story.

In addition to county-by-county searches, additional digging can locate state-wide crime statistics. These numbers allow comparisons between different years, criminal offenses, or the Statewide Crime Rate per 100,000 population. Armed with these statistics, a reporter can create an engaging story about

FIGURE 4.8

Community crime statistics are available from county sheriffs or bureaus of investigation. For example, visit the Georgia Bureau of Investigations at http://gbi.georgia.gov.

crime, safety, and prevention. As an example, the GBI Statewide Crime Rate reveals that overall crime actually dropped roughly 40 percent across Georgia since its peak in 1989. Statistics like these can result in a lead package, a series of reports on crime, or even a promotable news item during a ratings week.

BIRTH AND DEATH RECORDS

The facts of a person's birth often can be important to a reporter. A birth certificate lists the names of the parents, the date of birth, the name of the doctor who delivered the child, and the name of the hospital. Death certificates also provide information that may be important to a story. They show the cause of death and the date and time it occurred, but these records are not always public. If an individual left a will that involved real estate, reporters may also obtain a copy of the death certificate attached to mortgages and deeds found at the property tax office.

LICENSES

Nearly every community issues licenses of many kinds, and sometimes knowing who received a license can be important to a newsperson. In a large city, little goes on in business that does not require some sort of a license, even selling hot dogs on the street. Such licenses list names and other personal information about the grantee. Such information would be valuable, for example, if a reporter was working on a story about a junkyard that was an environmental or safety hazard.

The licensing of guns has been an ongoing issue throughout the nation. Because there is no national gun-control law, the ability to check on people who may own guns depends on where the reporter is doing the checking.

Many professional people, such as doctors, architects, and engineers, also must hold licenses. The state agencies or boards that issue those licenses have biographical information, including education and the applicant's specialty.

LAND RECORDS

The county assessor's office and/or the property tax office can provide a lot of information to an investigative reporter. It has records on who pays the taxes on property and, presumably, but not always, on the owner of the property. The records also reveal the former owners' names and the purchase price of the property, as well as who holds the mortgage on the property, if there is one. The names of the real-estate brokers and lawyers who were involved in the sale are also indicated. This information might be important to know if, for example, a reporter was checking on a city judge who seemed to be lenient with drunk drivers and it was discovered in the property tax records that the judge was living in a million-dollar home in the suburbs.

FINANCIAL RECORDS

It is easy to check a person's financial record. Many people, except perhaps reporters looking for such information, believe that it's too easy to find out how Americans handle their finances. Reporters need only ask the station's business office to call TRW or some other credit bureau, and the person's computer-produced financial record will be on the reporter's desk in minutes. The record shows credit histories for 10 years or more, the names of those holding mortgages, where individuals shop, and whether they pay their bills on time. The report also shows any bankruptcy declared during the past 10 years.

Any time an individual moves and establishes credit of any kind, the new address is recorded, which can be useful to a reporter trying to find the person. Other firms provide a person's new address as long as the reporter supplies a social security number. These numbers are increasingly difficult to obtain in this age of identity theft, although it remains an option for reporters.

TAX RECORDS

Tax records are among the most difficult documents to obtain. Reporters do, from time to time, obtain information about a person's tax returns from the Internal Revenue Service (IRS), but almost always as the result of a leak initiated by someone inside the agency. Some reporters manage to develop sources inside the IRS, but it is not easy; the penalties for IRS employees who leak information are severe.

PUBLIC RECORDS

Given the amount of data available in both real and virtual documents, the concept of privacy is more elusive than one may imagine. Aside from self-promotion via social networking Web sites (Facebook, MySpace, LinkedIn, and the like), information on private individuals and companies is both prodigious and readily accessible. For this exercise, remember that people have a fundamental right to be left alone; just because you can find out information on a private citizen does not give the right to broadcast the details on the news.

First, start with your home address, which is easily seen from the street. Assuming you own the property, you can quickly access your county's assessment office for information on price, square footage, ownership, and even how many bedrooms are in the house. Note that you do not start in the county's taxation office, as the assessor determines the value of the property, thus there is often more detail there. The tax office chiefly collects the money.

The assessor's office will sometimes also provide exterior pictures of the home. If you cannot find pictures there, broad search engines such as Google Earth can show the images of most homes or neighborhoods. This is not consistent across the country, as new development and some rural areas have yet to be put on the Internet.

We started with a simple home address, but the assessor's office has provided the name. Next, run a quick check of that name through Facebook and MySpace. Because the number of people who are on social networking Web sites increases daily, you may be able to find a picture, a resume, or other background information. Most reporters have an account with these sites for this very reason.

Whether information is found through that step or not, the vital components you possess for the background check are in your hands. With the name and address, you can check the city, county, and state Web sites' personnel records to see if that person has a municipal job—a number of these sites also publish the employee's salary. You can also search other property records to see if the person owns other land in the area, track down business licenses, and find out memberships in local organizations.

Additionally, one way to expand your research beyond an individual person is to research family members. This is much easier done than expected. A quick online search of the local newspaper's archives (again, usually available online) will access obituaries. These articles typically list survivors of the deceased, thus presenting an entire family tree in one compact location.

ADDITIONAL REAL AND VIRTUAL DOCUMENTS

The number of paper-based data sources and online Web sites increases on a daily basis, making it impossible for reporters to maintain a comprehensive list. With so many government resources (and endless Web sites of individual companies, social networking pages, and the like), a handful of touchstones can make finding documents less daunting.

DATABASE SERVICES

We have made numerous references in this book to the information explosion that has had a major impact on all types of communications. It already is a boon to journalists. The Internet, in particular, has invaluable tools for searching all types of subjects.

Most libraries have computerized the catalogue of the information that's housed in them, which makes locating the information much faster. Many libraries subscribe to database services such as LexisNexis, InfoTrac, and others that index hundreds of newspapers, magazines, academic and scientific journals, and trade publications.

Broadcast newsrooms usually have dedicated software platforms for word processing, creating assignment lists, and producing rundowns. Some of these programs also interface (via subscription) with database services, such as LexisNexis. Reporters routinely use LexisNexis for tasks such as researching stories, indentifying contacts, and obtaining story ideas.

CITY DIRECTORIES

The city directory is often helpful if you want to find out where a particular individual lives. The directory lists a person's name, address, spouse, children, employment, and several other useful pieces of information. The directories are particularly helpful when a reporter is trying to talk to relatives of someone who is in the news.

Telephone books are also useful; they would be the first place to look when trying to locate someone if you know the town or city in which he or she lives. In some communities, the telephone company also prints telephone books that list people and companies by their addresses. They are extremely useful, for example, if a major fire breaks out on the 1500 block of Main Street. There are listings for all of the phones on Main Street that are not restricted, so all the reporter or assignment editor has to do is try to locate a phone near the 1500 block. A call to a phone listed at 1550 Main Street, for example, might find someone who can see the fire from an apartment window. It's then simple to put the person on the air while he or she describes the fire and answers the reporter's questions.

The limitation of telephone books is the proliferation of cell phones. Cell phone numbers are not listed in traditional phone books, plus users can add or drop phones (and their respective numbers) frequently. Even Internet Web sites that promise success in providing phone numbers for people are stymied by the great strides made by cell phones. There are no accurate third-party sources with omniscient cell phone number lists—the only accurate way is to ask someone for their number.

CREATING CONTACT LISTS

For any journalist, the best database is the one created by the reporter. Naturally, a reporter who covers a specific beat will concentrate on their own field. A business reporter, for example, will list the local chamber of commerce (handy for business openings and broad business news), the city manager (who will know about businesses expanding or neighborhoods rezoning for business locations), and the spokespersons for the top businesses in the region. Health reporters will concentrate on local hospitals and clinics, whereas education reporters will need school principals and school board members on their list.

General assignment reporters, who cover a number of different topics, cast a much wider net for news sources. It is important to note that these contact lists do not include the names and numbers of competing stations. It is standard practice to monitor the competition, but you will not rely on them to find stories for you.

In addition to public information officers for the city, county, and police stations, your contact list should contain:

- Local and state health departments, as well as the Centers for Disease Control and Prevention

- The local school district, nearby universities and technical schools, and the state department of education

- The Chamber of Commerce, Better Business Bureau, and any leading unions

- County, circuit, and state courts

- The state legislature and governor's office, plus the contacts for the representatives and senators who represent the area in Washington

- City departments, including parks and recreation, the visitors' bureau, historical society, social services, public works, and the public library

- Nearby military bases

- Regional airports

- Local nonprofits, including the Red Cross, Salvation Army, and Habitat for Humanity

- Federal departments that may be of interest, including the Census Bureau, the Treasury Department, or National Aeronautics and Space Administration

It is poor journalism to simply revisit the same sources newscast after newscast, so you must resist having the mayor or another local figure pop up repeatedly for various stories. While some interviewees are simply better on camera than others, you perform a disservice to your audience by merely relaying the same person's viewpoints. You are a journalist, not a cheerleader—check your Web sites and sources frequently, but make sure you do not give the same people a soapbox for themselves.

FIGURE 4.9

SUMMARY

Unfortunately, most radio or TV news organizations do not give their reporters enough time to use the various information sources described in this chapter. Reporters spend most of their time working on breaking news stories. Investigative stories require a lot of research time and are expensive to produce. Most stations want at least one story a day from their reporters, which doesn't allow much time for checking court records or filing FOIA requests.

If you do have an opportunity to work on stories that require in-depth research, the information in this chapter should be extremely helpful. The FOIA is an important asset if you want to examine the actions of government at any level—town, city, state, or federal. The library at your college or university has numerous documents that will reveal more about the federal government, how it works, and what mistakes it makes. The report of the GAO, a congressional watchdog, and the *Congressional Directory* are also useful.

You should also familiarize yourself with the various business publications, indexes, journals, and magazines in your library and learn about the ability of the Internet and databases such as LexisNexis, which have cut reporter research tremendously.

Finally, the undisputed best resource for investigative journalism in this country is the Investigative Reporters and Editors (IRE), located at the University of Missouri's Journalism School. In addition to publishing books, tip sheets, and resource guides, IRE sponsors boot campus, scholarships, fellowships, and other programs for those interested in investigative journalism. Its Web site is www.ire.org.

Test Your Knowledge

1. What is the Freedom of Information Act?
2. Why is the FOIA so important to journalists?
3. List the different points that should be made in a letter requesting information under the FOIA.
4. Journalists can learn about the government and how it operates through various records and publications. List some of the most important ones and explain how they are useful.
5. How can computer databases be useful to reporters?
6. What kind of information can reporters obtain from police and court records?
7. What is the greatest limitation of city directories?
8. How can social networking sites help reporters find out information about individuals?

EXERCISES

1. Suppose that you are filing an FOIA request with the Defense Department because you have a source that claims that when he worked for the Acme Tool and Die Company in Centerville, a government contractor, as many as 60 percent of the products produced in the plant were rejected for various reasons. Prepare the FOIA request.
2. Pick three corporations among the *Fortune 500* list and find out the names of the top officials who run them. Also list any other companies that are owned by one of these parent corporations and find out the names of any corporations or individuals who own a substantial number of shares in a parent company.
3. Use a database service to find out how many articles were published last year about Diane Lane. List the names of the publications along with the titles of the articles and the dates they appeared.
4. Visit the local courthouse and find out the names of those who were convicted of drunk driving during the past month.
5. Create your own list of contacts, including the names of sources, their phone numbers, e-mail addresses, and business information. You will frequently revise this list, but expect to start with at least 30 contacts.
6. Research yourself or a family member by starting with only a name or address. Document your steps so you can track how you "discover" the information.

Beats, Spot News, and Reporting Assignments

INTRODUCTION

Reporters spend most of their careers covering spot news, which dominates the contents of all radio and TV newscasts. Spot news includes fires, accidents, holdups, and other incidents that occur every day, with varying frequency, in every city and town in the nation.

Chapter 1 discussed *how* stories are located for newscasts. Regardless of whether stories are planned, spontaneous, or enterprised, the newsroom must also decide *who* will cover a given assignment. In some situations, this is fairly straightforward; a basketball piece will fall to the sports reporter, whereas a medical update is given to the health reporter. This chapter covers these specializations, as beat reporters are looked upon as the newsroom's resident experts on a topic. There is also a discussion on the theories of how to cover spot news appropriately, especially those stories that may trigger an emotional response.

Further, this chapter discusses the most common types of spot news stories. In a fast-paced newsroom, the producer or assignment editor may have limited choices regarding who can be dispatched to a breaking story. Although it is not ideal for a business reporter to cover a crime story, it is not uncommon. The ability to cover a broad number of spot stories, in addition to having a solid background in a given beat, makes any reporter a more valuable addition to the newsroom.

FIGURE 5.1

BEATS

During their careers, reporters cover most of the types of news stories just discussed. Some reporters may have one particular type of story assigned to them as their *beat*. Unfortunately, not too many radio and TV newsrooms use the *beat* method of reporting, which was developed by—and is still a tradition at—newspapers. Most broadcast managers argue that they do not have the budgets necessary to assign reporters to beats. They note that news is only a small percentage of what is viewed on television every day, whereas newspapers devote most of their attention to it. Many people believe broadcast news suffers because it does not have enough beat reporters who can concentrate on and become an expert in a particular subject. But the networks and some large-market stations employ beat reporters—journalists assigned to such special areas.

Cliff Williams, managing editor of WFFA–TV in Dallas, says his station is dedicated to beat reporting. "It's very much a part of who we are," he says, adding that it "builds relationships" with news sources. Beat reporters develop an expertise and cultivate sources in the area he or she covers. This gives them an advantage when competing with general assignment reporters on breaking news stories.

A disadvantage to beat reporting, Williams says, is the reporter gets locked in, "too comfortable" and doesn't want to go outside the beat. Another disadvantage is the reporter can get too close to the people on the beat he or she is covering and lose objectivity. This may lead to the reporter's wanting to put the source in only a good light—to do otherwise would adversely affect the relationship he or she has cultivated.

WFAA–TV beats include police, city and county government, the state capital, transportation, education, economy/business, the environment, health, and entertainment. Even for a large-market station, that's an impressive assortment of beat reporters, and not that common. In addition, WFAA has two investigative reporters.

The beat system at the station was developed by the late Marty Haag, who was vice president of news for the A.H. Belo Corporation, which owns WFAA and four other stations. Haag also said he believed in the beat system because the world is getting too complicated. Beat reporters know what they're writing about; you have reporters who are familiar with the players. Haag said the beat system also allows stations to compete with newspapers. "We don't want to be clipping stories out of newspapers and then covering them," he says. "We want to be ahead of them, not behind them."

Another believer in the beat system is Jeff Hoffman, news director of WAVE–TV in Louisville. Yet his station's reporting staff numbers only 11, half the number of WFAA. Of course, Louisville is much smaller than Dallas. Hoffman has beat reporters covering city hall, medicine, and consumer news. He agrees that beat reporters give a news operation two important advantages: they can enterprise and cultivate sources.

Former WAVE news director Ed Godfrey, now retired, who was also very supportive of the beat system, noted that such reporters sometimes "get too close to their beats and wind up with stories not interesting to a general audience or get too close to their sources and can lose their objectivity." But he quickly added that the advantages of beat reporting "far outweigh the disadvantages."

Diane Doctor, the news director at WCBS–TV in New York, has a flock of beat reporters along with bureau chiefs in New Jersey and Long Island. Her beat reporters cover education, technology, and consumer issues; plus she has an investigative reporter and two people assigned to political reporting. She's very supportive of the beat concept, stressing that such reporters are able not only to focus on a particular subject, which makes them more effective, but also are able to enterprise more stories because of the contacts and sources they develop.

The following list of beats is not all-inclusive, although they are the most likely to be found in newsrooms that still maintain specialized reporters. A rural area, for example, may have an agriculture specialist who concentrates on farmers and crops, whereas a large metro area could deploy a traffic and transportation reporter. However, the beats listed here can provide a starting point for those who wish to specialize in a given field. They are:

Business/Consumer	Local Government
Crime	Military
Education	Science/Technology
Entertainment/Community	Sports
Environment	Weather
Health	

Chapter 3 discussed how to develop a contact list for a general assignment reporter; this broad list should include the local chamber of commerce, the city's public information officer (PIO), and a wide variety of local contacts. While beat reporters have a narrower focus, they require a deeper list of local experts to call upon for their particular field. The following pages provide a glimpse of how a beat reporter can develop his or her specialization.

FIGURE 5.2

Business/consumer

The business reporter uses the same basic techniques as a general assignment reporter—developing good sources and cross-checking information for reliability. Covering business is a little like covering politics. Because there's a lot of speculation, a good reporter soon learns to be skeptical about any predictions concerning the economy, interest rates, and the stock market.

Reporters thinking about specializing in business news should remember that the opportunities are not as great as in some other beats. This is largely because local newsrooms do not normally spend as much airtime on business subjects as on other issues. This lack of coverage results partly because many news directors think that most business news is either too dull or too complicated to explain to the public. At the same time, many stations that do have business reporters say they get good feedback from the public on business news.

For those who think business is fascinating and would like a future in reporting such news, we have these suggestions: Take courses in economics, marketing, and other business-related subjects and, perhaps, consider graduate work in business. An MBA degree carries a lot of weight with many news managers.

As always, research is a necessity. Broadcasters specializing in business reporting should read periodicals such as *Barron's*, *Business Week*, the *Economist*, *Forbes*, and *Fortune*. The *Wall Street Journal* is the bible for the business world. Similarly, The *New York Times*, The *Washington Post*, and their counterparts in other large cities have excellent business columns and reports that business specialists should follow.

Many good trade publications are also devoted to business and industry. Although many of these publications have biases that the reporter must consider, they should by no means be discounted. They are full of information that helps reporters learn about industries and new systems, techniques, and products.

Also, note that the business beat has gradually evolved into the business/consumer beat, boiling down arcane financial data into information that can be used by the typical homeowner, taxpayer, and average consumer. Because of this shift, there are now ample stories of clipping coupons, refinancing mortgages, paying bills, and saving money. This subtle tonal change allows business/consumer reporters greater access to newsrooms.

Consumer reporting works best when the reporter investigates serious problems and scams that affect many people. Reporters provide a real service when they alert the audience to beware of a company that guarantees consumers credit cards for a fee and then doesn't produce, a home siding company that's tricking retired couples into paying double what they should to repair their homes, or a garage that charges customers for unnecessary repairs.

These reporters also provide other services to the public. They often report on new products that may be useful to the physically disabled, a new low-cost prescription service for senior citizens, or the best way to discover low-cost airfares.

A sampling of their contact list would be based on some of the following:

- Banks and credit unions
- Chamber of commerce
- City/county business license department
- Industrial authorities
- Labor unions
- Realtors

Another professional strategy is to identify the top 10 businesses in the area (think of large local employers) and monitor their quarterly reports and stock prices. If a company has publicly traded stock, they will appear on the U.S. Securities and Exchange Commission Web site, www.sec.gov, where filings by companies are kept in a searchable database called "EDGAR."

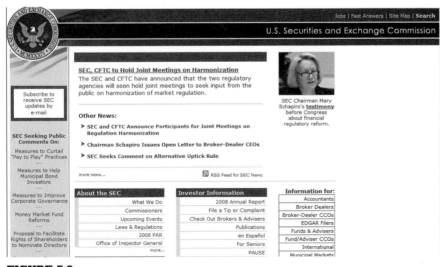

FIGURE 5.3
Find company filings at the Securities and Exchange Commission (www.sec.gov).

Crime

As noted in Chapter 1, PIOs are appointed within law enforcement divisions to provide a liaison between the police and the press. Maintaining a working relationship with the PIOs in your area (remember, there will be one for the city police, another for the county sheriff, and so forth) is key to covering crime. Of course, monitoring police frequencies on the scanner, performing beat checks, and reviewing the police activity logs are also important.

The process doesn't stop once there is an arrest. After the suspect is arrested, the local district attorney (DA) will file charges; a rookie mistake is to say that police have charged a suspect with a crime. They don't. Remember that police arrest, the DA charges.

Because covering the courts is a specialization unto itself, the following is a brief overview of what you may expect when you're called upon to cover a courtroom case. Remember that no two courts are alike, as judges may institute gag orders or move into closed session. Also, military courts operate under a different code and typically do not allow video cameras, thus necessitating the need for a courtroom sketch artist. Finally, despite the constitutional right of a speedy trial, the word "speedy" means different things to different people. Depositions, evidence discovery, pretrial motions, testimony, trials, and appeals can lead to endless days of courtroom tedium and possibly years of story coverage for a single case.

The courts

Those arrested by police wind up in criminal court unless the defendants are younger than 16 years old, who are then handled by the juvenile courts. Domestic relations courts also get some cases involving marital disputes.

A second court system, the civil courts, handles noncriminal matters—civil suits between individuals, between individuals and corporations and other institutions, and between two or more companies. These suits, for the most part, are about money. Someone wants payment for damages. It could be for libel, an unpaid bill, shoddy workmanship, an auto-accident injury, or numerous other reasons.

Federal courts deal with matters that in one way or another involve the federal government or federal laws. This section concentrates on the courts that most reporters cover—criminal and civil.

Criminal courts

Depending on the state, city, or town involved, a variety of court procedures take place before a defendant comes to trial. In small communities, a defendant may appear first before a justice of the peace, or he or she may appear in a county court. The defendant could be released on bail or remanded to jail to await a court hearing. In minor cases, a judge may hear the case and render a verdict, unless the defendant requests a jury trial.

In cities, the defendant usually is brought first to a police station, where he or she is booked, formally charged, photographed, and fingerprinted. Depending on the time of day of the arrest and booking, the defendant appears in court the same day or the next, where he or she enters a plea and is released on bail or sent back to jail to await arraignment and the setting of a trial date. More serious crimes are sometimes turned over to a grand jury, which examines the evidence and decides whether the accused should be indicted and stand trial or be released.

If the defendant is a celebrity, radio and TV reporters usually cover the court appearances, even if the charge is relatively minor. More serious crimes, such as rape or homicide, draw a crowd of reporters. As noted earlier, because so many killings take place in large cities, radio and TV reporters virtually ignore many of them. Assignment desks send reporters to homicide arraignments only if there is something unusual about the killing or if the defendant or victim is well known.

Reporter access

Although many courts are easing restrictions on cameras and recorders in court-rooms, many still bar such equipment. When they are allowed, access is usually obtained on a pool basis. Some courts allow reporters with cameras and tape recorders to question lawyers, prosecutors, defendants, and others in the corridors, whereas others restrict the media to remaining outside the courthouse.

Good reporters attend the court hearings and trials even if the equipment is barred. They take detailed notes on what goes on for use in their reports. The reporter not only looks for important remarks and choice quotes from the judge, prosecutor, defense counsel, and witnesses but also makes note of facial expressions and other signs of emotion. If it's a jury trial, the reactions of the jury members are particularly important because they may give some clue about how the case is going.

When cameras are not allowed in the court during an important case, an artist is usually assigned along with the reporter to render sketches of the principal figures.

Civil courts

When people believe that they have been damaged in one way or another by individuals, professionals, or companies, they may seek redress by suing in civil court. The suit may be for libel, malpractice, failure to live up to a contract or to pay a bill, or divorce (just to name a few). The loser in civil court usually ends up paying money. No one goes to jail as they once did when debtor prisons existed. But refusal to pay court-ordered alimony or child support is considered contempt of court, which could put the guilty party in jail.

Radio and TV newsrooms do not assign reporters to civil court trials because most of the cases are dull and relatively unimportant. But an unusual malpractice case involving millions of dollars or a class action suit against an automobile company for allegedly building an unsafe vehicle attracts broadcast media to the courthouse. Reporters also cover civil cases when celebrities are seeking damages for libel or are involved in a scandalous divorce or paternity suit.

As far as reporting assignments go, the rules are the same as those for covering the criminal courts. Attend the hearings and trials, take notes (particularly if you can't use equipment inside), and try to speak with both sides outside the courthouse.

To cover crime efficiently, some of the basic contacts needed include:

- Bureau of Justice statistics (www.ojp.usdoj.gov/bjs)

- City police's PIO

- Civil and criminal court clerks (for obtaining dockets of cases to be tried)

- County sheriff's PIO

- District attorney's office

- Federal Bureau of Investigation (www.fbi.gov) as well as your state's Bureau of Investigation

- State Highway Patrol

FIGURE 5.4

Visit the Bureau of Justice statistics (www. ojp.usdoj.gov/bjs).

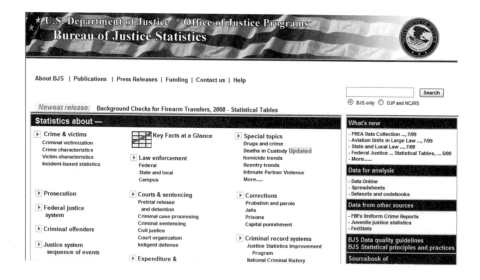

Also, the Census Bureau at www.census.gov links to the Federal Statistical Abstract, which provides searchable statistics on crime.

Education

Reporters within the education beat have a wealth of information at their fingertips on an ongoing basis, as teachers, administrators, state review boards, principals, and a score of other stakeholders generate reports at a nonstop clip. The downside is that the journalist must pore over piles of documents that correspond to annual (January to December), academic (August to May), and fiscal (July to June) calendars, as well as keep up with an ever-changing list of personalities. Done correctly, the education beat can become one of the pillars of the newscast. Done poorly, the beat will drown in missed opportunities and forgettable stories.

The following list is a good starting point for compiling a contact list:

- Board of education (and superintendent)
- Colleges and universities
- Libraries
- Home school advocacy groups
- Private schools
- Public schools
- Teachers' unions
- Vocational–technical schools

Entertainment/community

With the exception of a handful of large markets such as New York and Los Angeles, it is extremely difficult for a newsroom to justify an entertainment reporter. Most reporters don't live in metro areas packed with television stars, movie studios, recording artists, and red carpet debuts of feature films.

Instead, a reporter can carve out a niche as an entertainment/community reporter, thus concentrating their efforts on filing feature stories for the E block, where the *kickers* are slated. Kickers are feel-good pieces placed at the end of the newscast to leave viewers in a good mood and to serve as a springboard into the next program. No producer wants to end a newscast on a down note about a double murder, only to then ask the anchors to gleefully promote *Wheel of Fortune, The Tonight Show,* or whatever light-hearted fare follows on the channel.

Thus, a strong E block is an integral part of any local newscast. Even though the stories may not have the hard-hitting news impact of an A block crime report, journalists should still dedicate their best efforts to compiling a solid contact list. Some basics include

- Amusement parks
- Art galleries
- Comedy clubs
- Conference centers
- Dance schools
- Historic districts
- Movie theaters
- Museums
- Parks department (administered by the city or county)
- Playhouses and stage theaters

There are two distinct disadvantages to being an entertainment/community reporter. First, every local civic group, proud parent, bake sale sponsor, and wannabe actor will expect a fawning story; the list of demands can become unwieldy, the reports are expected to be universally glowing, and each story subject may very well expect a video copy for their own. Second, E block reporters will quickly develop a reputation as someone who can only produce a puff piece at the end of the show. While there is merit to having a strong E block, the day will inevitably come when a "hard news" story, such as a deadly car crash or blazing fire, will demand coverage in a short-staffed newsroom. Even when such a crisis occurs, producers are leery of sending an entertainment reporter to file a critical report.

Environment

The growing concern for the environment in the past decade has encouraged broadcast news managers to allocate more news to the subject. In many newsrooms, the environment is still covered by general assignment reporters, but more and more news managers are hiring broadcast journalists who have become familiar with environmental problems. Knowledge of the subject can be acquired in college, but reporters often gain their expertise simply by taking the time to learn about the complex issues.

Numerous periodicals deal with every aspect of the environment, and reporters intent on learning about environmental issues should spend many hours in the library reading these publications or should subscribe to them. A wide variety of environmental seminars also are offered throughout the country by private and government groups. The Environmental Health Center issues a newsletter; "Greenwire" is a news service offering stories about the environment; and the Society of Environmental Journalists provides help and resources for journalists trying to improve their knowledge of environmental issues. The Radio and Television News Directors' Association (RTNDA) often discusses the environment at national and regional meetings. Helpful computer databases, such as the Toxic Release Inventory, which stores information on 366 toxic chemicals, are also available.

Bob Engleman of Scripps-Howard newspapers says that covering the environment is like covering any other complicated, important issue. He advises following these steps:

1. Learn the issue.
2. Maintain skepticism.
3. Seek out all viewpoints.
4. Ask probing questions.
5. Report the story as accurately and as fairly as possible.

The editor of the *Freedom Forum Journal*, Craig Le May, says environmental reporters must "look at what local industries are doing—how they make and transport products, how they do business." He also warns reporters that much of the environmental information available is from press releases, which are not reliable.

Le May says that reporters must search through all the public relations and make sense of the issues. He notes that the rule for cultivating sources is the same as for other types of assignments: "Get the best people and find out what they have at stake in what you are reporting." He warns, for example, that because researchers at universities are often funded by organizations with a fixed point of view, reporters have to be skeptical of their findings. Le May also urges reporters to beware of trade groups that "masquerade as environmental organizations." He notes that the National Wetlands Coalition sounds like an environmental group, but it is actually a lobby group for the largest oil, gas, and utility companies.

Robert Logan, the director of the Science Journalism Center at the University of Missouri, also urges reporters to be "skeptical of everybody. Everyone is selling something," he warns, "even if they are not into making money." Logan says reporters should remember that the investigative rule "follow the money to get to the bottom of something" is bad advice for environmental reporting. He suggests instead to "follow the best scientific evidence first, and then look for the money."

In addition to local sources, environmental stories thrive online with numerous Web sites dedicated to climate change, biodiversity, pollution, recycling, and assorted environmental issues. As a starting point, the following contacts should be collated:

- Civic groups that sponsor clean-ups (Boy Scouts, Keep America Beautiful)

- Department of Natural Resources (or its equivalent in your state government)

- Dumps and landfills

- Environmental Protection Agency (www.epa.gov)

- Municipal sewage, refuse, and water departments

- National Resources Defense Council (www.nrdc.org)

- Recycling organizations

- Sierra Club (local chapters are listed at www.sierraclub.org/chapters)

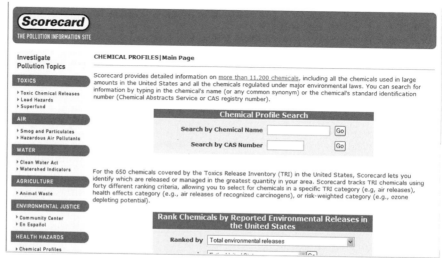

FIGURE 5.5

Find pollution information at www.scorecard.gov.

Health

Health and medical subjects rank high in interest among radio and TV audiences for obvious reasons—we all want to remain healthy. Reporters with knowledge of health and medical issues are assets to news managers. Most large news staffs have someone assigned to a medical and health beat. Many broadcast news producers regularly include health and medical stories in newscasts. Reporters do not have much trouble selling producers on a good medical story. Likewise, depending on the size of the market, good health and medical stories are usually not difficult to find.

Because they are public relations conscious, hospitals and research centers often bring stories involving their facilities or research to the attention of radio and TV newsrooms. Listeners and viewers also provide tips on medical-related stories, usually when someone close to them has been involved in something good or bad at a medical facility. Many tips concern malpractice, but some involve lifesaving techniques and appealing human-interest stories about children waiting for organ transplants and the generosity of people who contribute hundreds of thousands of dollars to make the surgery possible.

Objectivity is always an essential part of all reporting, but sometimes medical reporters must be particularly sensitive about their reports because providers often appear to be in the wrong. Doctors are accused of charging too much or refusing to accept Medicaid patients. Hospitals are criticized for turning away some patients and price gouging others. Many of these stories are true, but reporters must examine both sides of any issue. Reporters sometimes discover that hospitals are on the verge of financial collapse because of rising costs and heavy investment in equipment. They find that the government is slow in paying Medicare patients' bills and is often unrealistic when deciding on the amount doctors can charge.

Good medical reporters look for positive stories about doctors and hospitals to balance the negative ones. If and when reporters find they are beginning to dislike the medical profession as a whole, it's probably time for them to start looking for another beat. Health and medical reporters also cannot allow themselves to be duped. They must constantly ask tough questions about the medical establishment and whether it is meeting the needs of the American people.

Science and health-related courses in college help journalism students prepare for medical reporting. These students also should read the many health and medical magazines that are available. Teaching-hospital libraries also have stacks of journals from major research centers. Although these resources are provided primarily for medical students, persuasive reporters usually have no difficulty gaining access to the journals once the staff is convinced the reporters are not malpractice attorneys.

A basic contact list should include the following starting points:

- Hospitals

- Local and/or regional health departments

- The Centers for Disease Control and Prevention

- Local nonprofit chapters that specialize in health, such as the American Red Cross, the American Cancer Society, or the National Kidney Foundation

It is also prudent to compile a list of local specialists, such as a pediatrician, an allergist, a dentist, and one or two experts in their fields. They can provide an abundance of specialized information, but beware that you do not call upon them too frequently; using the same doctor on the air month after month smacks of both favoritism and laziness.

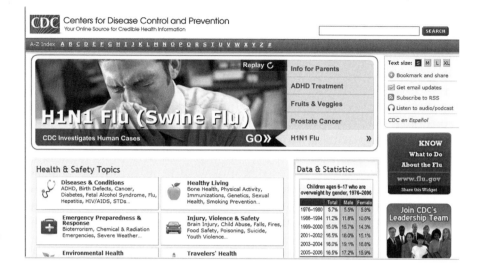

FIGURE 5.6

Visit the Centers for Disease Control Web site at www.cdc.gov.

Local government

Notice that the emphasis on this beat is for local government. Unless a reporter lives in a state capital or Washington, DC, covering politics tends to focus upon those jurisdictions within the viewing area. Of course, there are always national bills and laws that impact local viewers; the best Web site for tracking that activity is http://thomas.loc.gov/. Additionally, knowledge of state government is vital, as a reporter will interact with the governor's office, state representatives, and state agencies such as transportation and health.

FIGURE 5.7

Track the national bills that affect local governments at http://thomas.loc.gov/.

There are also ample stories to be covered at the local level, spanning city council meetings to planning and zoning public forums. Indeed, if the city's television station does not cover the working of the city council, who could argue that the public need for news is being addressed?

Like a police station, most municipalities have a PIO who interacts with the media. The PIO may serve as the default on-camera interview subject or may coordinate availability for city leaders to meet with the press. In addition to the local PIO, other useful contacts with local government include:

- Advisory boards
- City council
- County commission
- Planning and zoning commission

Additionally, the local government may have oversight regarding the airport, the animal shelter, and a host of other entities. If the government provides a budget or personnel, expect that agency to fall under this beat's responsibilities.

Military

Of all of the beats listed, the restrictions placed upon military reporters make it the most difficult to cover. The personnel involved are extremely limited in what they can say on-camera; even a military base's PIO may not be able to say much. Also, if reporters have limited military knowledge, their civilian background will hamper their reporting. After all, why should a serviceman trust a reporter who can't even tell the difference between a lieutenant and a sergeant?

FIGURE 5.8

A military beat can be the hardest to cover.

In addition to the following sources listed, some stories may be found at local businesses that serve military personnel. If the base is closing or the soldiers are being deployed, the businesses suffer. Conversely, when the soldiers come home, those shops and restaurants are among the first to benefit. For starters, the military contact list should include

- Collegiate ROTC groups
- Military bases' PIOs
- National Guard units

FIGURE 5.9

Members of the U.S. media embedded with U.S. Marines (courtesy of Richard Ellis/Getty Images).

- Recruiting offices
- Veterans' groups

The Department of Defense's official Web site, www.defenselink.mil, provides a wealth of data sources. It is also a good idea to bookmark the branch of the military that impacts your area. For example, if you have an Air Force base in your region, you should add both www.af.mil and the base's individual Web site to your list.

Science/technology

Science and technology are both broad categories, spanning fields ranging from astronomy to zoology. Most reporters specialize in technological advances that impact consumers directly. Because cell phones, high-definition television, and computer software stories evolve on an almost-daily basis, there is ample opportunity for reporters who can keep up. One successful nationally syndicated radio program, *The Kim Komando Show*, thrives on such technological stories.

The greatest challenge with developing a list of local contacts is that many will be vendors of specific products. For example, because those most knowledgeable about cell phones will likely be those who sell the phones, the stories can quickly become nothing more than thinly cloaked advertisements for one product over another.

One good starting point would be a local university, where the faculty will have specialized training in the technological fields and can give impartial interviews. Otherwise, proceed very cautiously, lest you become a cheerleader for one store or another.

Sports

Covering sports is the same as covering any other beat, except that viewers have come to expect it in their nightly newscasts; there may very well be a newscast without a health story, but sports never gets a day off. Sports reporters must have an in-depth knowledge of all local sports teams, rivalries, star players, coaches, playing venues, and countless other details to make their reports better than competing sportscasts. Additionally, they're expected to know about national teams who represent the region in the NFL, NBA, MLB, and NHL.

Many people are attracted to broadcast sports reporting because of their interest in sports and because they think it's more fun than covering city council meetings. The problem is that so many beginners have the same idea that not enough opportunities are available to provide jobs for them all. TV stations that may have six or more general assignment reporters usually have only one full-time sports reporter–anchor.

Sports reporting also requires some additional skills that general reporting does not. Personality has become important; knowing sports inside out is not enough anymore. Most news managers look for sports people who can attract an audience with their style of delivery.

FIGURE 5.10
Dan Patrick of ESPN Radio Network (courtesy of Ray Martin, ESPN).

Good organizational skills also are important. Sports reporters, particularly in small markets, are expected to cover local games and to be able to cut a lot of video quickly from a variety of sports contests that are being recorded throughout the evening. Sports seasons tend to overlap, which means that college and professional football and basketball games are often held at the same times as professional hockey matches, amid a variety of other sports. Many stations also cover high school sports. Collecting all this information and cutting video of all these activities are demanding.

How does a journalism student prepare for a sports reporting job? The best way is probably through an internship. Sports reporters look for sharp college students who know sports and know how to edit videotape. Quick learners may find that they soon cover high school games and even anchor on the weekends. Because most sports anchors, like news anchors, are looking for opportunities in larger markets, frequent turnovers sometimes occur at the sports desk. The weekend sports person who learns the job well sometimes gets the sports anchoring job during the week.

Sports anchors with a lot of talent and personality can demand good salaries in large markets. Like other anchors, they often are subject to the ratings and whims of management. Job security is less certain for sports anchors than it is for most beat and general assignment reporters.

Sports reporters have possibly the easiest list of contacts to compile, especially since all professional teams (as well as most universities) have a sports information director (SID) who serves as a gateway to stories. In addition to these SIDs, the basics of a contact list should include the coaches and star athletes from:

- Local high school teams
- Regional university teams
- Regional and state professional teams
- Stadium and arena officials

FIGURE 5.11

Weather

While none of the previously listed beats requires formal training, weather is its own special niche that has a certifying association. The American Meteorological Society (AMS) oversees a Certified Broadcast Meteorologist (CBM) program. This certification means the holder has both the experience and the educational background necessary to accurately provide weather information to a viewing audience. The AMS previously sponsored a Seal of Approval program, although that was discontinued in 2008.

The current CBM certification is not something to be entered into lightly. Successful applicants must hold a Bachelor's degree in Atmospheric Science, pass an AMS test, and provide a DVD of their weathercasts to the Board of Broadcast Meteorology for review. There is also a fee for the testing: $300 for AMS members and $600 for nonmembers.

Of course, AMS certification is not required to provide the weather outlook to the audience. Those who do not pass the certification go by the title "weatherman," whereas those who have passed the AMS criteria can call themselves "broadcast meteorologists."

If weather reporting is your goal, you also have to learn about computer and chroma-key (special effects) technology. Jerry Brown, a meteorologist for KVVU in Las Vegas says: "The [reporter's] discomfort level in front of the chroma board too often is readily apparent. It's not that the weathercaster doesn't know what to say. The problem is how to visually integrate a storyline and chroma-key graphics into a cohesive 'show-and-tell' presentation."

Brown says weathercasters must "maintain continuous eye contact with one of three monitors, ad-lib and synchronize hand and body movement, all the while pirouetting across the screen. Done right," he says, "it looks effortless." But it's not easy.

Station managers look for personality along with a knowledge of maps, computers, and chroma-key technology. The auditions for weather anchors are considerably different from auditions for beat reporters. Although the news director looks for good writing and reporting skills, the general manager looks for a great smile and a quick wit.

Web sites for those giving weather information are fairly limited, although they can be expanded by adding local farmers, pilots, or others who are directly impacted by the weather. The usual internet bookmarks are

- The American Meteorological Society
- The National Weather Service

It should be noted that most newsrooms have dedicated software for designing weather maps and forecasts; these may also be linked to sources for accurate weather information.

FIGURE 5.12

Jerry Brown, meteorologist, KVVU–TV, Las Vegas, Nevada (courtesy of Eric Foerch).

SPOT NEWS

Chapter 1 discussed spot (spontaneous) news as it relates to traffic accidents, crimes, and breaking stories. Some of these stories, such as the burning of a vacant house, are comparatively simple to cover; a fire blazes, the firefighters arrive, the blaze is extinguished, and there is an investigation over whether the cause was arson. Other stories, such as riots or disasters, have far deeper consequences, impact many more people, and can endanger the reporting crew. For this reason, we'll outline typical spot news scenarios that a reporter may face.

Accidents

Accidents are another common type of spot news stories. Reporters cover a variety of accidents during their careers. When people talk of accidents, they tend to mean traffic accidents, which certainly do provide a lot of news. But many other accidents occupy a reporter's time as well: trains jump tracks, cranes fall at construction sites, children fall out of windows, small planes collide, and buildings collapse. Most of the time, such accidents—and many others—require reporter coverage.

Traffic accidents get the most attention even when they do not result in deaths or injuries. A chain-like collision involving a dozen or more cars on a snow-covered major highway is certain to attract reporters. Radio reporters know that drive-time audiences will be interested because of the effect such a pile-up may have on getting to and from work, and TV reporters and crews want to be at the scene for pictures and interview possibilities. TV audiences, at least in the minds of news directors and assignment editors, are fascinated by the sight of a dozen cars wrecked on a highway. Fortunately, most of those chain-like accidents produce more totaled cars than deaths and injuries.

Other accidents involve airplanes, trains, or other forms of mass transit, but these occur with less frequency. In addition to covering the actual accident, reporters should bookmark relevant Web sites for background information. For example, the National Transportation Safety Board's Web site at www.ntsb .gov provides information for aviation, highway, marine, pipeline and hazardous materials, railroad, and transportation disaster assistance.

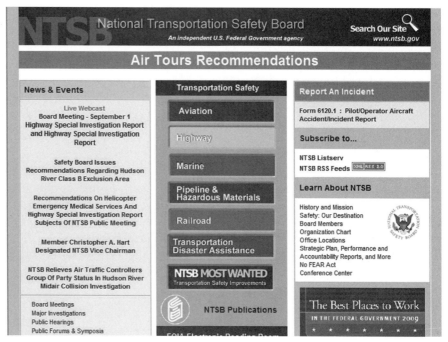

FIGURE 5.13

The National Transportation Safety Board (www.ntsb.gov) provides information on everything from highways and aviation to disaster assistance.

Crime

Depending on the size of the city or town, reporters spend a lot of time covering crime. Wherever police turn out at gang battles, homicides, drug busts, and numerous other criminal activities, you will find reporters and cameras.

The crime that gets the most coverage is homicide. Americans kill one another more than people in any other country, and most of the killings will be reported on radio and TV. Reporters working nights in a large city often get "burned out" covering murders night after night. The scripts all tend to sound alike after a while. Reporters talk to police in an effort to find out what happened and, more often than not, the word *drugs* is in the sound byte. There are sound and video of crying relatives, questions to witnesses, and shots of the body bags.

Crimes other than murder are also news. The decision whether to cover other crimes, such as holdups and gang battles, depends mainly on the circumstances. In a large city, a holdup would warrant a reporter only if people were seriously injured or taken hostage. In a small community, even an injury-free holdup of a convenience store might attract a broadcast reporter to the scene.

It may sound obvious, but reporters must remember that a person charged with a crime is considered innocent until proven guilty. Police arrest a suspect, the district attorney files a charge, and then it's up to a judge or jury to decide whether someone is guilty or not guilty. It is important to remember that many accused people walk out of court free.

Before the courts reach a verdict, a reporter must always say the defendant is "accused of" or "charged with." A reporter must never take on face value what a police officer or detective says at the scene of a crime. A reporter may be told that Kelly Hammer was stopped in his car and a pound of heroin was found in the trunk. It is irresponsible reporting to go on the air and say: "Police find a pound of heroin in a Springfield man's car trunk. Details in a moment."

The words "police say" or "the district attorney charges" are critical, even in a headline. If Hammer is innocent, the station can expect to receive a lawsuit alleging slander. If Hammer is proven guilty, the defending attorney can file for a mistrial, as the station's newscast may have tainted the jury pool. Given these two outcomes, the reporter must ensure that the defendant is treated fairly in any broadcast about a crime.

Demonstrations

The right to demonstrate is a freedom enjoyed by all Americans, and hundreds of thousands of us (maybe more) take advantage of this freedom each year. Radio and TV reporters do not cover every demonstration, but if the organizers know their business, they can almost always orchestrate a demonstration to guarantee media coverage. Regardless of the nature of the demonstration, the primary responsibility of the reporter is to avoid being "used."

With the possible exception of issues of civil rights and U.S. involvement in the Vietnam War, the battle over abortion has brought out more protesters than any other controversy. Americans on both sides of the issue are dedicated to their cause, and they spend a great deal of time either defending or marching against abortion clinics. Because the picture and sound possibilities are always good at such demonstrations, a high percentage of them get radio and TV coverage. The right-to-life demonstrators are likely to have their children in tow and an assortment of picket signs accusing abortion clinics of murder. The pro-choice advocates have their share of signs and are extremely vocal in pleading their case that a woman should have control over her body.

Reporters cannot allow themselves to get caught up in this frenzy. Once the media arrive at the scene, the crowd gets louder and more agitated; the arrival of the TV cameras brings the noise to a peak. If you see this happening, wait until the crowd gets back to normal. Turning the camera off and moving away from the crowd for a few minutes is often effective.

FIGURE 5.14

An antiabortion demonstration in Baton Rouge. Reporters should always present both sides of a controversial subject (photo by James Terry).

The reporter should find a spokesperson in the group and get a statement. It is not the reporter's role to debate the merits of the controversy with the individual. In a demonstration involving a specific facility (such as an abortion clinic), the reporter should also try to talk with someone inside.

Often, both sides show up at the same site, which makes the reporter's job of being fair even easier. Remember that regardless of what the demonstration is about, the reporter must always get the views of both sides.

Disasters

Some reporters never experience a disaster, but those reporters working in tornado or hurricane areas and in cities with major airports will probably cover one eventually. The horror of disasters creates an emotional and trying experience for reporters.

Although it's often difficult, reporters covering a disaster must get the facts straight. That may sound obvious, but because of the magnitude of a disaster,

FIGURE 5.15

Reporters must be careful to check facts when reporting on a disaster.

a lot of confusion ensues. Because so many residents, witnesses, government officials, law enforcement personnel, and various people will want to talk to the press, it is often difficult to tell which version of a story is accurate. A reporter must check and double-check all information. If something sounds suspicious, it should be reported with specific attribution. If there are two versions of casualty figures, for example, the reporter should give both figures (with attribution) and advise the audience of the discrepancy. This approach is better than trying to guess which figures are accurate and running the risk of having to make a correction later. The key point: When in doubt, be cautious.

Fires

The decision regarding whether to cover a fire usually is based on the amount of destruction it is causing. Sometimes a relatively small fire can have tragic results if it occurs in an occupied house, particularly in the middle of the night when people are asleep.

These considerations are on the news director's or assignment editor's mind when news of a fire first breaks. In a large city such as New York, there would not be enough reporters to cover

FIGURE 5.16

other news if reporters were assigned to every fire. There are just too many of them. A cameraperson may be sent to cover a burning, empty warehouse, and the video may provide 20 seconds of footage on the six o'clock news. In the same city, such a fire may not even be mentioned on radio newscasts unless the blaze lasted for hours or caused some tie-up in traffic or injuries to firefighters. In a small town, a fire of any kind may be a major story and may need a reporter at the scene. A fire in a residential area is almost always news, regardless of the size of the community, once it has been determined that the dwelling is occupied and lives are in jeopardy.

Once at the scene, the radio and TV reporters look for the same kind of information: Have any injuries or deaths occurred? Are any people in the building? If it's an industrial building, what is burning? Is the material hazardous? How many firefighters and pieces of equipment are at the scene? How did the fire start? Finally, is arson suspected? Reporters get most of this information from the fire official in charge.

The radio and TV reporters at the fire scene also look for other people to interview—those who escaped from the building, those who might have seen

FIGURE 5.17

A fire in this warehouse in Madison, Wisconsin, caused tens of millions of dollars in damage and kept broadcast news organizations busy for days (photo by Kathy Ozatko; used by permission of the Capital Times).

the fire start, or, in the case of fatalities, friends or relatives of those who died in the building. The radio reporter also records the natural sound of the fire and the battle to put it out, and the TV videographer does the same on videotape.

Rape

This is one of the most controversial crimes that appear in newsrooms as a potential story. Some question the fairness of naming the alleged rapist but not the victim. In the courtroom, one law says a defendant's sexual history is typically considered to be valuable information and should be presented to a jury. The other "rape shield" law says the defense has to prove an alleged victim's sexual history is relevant in order to present it to the jurors.

Rape and sexual assault are common in the United States. Rape can be measured by counting the victims or the assailants and by calculating the financial impact or the emotional devastation. This may be the occasion to document exactly how common rape is and to explore the toll the phenomenon is exacting.

The Poynter Institute suggests that if journalists want to better the public's understanding of the crime, they should look for stories about rape where the victims agree to be named. Finally, reporters should dedicate themselves to reporting on the judicial process. Recognizing the different stigma that comes with being falsely charged with rape, journalists should strive for balance and accuracy in stories about cases where the court system has yet to determine guilt or innocence.

Ultimately, stand for the principles of a noble profession rather than racing your competitors to the depths of an anything-goes-as-long-as-it-sells contest. There is still no justification for journalists to deviate from the standard practice of granting a woman anonymity along with millions of other rape victims.

Riots

Demonstrations sometimes get out of hand and turn into riots. And sometimes riots just break out on their own—in prisons, among workers involved in a strike, or on city streets following a racial incident. The most important guideline is that reporters should never put themselves or their crew in unnecessary danger. It is impossible to determine, or even guess, what an unruly mob will do, and it could just as easily as not turn its anger on the media.

Nighttime is particularly dangerous. Camera lights invite trouble, and most news directors tell their crews not to use them. Today's cameras do a credible job with just streetlights. News managers suggest that crews use telephoto lenses if the situation shows the least sign of becoming dangerous. Helicopters have eliminated some of the danger from covering potentially explosive situations.

FIGURE 5.18

Tragedies

A tragedy is a form of disaster but on a smaller scale. For the friends and relatives of a couple and five children who were killed in a fire, the event is no less a disaster. For reporters, tragedies are often more difficult to cover than full-blown disasters because they become more personal. Regardless of how tough a reporter thinks he or she is, the sight of five small body bags being removed from a burned-out building has a strong emotional impact. Reporters can cry, and sometimes do, alone. They must report such stories as dispassionately as possible and move on to the next one. For some, the emotion is too strong; more than a few reporters quit as a result.

Guidelines for covering violent stories

It sometimes seems as though violence is an inescapable part of our lives. In one form or another, violence touches millions of Americans each year. Even those who escape such horror often know some friend or relative who is a victim of it.

There have been many reports about violence and television, and sometimes it seems as if the two words are synonymous. The debate about too much violence on TV has been continuing for more than two decades. Although most of it deals with violent entertainment and the impact such programs have on children, there is great concern among journalists and nonjournalists that television news also shows too much violence.

FIGURE 5.19

News directors defensively point to society and argue, as we pointed out earlier, that the world is violent and journalists are just reporting what is going on. Much of that argument is valid, but critics maintain that too much emphasis is placed on violence in the news and that it is not necessary to report every violent incident, as it sometimes appears to TV viewers.

News directors counter that they do not cover all violence, and if they did, there would not be enough room in the 30-minute newscast to cover any other news. This discussion examines the problem of violence in the news and how journalists try to deal with it—not only the reporting of it but also how they handle the often gruesome details of the crime, those who commit the violence, and the often-forgotten victims.

One case study involves a school shooting of 25 people in Jonesboro, Arkansas. Although some considered the news coverage excessive, several lessons were learned from the tragedy. The Freedom Forum compiled an extensive report on the shooting coverage and offered the following "lessons for the media:"

- Be wary of unsubstantiated information. Anything not observed by a reporter should be scrupulously attributed.

- Avoid demonizing or glorifying suspects or victims.

- Correct errors promptly and prominently in full detail.

- Obey the law, don't trespass on private property, and respect the privacy of those involved.

- Appreciate the value of veteran journalists who know the community and who have built relationships over the years based on trust.

- Remember that when a disaster or tragedy occurs, coverage should reflect the fact that the entire community may feel victimized, not just those affected directly.

- Understand that viewers are better able to handle the grim details when they are reported in a larger context of sympathetic and extensive coverage that embraces the experience of the entire community.

- Don't hype an already powerful story or tell it in florid language.

- Avoid drawing quick conclusions, making unsubstantiated assumptions, or creating stereotypes.

- Never misrepresent yourself or engage in deception to get the story.

- Report on what went right and what worked when government and the public responded to a major, newsworthy event.

- Remember that trust is the bedrock in the relationship between the news media and the community. It enables public officials to deal openly with the media by providing information that allows the story to be told quickly, completely, and accurately. Trust also helps the community understand the purpose, needs, and duties of the news media.

Further, the RTNDA has a keen interest in how journalists present stories on-air. The Iraq War has presented newsrooms with countless violent images and frequently vocal newsroom debates on what can be shown to the public. RTNDA's ethics committee offered a number of suggestions for news managers for their consideration in deciding whether to use such images and, if so, how. Here are some of the highlights of the guidelines:

- What is the journalistic purpose behind broadcasting the graphic content? Does it materially clarify and help the audience understand the story better? Is there an issue of great public importance involved, such as public policy, community benefit, or social significance?

- Is the use of the graphic material the only way to tell the story? What are your alternatives?

- If asked to defend your decision to show the pictures to your audience, such as family members or stakeholders in the story, how will you justify your decision?

- When is the story important enough to justify replaying graphic material?

- Should you have guidelines or discussions about how to use the graphic material in promos and teases?

- When is a notice to the audience warranted that they are about to see or hear graphic material?

SUMMARY

Most reporting jobs in radio and television are general assignment positions. Reporters with these jobs cover everything they are told to cover, but most of their stories are spot news stories. Spot news deals with everyday breaking stories—fires, accidents, crimes, disasters, and so on.

Some stations and the networks assign beat reporters to cover specific topics, such as entertainment, education, and health. The burden on these reporters is that they must justify their existence with every newscast, unearthing stories in their area that are relevant enough to earn a spot in the news rundown.

Of course, a reporter can try for the best of both worlds: have the competence to cover a spot news story while also being the "go-to" reporter for a beat such as education or local government. This can be difficult to pull off well (nobody wants to see the sports reporter at the scene of a double homicide) but reporters who are adept at producing stories may find themselves as an invaluable part of the news team.

Test Your Knowledge

1. What are spot news stories? Give some examples.
2. What factors are considered when deciding to cover a crime or a fire?
3. Journalists must be especially careful with stories about defendants in a criminal case. How is that done?
4. What are some of the advantages and disadvantages of having beat reporters in a newsroom?
5. Out of the beats listed in this chapter, which one do you think would be the easiest to cover in your market? Which would be the hardest? Why?

EXERCISES

1. Arrange with a news director or assignment editor to follow a reporter when he or she is assigned to a breaking news story. Report on what happened at the scene and how the reporter covered the story.
2. Monitor a local TV newscast and see how many spot news stories were reported. What other types of stories were in the newscast?
3. Watch a week of TV newscasts on the same channel and identify which reporters have a beat, such as health, education, or local government.
4. Pick a beat and create a local database of news sources. Expect to compile a list of at least 10 names, complete with phone numbers and email addresses.
5. Focus on one spot news story, such as a fire or crime, which has received both television and newspaper coverage. Analyze how the two media varied in their coverage of the same event.

PART

2

Writing the News

CHAPTER 6

Newswriting Mechanics

KEY WORDS

Conversational Style
Slugs

Split Page
Teleprompter

Timing
Wire Copy

CONTENTS

INTRODUCTION

The mechanics of crafting a broadcast news story are unlike the parameters of most other writing formats. Here, brevity is cherished, holding the audience's attention is vital, and accuracy is absolutely paramount. Many stories last no more than 30 seconds, while some bumps and teases are a quick 5 seconds. Even more daunting for broadcasters is they have but one opportunity to unveil the story; unlike print media, the consumer cannot go back and reread the story.

Moreover, viewers and listeners of broadcast news are often distracted and only give partial attention. Radios offer news while drivers motor along at high speeds in one-ton vehicles. Television newscasts are watched by viewers who may be eating, cleaning, or simply walking through the room. There is no captive audience; thus delivering the news must be crisp, clear, and easily understood.

The broadcast industry's style of newswriting deals with how to attribute quotes, round off numbers, avoid clichés, and a number of other techniques—these are explained in the next chapter. Here, we address the small but essential details of preparing a script correctly, starting with how to format the script's page correctly.

SLUGS

Every page of the news script must be identified. These identifications are called slugs and are placed in the upper left-hand corner of the page. The slug

FIGURE 6.1

includes a one- or two-word description of the story, such as Forest Fire, Newspaper Strike, or Missing Boy. The slug also includes the date, the time of the newscast, and the writer's initials. Here's an example:

Kids' Band
4/25/10
6 p.m.
FB

Slugs are important because they allow the writer, producers, anchors, director, and a variety of other people involved in putting a newscast together to locate a particular story in the script quickly. This can be vital when, for example, the position of the story in the script must be changed or the story must be dropped just as the newscast begins or when it is already on the air.

THE SPLIT PAGE

Preparing a TV script is somewhat more complicated than preparing a radio script. A TV script is divided into two vertical sections and is known as a split page. All technical instructions and identification of video and graphics appear in the left portion of the split page, while the script to be read by the anchor or reporter appears in the right column along with sound byte out cues and times. There are a number of examples of split pages, and how they are used, throughout this book. As you examine those scripts, you will notice that each station has its own way of using the split page. Experienced broadcast journalists adjust easily to the slight variations as they move from station to station.

AVOIDING SPLIT WORDS AND SENTENCES

If there is not enough room on a line of copy to complete a word, the entire word must be carried over to the next line. Words should not be hyphenated because splitting words at the end of a line could confuse the anchor. The same is true with sentences that cannot fit on one page. Part of a sentence should not be carried over from one page to another. Forcing anchors to jump from the bottom of one page to the top of the next when they are in the middle of a sentence invites trouble. It cannot be stressed too often that writers must avoid anything that increases the chance that anchors will stumble over copy.

If a sentence cannot be completed on a page, it should begin on the top of the next page. Type the word MORE at the bottom of the page so the anchors know that there is more to the story on the next page. Otherwise, they may pause unnecessarily, believing a new story starts on the following page. Some newsrooms prefer to use an arrow at the end of the page to indicate more copy is coming.

PUNCTUATION

One of the most frustrating aspects of writing for broadcast journalism is that the traditional punctuation taught in English composition may be discarded. For example, you will use commas to indicate a pause, not simply for grammatical reasons. Some writers use a dash instead of a comma to indicate a pause, but dashes should be used sparingly, usually to indicate longer pauses. Unless you are writing for yourself (when you can do whatever is comfortable for you), you should not use an ellipsis (three dots) to indicate a pause or as a signal that you have eliminated part of a quotation because those dots could confuse anchors. Never use a semicolon.

Capitalize certain words, such as Not and other words you think the anchors should emphasize. This is especially helpful when the anchors might not have an opportunity to go over the copy before they read it on the air. Keep such emphasis to a minimum, as the anchor is usually the best judge of which words to stress.

Additionally, some newsrooms prefer the copy to be written in ALL CAPS, although others want upper- and lowercase letters. This can be done with a click of the mouse in word processing programs, plus teleprompter systems can be preset to offer one style over the other.

REWRITING WIRE COPY

The essence of rewriting news stories from wire services is in relaying the relevant information as concisely as possible. A prime source for information in the newsroom is the wire service. The stories offered may be far too long for your program, thus prompting a quick rewrite. Unlike the inverted pyramid style of writing favored by newspapers, you simply do not chop off the final paragraph of the story for broadcast. Instead, an entire rewrite of the story is in order.

One strategy is to read the story from the wire copy, digest it, and then discard the copy. Then rewrite the story based on what you remember. This allows you to focus more on the essentials of the story. Once you are finished writing, review the wire copy again to check your facts.

You may find it difficult to surrender the wire copy and rely only on memory, but that is the only way to be certain that you rewrite newspaper-style wire copy into conversational broadcast copy. There are wire services that offer a broadcast wire written in a conversational style, but those are not always available in all newsrooms.

Getting accustomed to reading and absorbing material and then expressing it in your own words takes practice. Once you have conquered the temptation to refer to the original wire or newspaper copy as you write, you will discover that your broadcast copy will be easy and natural for you, or anyone else, to read on the air.

CONVERSATIONAL STYLE

Writing in conversational style means writing for the ear. Newspapers, obviously, are written for the eye, which means that if readers do not understand something, they can return to the paragraph or sentence and read it a second time. In broadcast news, the audience has no such luxury; they hear the copy just once. As a result, broadcast copy must be written clearly and simply. Thoughts must be expressed quickly with brief, crisp, declarative sentences. They must be aimed at ordinary people, which means the words must be understood immediately, without second thought. If the audience does not understand the copy, nothing else matters.

READING YOUR COPY ALOUD

Reading copy aloud helps you determine when words should be contracted, which words should be emphasized, how clear the sentences are, and how well the copy flows from sentence to sentence. Writers should not be embarrassed about reading copy aloud in the newsroom. The ear, not the eye, is the best judge of well-written broadcast copy. It is almost impossible to catch some poorly written phrases or sentences without testing them on the ear. In particular, you may not realize how complicated a sentence is until you read it aloud. There may also be a case of poor sentence structure or phrasing or you may encounter a situation like this:

> The school superintendent says the new teachers' contracts are the best that can be offered in this tight budget year. When the veteran teachers finally received the paperwork in the mail this week, almost half of them promptly resigned.

Do you see the problem with the final word in the sentence? Did they resign the contracts, binding them to their jobs for another year, or did they resign from their jobs, meaning the school needs to find a new crop of teachers? By reading the copy aloud and hearing how the change in inflection can alter the story, you prevent the anchor from fumbling the story away.

AVOIDING INFORMATION OVERLOAD

Often, copy that is difficult to understand contains too much information in any one sentence, a situation known as information overload. Some of the nation's finest newspapers are guilty of overloading sentences, but, as mentioned earlier, readers can always reread complicated passages. Here's an example of some copy from a major city newspaper and how it could be simplified for broadcast:

> Two weeks into the Congressional debate on taxes, and with at least two more weeks to go, it is clear that Congress will eventually approve a big tax cut, smaller than the $726 billion, 10 year reduction the President proposed but still the third largest in history, on top of the largest, enacted just two years ago this month.

Quite a mouthful. It is not well written even for a newspaper, but in its present form, it would be outrageous to read on the air. For broadcast, we must chop that unmanageable paragraph into separate new short sentences that can be easily understood by the listener.

Our first sentence could start out this way: "Two weeks into the Congressional debate on taxes, it is clear that Congress will eventually approve a big tax cut." Next, we could point out that the debate will go on for at least two more weeks. Our third sentence could deal with the amount of the proposed tax cuts: "The amount approved by Congress is expected to be smaller than the $726 billion, 10-year reduction proposed by the President." The next and final sentence would give these additional details: "The final tax cut is expected to be the third largest in history, on top of the largest, enacted just two years ago this month."

This copy, rewritten for broadcast, can now be understood easily. It would have been virtually impossible to understand the original newspaper copy if it had been read on the air as it appeared in print. Here's another newspaper lead that needs revising for broadcast:

> The Energy Department proposes to spend $2.4 billion next year and up to $3.7 billion in each of the following four years to bring the nation's paralyzed nuclear weapon production plants into compliance with environmental and safety laws, according to Energy Secretary Walter Gregg.

If you read that sentence to some friends and then ask them to tell you what it says, you would probably find that unless they have unusual abilities of concentration and recall, they would be unable to repeat all the details. That lengthy, involved sentence could be turned into good broadcast copy:

> The Energy Department wants to spend almost two and one-half billion dollars next year to improve the nation's nuclear production plants. The funds would be used to bring the paralyzed plants into compliance with environmental and safety laws. Energy Secretary Walter Gregg says the government is willing to spend almost 15 billion dollars over the next four years to continue the cleanup and safety checks at the nuclear weapon production plants.

If you read the new sentences to your friends, they would probably remember more about the story than they did when you read the newspaper version. Let's examine how the newspaper copy was rewritten. First, it was broken into three parts to reduce the number of details in one sentence. It is easier for listeners to understand the information if they hear it in small doses. The newspaper version mentions two large figures, $2.4 and $3.7 billion. In the broadcast version, the first figure was explained in the first sentence, and the second figure was mentioned in the third sentence.

The first figure, $2.4 billion, was rounded off to "almost two and one-half billion dollars." It is best to round off figures and to eliminate use of the decimal in broadcast copy because the result is easier for most people to understand. The second figure, "up to $3.7 billion in each of the following four years," was totaled and rounded off. The result, "the government is willing to spend almost 15 billion dollars over the next four years," is easier for listeners to grasp because they don't need to do the math in their heads. Notice, too, that dollars is spelled out in broadcast copy.

No attempt was made in the first sentence to discuss exactly how the Energy Department plans to spend the money. It was enough to tell the audience that the department wants to spend this money to improve the plants. Now that the audience has digested that information, it is told how the money is going to be used, "to bring the paralyzed plants into compliance with environmental and safety laws." Then, in the third sentence, the audience learns that the energy secretary wants even more money in the coming years to complete the job. Just in case the audience was not paying complete attention, how the money is to be used was mentioned again in the closing words "to continue the cleanup and safety checks" at the plants.

LOOKING AHEAD

Some newscasts alert the audience to events that are expected to happen in the future. The information should be as specific as possible. Two examples are:

The President is expected to leave the White House in the next 15 minutes or so for Andrews Air Force Base, where he'll board Air Force One for his trip to London.

At any moment now, members of the United Nations Security Council will consider new proposals on the crisis in the Middle East. We were told a few minutes ago that members were already beginning to arrive at the Security Council chamber.

This sort of specific time reference adds immediacy and drama. It's much better than offering little more than the bland *today* reference:

The Security Council meets today to consider new proposals on the Middle East.

One final note: Whenever you use a specific time reference, such as *tonight* or *a few minutes ago*, place the reference as close as possible to the verb whose action it describes.

FIGURE 6.2

TIMING STORIES

It is essential to know how to time copy. If you are writing for yourself, use a stopwatch as you read each page of copy aloud and then write the time on the page. Be sure to read the copy aloud because the timing would be different if you read it silently. If you are writing the copy for someone else, it is more difficult to estimate time because everyone reads copy at a different pace. On average, newscasters read at a speed of about 15 or 16 standard lines of copy per minute.

FIGURE 6.3

For television, because of the split page and the potential use of bold type for the teleprompter, most newscasters take about 1 second to read each line of copy; most teleprompter programs have built-in timers, which can be customized for individual anchors. As you become familiar with the equipment you use to write scripts, you'll learn how best to time the material. You must know this information so that you will be able to estimate how many lines of copy you need to write for a given story. You may often be told by a producer, "Give me about 20 seconds."

Test Your Knowledge

1. Why can't you use standard newspaper copyediting techniques when you are correcting mistakes in broadcast copy?
2. What is a slug, and where does it go on your copy?
3. What should you do if you cannot complete a sentence on one page?
4. Why is it important to rewrite wire copy?
5. Why is it important to read your copy out loud?
6. What are the advantages and disadvantages of writing your copy in ALL CAPS versus traditional upper- and lowercase?
7. For anchors delivering the news, how should you use commas, ellipses, dashes, and semicolons?
8. For an 11 p.m. newscast, what time reference would you give to a story about a lunar eclipse that takes place around midnight?

EXERCISES

1. Read through your local newspaper until you find three local stories to rewrite for broadcast. Type the material so each is no longer than 30 seconds.
2. Rewrite a one-page story from a newspaper and, after you have corrected the copy, time it and note the time on the page.
3. Watch two anchors on a local newscast and see how they manage to make pauses in their copy. Do they change their voice inflection, make dramatic pauses, or hurry through stories so they don't run out of breath?
4. Financial stories are notoriously difficult to rewrite in conversational style. Locate one online story from The *Wall Street Journal* and rewrite it for a general television audience with little financial background.

Newswriting Style

INTRODUCTION

Broadcast newswriting style differs from other styles of writing, principally because, unlike most other writing, broadcast copy is written for the ear, not the eye. Thus, it must be delivered in a conversational style that can be understood by a passive audience. Compounding the difficulty is that the audience is typically occupied with other tasks; the radio news audience is often driving a car, while the television audience is frequently eating a meal during the broadcast.

While the style must be easy to follow, it still must maintain its news impact as it fits into a small time frame. Because most newsbreaks are a few minutes long, most stories command less than a minute of air time. In a nutshell, broadcast news must be conversational, timely, easily understood, free from technical jargon, brief, and deliverable to an audience that is likely multitasking.

There are writing strategies for broadcast journalists to accomplish this formidable task. Verbs are constantly evaluated, the newsmakers' identities are shortened, and even the sentence structure lends itself to both accuracy and brevity. This chapter explains the techniques used in news copy that allow reporters to write stories cleanly and concisely for their audiences.

107

FIGURE 7.1

DESCRIPTORS AND IDENTIFIERS

Identifying those in the news poses a harder task than one may assume. Think of an interview subject who presents a business card reading TIMOTHY MOORE, VICE PRESIDENT AND SOUTHEASTERN REGIONAL COMMUNICATION COORDINATOR, FINANCIAL DIVISION, THIRD STATE AND TRUST BANKING, INC. By the time the news anchor reads that entire title, the audience is lost, the anchor is out of breath, and the story is halfway over.

As in the news copy itself, the descriptors and identifiers must be concise. This section reviews what's needed, what can be eliminated, and when the information is optional.

And for the above example? Just call the guy a banker.

Names and titles

Titles are always used before a person's name in broadcast copy; never after it. For example, Secretary of Defense Kenneth Daw should be used rather than, as newspapers write, Kenneth Daw, Secretary of Defense. Using the title first alerts the listener to the upcoming name and reflects conversational style. It is acceptable to break up the name and the title. For example:

> The Secretary of the Navy said today that joint maneuvers would begin in the Atlantic next week. Tony Jarvis told reporters that Canadian and British vessels would join part of the Atlantic fleet in the maneuvers.

If you use names in your copy, make sure you double-check their spelling and pronunciation. If you are reporting an accident or a fire in which there are injuries or deaths, ask the police officer or fire chief to confirm any names you're unsure about. Wire services are a good source for checking names and pronunciations.

Names are not always essential to a story. Scripts written at a small-town radio or TV station should certainly include the names of those who were killed or injured in a fire at the local paper plant. However, the names of three people from another state who were injured on the freeway would be of little interest to the local audience. It would be sufficient to say:

Three Missouri residents suffered minor injuries after their car spun out of control on the freeway and hit a guardrail.

If those three people live in a small town in the station's listening area, then the names and addresses should be mentioned. The story might read:

Three Wheatland people are recovering from minor injuries suffered this afternoon when their car went out of control on the freeway and hit the guardrail. Police identified the injured as Dennis and Samantha Rose of the 300 block of Slater Avenue and Peter Francis, who lives at 177 Sunshine Road.

Some news directors prefer to omit the house numbers, limiting the address to the street. In many cases, the determining factor is the size of the community. A radio station in a community of 5000 will give more details about the injured than a station in a city of 100,000. A newscast in a larger city might merely identify the neighborhoods in which the injured people lived. But in that community of 5000, the second paragraph of the story might give more details:

The injured were on their way home from a P-T-A meeting. The Roses both teach at Richmond High School. They were giving Francis a ride home when the accident took place.

The added details are of interest because in a small community the chances are that many of those listening to the newscast know the three people. If they do not, they may still be interested for other reasons: most of the audience will be familiar with Richmond High School, they may be members of the PTA, and some may have attended the PTA meeting.

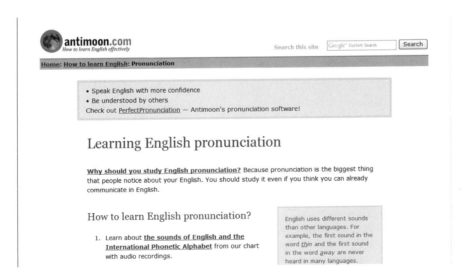

FIGURE 7.2

Correct pronunciation is important. Web sites such as www.antimoon. com can help.

Middle names, initials, and maiden names

Do not use middle names, initials, or maiden names unless (a) the person is known by that name or (b) they are needed in a story to identify people with similar names. Examples of correct usage include

- Former Supreme Court Justice Sandra Day O'Connor
- Edward R. Murrow
- The late President John F. Kennedy
- *Harry Potter* author J.K. Rowling

Foreign names

It is often embarrassing to hear radio and TV anchors trying to pronounce foreign names, whether they are covering distant wars, international summits, or even sports events from abroad. There will be more discussion on pronunciation in Chapter 15, "Delivering the News," but for now remember that foreign names are used in broadcast copy only if they are essential. The names of foreign heads of state, ambassadors, and foreign ministers who are frequently in the news must be mentioned, but secondary foreign officials can usually be identified by title alone.

Additionally, most wire services will provide phonetic spelling of difficult-to-pronounce names for newsmakers (as well as foreign places). It is vital that the anchor is warned in advance that a phonetic name will appear on the teleprompter, as even phonetics can trip up the best anchor on-air.

When a foreign name is used, it must be used according to custom. In some foreign countries, the first name is the important surname, not the last. Most current journalists do not file reports on the late Chinese leader Mao Tse-tung, who was referred to as Chairman Mao. But a recent Secretary-General of the United Nations was Ban Ki-Moon; his correct title was Mr. Ban, not Mr. Ki-Moon.

Ages

A person's age, which is usually irrelevant in a story, may be used if it is significant. There certainly would be no need to give the ages of Dennis and Samantha Rose or Peter Francis who were involved in the earlier accident example. But if the Roses' 5-year-old daughter had been involved in the accident, her age would be worth mentioning because she is so young; likewise, if Francis' 87-year-old mother was in the back seat, her age should also be given.

Sometimes it is also acceptable to give ages in crime stories. If two teenage boys were involved in a hit-and-run accident, their ages should be reported. If an 80-year-old man tried to hold up a bank, his age is the most interesting part of the story because it's unusual to hear of a senior citizen committing such a crime.

If a 75-year-old woman's vehicle crossed a divider and collided head-on with another car, give her age. It could have been a factor in the accident. Perhaps not, but until police determine the cause of the accident, the woman's age should be included. It also should be noted if, for example, police said one of the tires on the woman's car had blown out and possibly caused the accident.

Other reasons for giving ages include exceptional accomplishments or unlikely occurrences. For example:

- A 16-year-old graduates at the top of her law school class.
- A 60-year-old Hollywood actor marries a 22-year-old woman.
- A 44-year-old woman gives birth to quadruplets.

Marital status and children

It is not necessary to specify whether someone is married, divorced, or single unless the information directly relates to the story in some way. There would be no reason to say whether someone who was arrested for driving while intoxicated is single or married. However, when a candidate is running for mayor, most people want to know whether he or she is single or married. It may influence how some people vote. Of course, if an actress has been married seven times and is about to wed husband number eight, that is not only relevant to the story, it is likely the story's lead.

Children and other familiar relations are warranted on a case-by-case basis. If a single woman with 6 children gives birth to octuplets (as famously happened in California in 2009), then the human interest value of the 14 children *is* the story. A school board candidate who has 5 kids in the school system is important; voters want to know if the candidate has a vested interest in the school's success. As with marital status, unless the children have a bearing on the story, they should be removed.

Race

Race should be noted only if it is relevant to the story. For example, you would mention race or ethnicity if a city elected its first Hispanic member of the city council or if an African American graduated at the top of the class in a predominantly white college. Barack Obama's election to the U.S. presidency and the stories that noted his race provide ample evidence of how newscasters referenced his heritage in their broadcasts.

A person's race should be mentioned in a crime story only if it is necessary for identification purposes while police are still looking for a suspect. If a person has already been arrested for a crime, there is no reason to indicate the person's racial or ethnic background.

NUMBERS, CAPITAL NUMBERS, PUNCTUATION MARKS, AND WEB SITES

Nowhere is the difference between print journalism and broadcast journalism more acute than here. Newspapers have the luxury of offering large columns of numbers and figures for readers to pore over, frequently to the point where readers can reread the information to make sure everything adds up. Television and radio journalists simply cannot compete in this arena of news delivery.

Fortunately, there are methods to convey tricky information without sacrificing the news value. The specific details vary from newsroom to newsroom; for example, one news anchor wants the number eleven written as *11*, whereas another prefers *eleven*. These individual differences can be accommodated easily enough if you remember the underlying method for relaying numbers, capital numbers, and punctuation marks. You need to simplify.

Numbers

The fundamental rule regarding the use of numbers in broadcast copy is that they should be rounded off and spelled out when there is any chance for confusion. For example, a budget figure of $60,342,960,000 should be rounded off to "more than 60 billion dollars." Such a figure is spelled out because it would be virtually impossible for a newscaster to deal with all those numbers in the middle of the copy.

The convention is to spell out single-digit numbers, and eleven, and to use figures for 10 and for 12 through 999. For larger figures, use words or word–figure combinations. Here are some examples:

- There are only eleven days left until Christmas.
- There were 45 students in the class.
- There were three people at the table.
- There were 600 prisoners of war.
- There were 75-thousand people in the stadium.

Single-digit numbers with million, billion, and so on are expressed in words, such as: It will take another three million dollars to complete work on the project. Some figures reaching the news desk are expressed in decimals.

- The stock market was up 6.88 points.
- Unemployment was down .01 percent for the month.
- The Navy asked for an additional 5.5 billion dollars.

Some newscasters will say the stock market was up "six point 88," but most prefer to eliminate the decimal and round off the figure to "almost seven points." As for the other examples, recast them for broadcast copy to read, "Unemployment was down one tenth of one percent for the month," and "The Navy asked for an additional five and one-half billion dollars."

Capital numbers

On a computer keyboard, capital numbers are those symbols that are found when the SHIFT key is pressed simultaneously as a number. Moving from left to right, capital numbers are!, @, #, $, %, ^, &, *, (, and). Except for the @ sign, which is used frequently for e-mail addresses and should be written and pronounced "at," these should be avoided. For example, $15 is written "15 dollars"—this is how an anchor would read it on the teleprompter. Similarly, 15% is written "15 percent."

Capital numbers are avoided largely because not all anchors can read the script fluidly if these images are left in the script. Also, if read literally, $15 would be pronounced "dollar sign 15." If it is even remotely possible to confuse an anchor, by all means, spell the wording out precisely.

Punctuation marks

Like capital numbers, several punctuation marks should not appear in a tele-prompter script, such as + or =. While most of this seems intuitive, the trickiest punctuation marks are the quotation marks. Leaving quotation marks in the script may force an anchor to artificially inflect their voice or, even worse, make quotation symbols with their fingers in the air. How to deal with quotes is discussed later in this chapter, but for now, avoid quotation marks in your copy.

Web sites

Pity the newswriters from the 1990s when Web sites were just gaining traction in the media. Before the 1990s, no one bothered with announcing Internet Web sites on the air, simply because they didn't exist. As the Internet and the World Wide Web gained in popularity, 1990s newscasters were compelled to relay complex web addresses, such as "For more information, you can log onto the World Wide Web at H-T-T-P colon backslash backslash W-W-W dot...."

What seemed necessary at the time feels outdated today. It is now acceptable to eliminate all of the above and focus on the address, such as Red Cross-dot-org or White House-dot-gov. The three Ws should be dropped as well, as their commonplace usage makes spelling them out cumbersome. Also, avoid sub-menus that can confuse the audience—if you're giving lengthy Web site addresses full of backslashes, shorten it so only the Web site's home page is given.

As a rule of thumb, no one is watching the newscast with a handy pen and paper, eager to jot down a Web site address. If you keep it short and simple, the viewer can remember it easily enough. If the information is too complex, you have not performed a service to anyone who is watching.

LANGUAGE—USING THE BEST WORDS

Avoiding abbreviations

All words in broadcast news copy, with a few exceptions, must be spelled out. Abbreviations are not permitted because they would force anchors to interpret their meaning, thus inviting confusion and mistakes.

WRONG	RIGHT
Lt. General	Lieutenant General
Ass't. Sec. of State	Assistant Secretary of State
Union Pres. Kathy Bland	Union President Kathy Bland

There are two common abbreviations that are especially brutal to anchors. Read through the following sentence as an example:

Dr. Stanley Nelson of St. Louis lives at the intersection of Ashley St. and Pecos Dr.

Saving a few extra keystrokes, particularly by abbreviating "doctor," "drive," "saint," and "street" is setting your anchor up for failure.

There are exceptions to the rule, as abbreviations are used if the names of organizations are better known by their initials than by their full names, for example, FBI, NBC, and CIA. To make it easier for anchors to read, place hyphens between the letters, such as F-B-I, N-B-C, and C-I-A.

Contractions

Broadcast newswriters must write the way most people speak. When we have a discussion with another person, we automatically do a number of things of which we usually are not aware. For example, we almost always use contractions. We are more likely to say "I'm going to work now, Tim," than "I am going to work now, Tim." And we might add, "Let's get together for lunch again soon" instead of "Let us get together again soon." In other words, if we contract our words in conversation, we should do the same in broadcast copy. Here are some other examples:

- Good Morning, I'm Amy Jerrell with the early news.

- Here's a rundown of the top stories we're covering.

- We've just received word that teachers are walking out of classrooms at West Ridge Elementary School....

- If you're driving to work, expect serious delays on the freeway because of an accident at the Brookwood Street exit....

- There's no word from the mayor yet on rumors he'll resign....

- Those are the headlines. Now here are the details....

In the aforementioned copy, most pronoun–verb combinations have been contracted. However, sometimes—for emphasis—it is better not to contract words. For example:

The mayor says he will seek reelection.

Because the word *will* is key to this particular sentence, it would be better to avoid the contraction *he'll*. The newscaster would want to emphasize the word *will*.

Eliminating long words

Short words are usually easier to understand than long ones and, crucially for broadcast news, where time is precious, they take less time to deliver. For example:

Police *abandoned* the search.

is more difficult to say than

Police *gave up* the search.

Here are examples of long words and some shorter ones that could replace them in broadcast copy:

AVOID	USE
extraordinary	unusual
acknowledge	admit
initiate	start, begin
transform	change

Certain words should be avoided because they are difficult to pronounce on the air. Here are some examples:

AVOID	USE
burst into	broke into
coaxing	tempting
autonomy	independence
deteriorate	grow worse
intermediaries	go-betweens; negotiators

If you are unsure about other words you find yourself using, remember that reading them aloud is the best way to decide whether they are appropriate broadcast words. If a word is difficult to say or sounds strange or confusing to the ear, don't use it.

Conjunctions

Coupling pins such as *but* and *and* are often helpful in connecting sentences or parts of sentences. Using conjunctions to link ideas to one another can often help broadcast copy sound more conversational, although caution should be taken so that they are not overused. Remember also that some conjunctions that work in print, such as the word *however*, do not always work as well in broadcast copy. Use *but* instead of *however* in broadcast copy.

Prepositions

Prepositions can also help make copy more conversational, particularly when used to eliminate the possessive, which tends to make listeners work harder to follow the meaning. Here are some examples; the first uses the possessive:

> The Senate Armed Services Committee's spokesman announced a series of new hearings on budget cuts.

Here is a preposition used in the same sentence:

> A spokesman *for* the Senate Armed Services Committee announced a series of new hearings on budget cuts.

See how much easier it is to read the version with the preposition? It is more natural. The preposition is more likely to be used than the possessive in conversation.

Pronouns

We use many pronouns during conversation, and they serve a useful purpose in broadcast copy. They eliminate the need to repeat a person's name. Some difficulty arises when pronouns are used too far from the person's name or when more than one name is mentioned in the sentence or paragraph. Examine this troublesome use of a pronoun:

> The Boy Scout of the Year award was given to Mike Greene by Mayor Savoy. Immediately after the presentation, he slipped and fell on the stage.

Who slipped and fell on the stage, the mayor or the Boy Scout? The pronoun *he* does not work here because two males are mentioned in the sentence. The person who fell should be identified by name.

Adjectives and adverbs

Like good verbs, adjectives and adverbs sometimes add color to broadcast copy, but for the most part they should be avoided. Many adjectives add unnecessary detail, and rather than enliven the copy, they weigh it down. Here's an example with too many adjectives and adverbs:

> The *diesel-powered* train was quickly moving around the *very sharp* curve when the accident happened. Suddenly, there was a *loud, screeching* noise and the locomotive at the very front of the train *rapidly* started to leave the track.

The sentence would be more effective without most of these adjectives and adverbs because they add little meaning. It is not important to know that the train is *diesel-powered*, because most are. *Quickly moving* could be replaced by the strong verb *racing*, and the adverb *very* could be omitted because intensifiers are "filler" words that rarely add meaning. *Rapidly* could be eliminated because it is a given that the cars would leave the tracks quickly if the train was *racing* around the curve. Finally, *started to leave* could be replaced by the more vivid *jumped*. The cleaned-up sentence would read:

> The train was racing around the sharp curve when the accident happened. There was a sudden screeching noise as the locomotive jumped the track.

Screeching was left in the sentence because it is a strong, colorful adjective that describes the noise. *Loud* was eliminated because a screeching noise is, by definition, loud.

Avoiding clichés

We all use clichés from time to time, but you should avoid using clichés in broadcast copy as much as possible, even though some clichés are heard every night on news programs. For example, killers are often "cold-blooded," "slaughter" is always "bloody," and events "come on the heels of" other events. Broadcasts during political campaigns in particular inundate listeners with clichés, such as "hats in the political ring," "campaign trails," "political hay," and "political footballs." After disasters, rescue workers "sift through the rubble" and "comb through the wreckage." Other tired clichés that should be retired include:

- Airliners that become "ill-fated planes" after they crash
- Politicians and others who "take to the airwaves"
- Lobby groups and others who "are up in arms"
- People who end up "in the driver's seat"
- Facts that are "difficult to swallow"
- Plans brought to a "screeching halt"

- Comments or actions that lead to "a perfect storm"
- Troublesome situations that are a "can of worms"

Why are so many things "put on the back burner"? What is wrong with "delaying action" or referring to something as having "a low priority"? Say simply that people are "delaying" or "avoiding" something rather than "dragging their feet." Police should be "searching for," "looking for," or even "hunting for" a missing person, not "combing the woods" for him or her.

Broadcast writers who use "cooling their heels," "tight-lipped," and "Mother Nature" should be "tarred and feathered." Although some news makers insist on referring to something as being "miraculous," do not use the word to describe some spectacular escape from death or injury unless you are quoting the newsmaker.

"Rampage" is another "worn-out" word that will never go away. Instead of using the cliché to tell a prison riot story, describe what's actually going on inside the prison. For example:

> Prisoners at the Wheatland jail this afternoon took five guards
> hostage, burned cellblocks, and demanded that Governor Rollenhagen
> come to the jail to hear their demands.

A Miami TV station, in its story about the arrest of a suspect in the Florida State University serial killings, reported the following:

> People are breathing easier tonight because a suspected serial killer is
> behind bars.

As it turned out, the suspect was then released for lack of evidence, so we can assume that the breathing in the community became heavier again. Such writing is not limited to news; a network sportscaster reporting about a series of injuries in the NBA wrote this sentence:

> Officials are scratching their heads for an explanation.

These are examples of "lazy" writing. Whenever you are tempted to use a cliché, make the extra effort to think of a fresh way to express your point.

Good grammar and some exceptions

The same rules of grammar apply to both print and broadcast copy most of the time. Writers do take a few liberties in broadcast copy because of its conversational nature. Verbs can be dropped from some sentences, as is done frequently in conversation.

For example, if you are talking to your letter carrier and say, "Looks like snow today, Ally," no one is going to object because you did not say, "It appears as if we are going to receive some snow today, Ally." Therefore, it would be natural for a newscaster to say, "Three injuries tonight on the turnpike, that story when we return." Few people will take offense because the newscaster did not say "*There were* three injuries tonight on the turnpike."

LANGUAGE—USING THE BEST PHRASING

Active and passive voices

Eliminating words (and therefore saving precious seconds) is crucial in any news script. The active voice speeds up copy and gives it more punch because it focuses on the action rather than the receiver of the action. Nowhere is this forgotten more quickly than by writers who prefer the passive voice over the active voice. A few examples are:

Passive
Nine hamburgers were devoured by the hungry dog.
The motion was approved by the Senate.
The game was won by the Wildcats.

The easiest way to identify passive sentence structure is to find the word "by." If "by" appears in a sentence, see if a quick rewording will make it briefer and clearer.

Active
The hungry dog devoured nine hamburgers.
The Senate approved the motion.
The Wildcats won the game.

Modifying phrases

Some writers, in their eagerness to tell the story, often get the details right but confuse the meaning of the sentence. When you use modifying phrases, be sure to place them as close as possible to the word(s) they describe or identify, such as:

The two cars collided in heavy rain on Interstate 95 during the rush hour.

It's true that the "heavy rain" did fall on the highway, but it also fell elsewhere. When recast to be less ambiguous, the sentence would read this way:

The two cars collided on Interstate 95 in heavy rain during the rush hour.

Avoiding relative clauses

Other sentences that produce information overload are those that contain relative clauses. Relative clauses are introduced by the relative pronouns *who*, *which*, *that*, *what*, *whoever*, *whichever*, and *whatever* and add information to simple sentences. Newspapers often use relative clauses to stress one point about a person or thing over another in a particular sentence. Because relative pronouns refer to nouns that precede them, TV and radio audiences may have trouble identifying the noun and pronoun as the same person or thing. Take this example found in a newspaper:

> The comments from the State Department spokesman came in response to a report in the English-language Tehran Times, which quoted a source as saying Iran would definitely intercede to gain the release of the hostages if Washington gave assurances it would release frozen Iranian assets.

Whereas newspaper readers would immediately know that *which* refers to *Tehran Times* because the words are next to each other, a broadcast audience might have to stop and think about what *which* refers to. When this copy was rewritten for broadcast, the relative pronoun *which* was removed and the sentence was cut in two. The noun *newspaper* was used again instead of the pronoun:

> The State Department spokesman made the comments after a report appeared in the English-language newspaper The Tehran Times. The newspaper quoted a source as saying Iran would definitely help win release of the hostages if Washington promised to release frozen Iranian assets.

Other changes included recasting the passive construction in the first sentence as active and replacing the phrase *intercede to gain* with the single word *help*. Likewise, *gave assurances* was simplified to *promised*. The second version is better for a broadcast audience because it does not use pronouns or wordy phrases that could cause misunderstanding.

Which, when used as part of a clause that adds descriptive detail about a noun, also presents unnecessary problems for broadcast writers. Take this print copy:

> Two people were killed today when a small plane, which was on a flight from Key West to Miami, crashed into the ocean off the coast of Key Largo.

All these details will be simpler for your audience to digest if you give the number of dead and where the crash took place in the first sentence and explain the departure and destination of the plane in the second sentence. Here's a broadcast version:

> Two people died today when a small plane crashed into the ocean off the coast of Key Largo. The plane was on a flight from Key West to Miami.

Relative clauses introduced by *that* contain information important to the meaning of a sentence, not just additional details. For example,

The truck that jackknifed on the freeway today was carrying flammable liquid.

The *that* clause identifies which particular truck was carrying flammable liquid.

In some sentences, *that* can be omitted because the sentence sounds more natural and is clear without it. Compare the following two sentences.

The governor says that he'll leave the capital by plane this evening.

The governor says he'll leave the capital by plane this evening.

Dropping *that* makes the sentence more conversational. While you shouldn't always delete every *that* you see in a sentence, always double-check whether you need it.

VERBS

Without using a thesaurus or help from the Internet, imagine people walking down the street. But *walk* is a bland verb. Did they *shuffle, saunter,* or maybe *stroll*? If they were slow, they likely *dawdled* or even *wandered,* but a faster clip warrants a quicker verb, such as *hustle* or *stride*. Each of the just mentioned verbs is fine to use, yet the connotation conveyed by each implies a unique image.

Furthering complicating verbs is the fact that the tenses used in newscasts frequently shift, even within the same story. And since many news stories are *current* updates of *previous* events that may affect viewers *in the future,* it's easy to fall into the grasp of some truly tortuous phrasing. This section examines how critical it is to ~~use~~ have ~~utilize~~ apply ~~handle~~ employ the correct action verbs.

Be ...ing verbs

Some verbs are candidates to be the first words that may be excised from a news script with little difficulty. Compare the following sentences:

The Wheatland Middle School will be hosting an open house Friday.

The Wheatland Middle School will host an open house Friday.

The impact and factual information is the same, yet the second sentence is tighter than the first. The difference is the *be ...ing* verbs. Instead of "will be hosting," it is cleaner to write "will host." If a team "will be playing," write that the team "will play." As a quick guideline, when you see the word "be" followed by a verb ending with "...ing," check whether you can drop a few words. Not only does it clean up the written copy, it will also simplify the sentence for the audience.

Present tense

Broadcast news must always present an image of immediacy. Without deceiving an audience by treating an old story as if it were fresh, the broadcast newswriter's job is to tell the news as though it is in progress or has just recently happened. If a story is still developing or has just cleared the wires, a newswriter should make it sound as new and exciting as possible because most of the audience will be hearing the story for the first time. Use of present-tense verbs, particularly present-progressive verbs, which suggest ongoing action, adds to that immediacy. For example, in covering a meeting at the White House that is still in progress, a writer would best say:

> The President is meeting with his cabinet this morning to discuss the budget.

Only if the meeting had ended by the time of the newscast would the writer use the past tense:

> The President met today with his cabinet to discuss the budget.

When writers use the past tense, they tell the audience that the event has already taken place, even though some aspect of it may actually still be in progress. Look at the following examples to see how the present-tense verbs focus on the continuing action:

> *Poor:* Members of Congress ended their session today and headed for home.
> *Good:* Members of Congress are on their way home today after ending their session.
> *Poor:* A hurricane warning was issued tonight for Florida and Georgia.
> *Good:* A hurricane warning is in effect tonight for Florida and Georgia.

Present perfect tense

Another verb tense that gives a sense of immediacy is the present perfect, which suggests that an action started in the past and is continuing into the present. For example,

> The President has left Camp David for Andrews Air Force Base.

The present perfect tense is useful when the status of the story is not certain. In this case, it may be known that the president left Camp David, but it may not be clear when he is going to arrive at Andrews Air Force Base.

Mixing tenses

Because a news story may mention events that happened at different times or may report a statement that still holds true but was made earlier, it is acceptable to mix tenses in broadcast copy. For example, a story may begin with the present tense and then change to the past tense in later sentences so that the story makes sense. Here's an example of changing tenses:

> Mayor Savoy says he hopes to keep property taxes at their present level. He made the comment during a speech earlier today before a meeting of the Chamber of Commerce. The mayor told the group he expects an improving economy and a reduction in city expenses will eliminate the need for higher property taxes.

The first sentence uses the present-tense verb *says*, but the rest of the paragraph uses past-tense verbs because it would sound strange to continue the present tense once it is established that the mayor made the comments earlier in the day. But suppose the mayor has not yet delivered the speech. The story might be handled this way:

> Mayor Savoy says he hopes to keep property taxes at their present level. He will say this tonight in a speech to the Chamber of Commerce. The mayor says he believes that an improving economy and a reduction in city expenses will eliminate the need for higher property taxes.

In this case, the present tense is used to describe opinions the mayor holds now, and the future tense is used to describe when he will express those opinions. The fourth and fifth sentences might continue with the future tense:

> The mayor will also tell his audience that he expects to attract new business to the city. He'll say he has a promise from Governor Rollenhagen for extra state funds to take care of the city's needy.

Says and related verbs

Don't be afraid to use *says*. Many writers think they have to find different ways to avoid using a form of *say* because they think it is a boring verb. As a result, they will use forms of *exclaim, declare, assert, announce,* and other words that they believe mean the same thing as *say*. The problem is that these other words are not synonyms for *say*; each has a different connotation.

Although these verbs should not always be used in place of *say*, sometimes they do describe the situation accurately. For example,

> Serbia declared war today.

> The White House announced that Peter Morgan would become the new Secretary of the Interior.

As for *assert*, it is difficult to think of an occasion when it would be appropriate to use that word in broadcast copy. In writing broadcast copy, look for strong verbs that describe the action vividly:

> *smother*, rather than *put down*, an uprising
> *snuff out*, rather than *defeat*, a rebellion
> *echo*, rather than *repeat*, an opinion
> *clash*, rather than *disagree*, over strategy
> *lash out at*, rather than *attack*, opponents
> *muster*, rather than *collect*, enough votes

When choosing verbs, think about the image you want to create. For example, a tornado *roars*, but it also can *sweep* through a neighborhood. A hurricane can *hit* a beachfront, but *demolish* gives a stronger picture. A high-school student might be *expelled*, but a deposed leader would be *exiled*. Battalions can *move* through the desert, but if they are doing it quickly, they might be *racing* through.

ATTRIBUTION, QUOTES, TIME, TRANSITIONS, AND LOCATIONS

Attribution

Proper attribution is one of the basic requirements of good newswriting and reporting, whether for newspapers or broadcasts. For the most part, newspapers use attribution at the end of a sentence, what is called *dangling attribution*. For example,

> Hundreds of people have been killed in Russian army attacks, according to the Associated Press.

Attribution in broadcast copy, if used in the lead sentence, is always at the top of the sentence. This makes the writing crisper, creates a sentence structure in which active verbs are more prominent, and requires fewer words. The same information in broadcast copy reads:

> The Associated Press reports hundreds of people have been killed in Russian army attacks.

The attribution can also be *delayed*, that is, it can be mentioned in the second sentence. For example,

> Hundreds of people reportedly have been killed in Yugoslav army attacks on Croatia. That report comes from the Associated Press.

Using quotes

Most of the time, quotes are paraphrased in broadcast copy. Newspapers have the luxury of providing long, detailed quotes of politicians, government officials, and other newsmakers. But broadcasting time restrictions require a distillation of such information. There will be times, because of the importance of statements, when direct quotes can be used. Even then, the writer must keep them to a minimum. Here is a sample of a quote that appeared in a newspaper:

> "This is an example of the worst brutality I have ever come across," was the way the judge described the beating of a man arrested by police.

There are two viable options for broadcast copy. In the first, the quote is maintained. In the second, it is paraphrased.

> The judge said the police beating of a man under arrest was—in his words—"the worst brutality I have ever come across."

> The judge described the beating of the arrested man as the worst brutality he had ever come across.

If a quote is too important to paraphrase, the actual words must be used. Most broadcasters avoid saying "quote" and "unquote" at the beginning and end of a direct quote, but you may sometimes hear them on the air. There are better ways to handle a direct quote, such as

> The Senator said the Republican sponsored welfare reform bill would—and this is a direct quote—"take food out of the mouths of poor children."

Some newscasters will use a direct quote after saying "and these are the president's exact words." Other anchors will simply pause a second before a direct quote and change the inflection of their voices, but not all newscasters do this effectively. If you are writing the script, be explicit and use an introductory phrase to indicate you will be quoting someone directly.

Expressing time

Because broadcast news usually reports or describes events that are currently happening, it is not always necessary to use the word *today* in broadcast copy. If events are not current, point that out quickly.

If a story says that 18 people have been injured in a train crash in Wheatland, listeners are going to assume that the accident occurred today unless the broadcaster explains that it happened last night or

FIGURE 7.3

at some other time. Repeating the word *today* throughout a newscast, then, would become tiresome.

Those writing or reporting for an evening or late-night newscast should be specific. If the story is about something that is happening while the newscast is on the air or took place a short time earlier, the copy should stress the word *tonight* or use a phrase such as *at this very moment, a short time ago, within the past hour,* or *earlier this evening* to alert the audience that this is fresh news.

A story should never lead with the word *yesterday*. If a story happened the day before, something new must be found to freshen the story and eliminate *yesterday* from the lead. Otherwise, it simply isn't news.

Finally, there is a danger in overwriting time elements regarding future events. You need not say that an event will occur at *seven p-m in the evening*; either *seven p-m* or *seven in the evening* will work. Or what about a football game scheduled for this Saturday? Just say it's coming up *Saturday* without the date. It's pointless to say *Saturday, April 26th*, unless there are a number of Saturdays between then and now. However you would say the day conversationally to a friend is probably right.

FIGURE 7.4
Newsroom at WAFB-TV, Baton Rouge (photograph by Christopher J. Rogers).

Transitions

Transitions are phrases and words that signal relationships between sentences. Some broadcast newswriters use transitions to carry listeners from one story to another; however, in a newscast, transitions should be used with care and in moderation. If a transition is natural, it can be effective, but most transitions tend to sound contrived. Here's an example of good use of a transition:

> Wheatland Mayor Paul Savoy is flying to New York City at this hour to take part in talks with other mayors on how to deal with Washington's cut in funds for American cities.

> Also traveling today is Wheatland Police Chief Frank Aiman. He's on his way to Chicago to meet with officials in that city to discuss the fight on drugs.

The transition *also traveling today* works here because it links stories about similar events of equal importance. But here's a bad example:

> Wheatland Mayor Paul Savoy is flying to New York City at this hour to take part in talks with other mayors on how to deal with Washington's cut in funds for American cities.

> Also traveling tonight, Hurricane Dorothy. It's headed our way at about 10 miles an hour and could slam into the mainland in the morning.

In this example, the transition is forced. Unlike the natural connection of two city officials who are traveling on government business, there is nothing logical about connecting the movement of the mayor and that of a hurricane. That example was not made up. The names have been changed, but the transition tying together the movement of an official and a hurricane was actually broadcast. Here is another example of an effective transition:

> The Justice Department wants to know if there are patterns of police brutality anywhere in the country. The Department has ordered a review of all police brutality complaints filed with its civil rights division during the last six years. The order comes after the police beating of a motorist in Los Angeles.

> Los Angeles isn't the only place where authorities are investigating allegations of police brutality. In Georgia, witnesses say more than a dozen police officers pounced on a suspected prowler they caught after a chase from Atlanta to Stockbridge. The Atlanta and Clayton County police departments are conducting internal investigations.

Locations

Your viewers know where New York and Chicago are located, so don't waste their time with New York, New York, or Chicago, Illinois. The same holds true with smaller communities near you; if a suburb or nearby town is fairly well known, you can drop the name of the state.

Exceptions are rare, but they happen. There are a number of cities named Springfield, including those in Illinois, Massachusetts, and Missouri. If there may be confusion with your audience, it is better to be precise.

People, not persons

Our final style note concerns the use of the term *people* as opposed to *persons*. When more than one person is involved in a story, it is more conversational to refer to them as *people*, even though some style books continue to insist that a small group be referred to as *persons*. For example, in conversation we are more likely to say that "five *people*" are going to join us for dinner than we are to say that "five *persons*" will be joining us.

SUMMARY

This chapter suggests that you use conversational style in writing broadcast copy. The material in the chapter is meant to help you learn to write as you speak. Most of us use brief sentences, with few subordinate clauses, and choose easy-to-understand words in everyday conversation. Communicating information to a radio or TV audience is best done in everyday language, simply and with sincerity. As always, if you are unsure of your script, read it aloud to hear whether it sounds natural or forced. Your ears, not your eyes, will tell you if your copy is good.

The keys to solid newswriting must be broken down by how the overall story is phrased, which individual words are selected, and how those words flow in a sentence. Unlike traditional print writing, broadcasters must make sure their descriptors and identifiers are correct, their abbreviations are understood, their attribution precedes the information, adverbs and adjectives appear only when needed, appropriate verbs are used, phonetic phrases are dropped in at the right times, lists of numbers aren't confusing, and a score of other broadcast style rules are followed. If that weren't enough, the writers must also adhere to conversational style, make sure their news copy is accurate, and wedge all of the relevant information into a finite parcel of air time.

Done correctly, newswriting is natural, compelling, and "sounds" right. Remember, although it may feel counterintuitive for television newsrooms, a newscast can survive without compelling video footage as long as it has a strong script. But all the video in the world will not save poor writing.

Test Your Knowledge

1. Where would you use contractions in the following sentences?
   - The governor says he will leave on vacation tomorrow.
   - There will be a dozen people at the reception.
   - The workers say they will walk off the job at noon.
   - Here is the latest word from the Weather Bureau.
   - Now let us take a look at what happened in baseball tonight.
2. What's wrong with the following sentence, and how could it be improved for broadcast?
   Two years after the crash of a helicopter into the Washington channel, the D.C. Fire Department has not provided scuba equipment and training for its fireboat personnel, despite an order from Congress to do so accompanied by an appropriation to pay for it.

3. Here is another complex sentence. How could you improve it for broadcast?

Higher rates for electricity could be one result of the miners' strike against the Pittston Coal Company, which has forced some utilities to curtail sales of power to neighboring companies and to buy more expensive types of fuel, according to an industry spokesman.

4. Here are words that are not particularly good for broadcast. Think of an appropriate substitute for each.

emblazoned   facilitate   ascent   perquisites

capitulation   stupefied   exodus   disperse

5. Keeping in mind the suggestions for using prepositions and conjunctions, how could the following sentence be improved for broadcast?

The circus' chief lion trainer did not take part in the show because he was sick. However, the apprentice trainer took over and his performance was loudly applauded.

6. There's a pronoun problem in the following sentence. Identify it and explain how the sentence should read.

The governor accused his opponent, Taylor Bean, of mudslinging. After the exchange, he predicted he would win the election.

7. What words and phrases could you use to replace the clichés in the following sentences?

- The prisoners rampaged for more than an hour.
- The White House announcement came on the heels of Iran's invasion of Iraq.
- The Republican candidate said he had no doubt that the tax issue would become a political football.
- The loss of the home team and the amount of alcohol sold to the crowd led to the perfect storm of a riot.

8. What's wrong with these sentences?

- There was applause when the birthday cake was brought out by the chef.
- The robber was grabbed by the sheriff as he tried to run from the bank.
- The financial report was improved by the price of silver.

9. How could the verbs in these sentences be improved for broadcast?

- The teacher declared that the student outing was postponed because of rain.
- The mayor asserted that she would seek another term.
- The president exclaimed that he would go to Camp David for the weekend.

10. What's wrong with the attributions in the following sentences?

- The nation's economy is going to get worse before it gets better, according to a leading economist.
- Hundreds of people were injured in rioting in Los Angeles, according to the police.
- The final football score will be reviewed due to an illegal play, says the head umpire.

11. What's wrong with the transition used to link the following sentences?

Forest fires swept through a number of states on the West Coast today, destroying hundreds of thousands of acres of trees. Also under fire is our town's police chief, who is accused of failing to control some of his officers.

EXERCISES

1. Rewrite the following wire-service sentence for broadcast.

   Thunderstorms that raged through the South, and bad weather elsewhere, have been blamed for at least 23 deaths and the presumed drowning of a North Carolina man swept away by a swollen creek the night before he was to be married.

2. Take a story from the wires or a newspaper. Read it carefully and then put it aside. Now rewrite the story in broadcast style without looking at the copy again. When you have finished, look at your copy and make a note of anything important that you forgot or any information that you wrote incorrectly.

3. Watch a program of any kind on television and then write a story about it, describing it as you would to a friend.

4. Read over your story from Exercise 2 or 3 and make any changes you think will improve the copy. Then read the copy aloud and note any changes you would make that you did not notice when you read the copy to yourself.

5. Using stronger verbs, rewrite the following copy.

   ■ An earthquake has hit San Francisco. Police say several people may have been killed. There is no report on injuries. But rescue workers looked through several wrecked buildings for possible victims. Hundreds of frightened residents left their homes. It was the strongest quake to hit the city in several years.

   ■ Power lines were down in some areas. Police say they fell when cracks developed in the pavement.

   ■ Utility company officials are in the area to examine damage. They said some power lines were broken during the quake and present a danger.

6. Find two related stories on the wires or in the newspaper. Rewrite them in broadcast style and use a transition to tie them together.

7. Using wire copy or newspaper stories, find three sentences that use the passive voice and rewrite the sentences in broadcast style.

8. Find as many verbs as you can on the front page of your local newspaper that you feel could be stronger or more colorful. Replace them.

9. Look through your newspaper for words that you feel are too long or might be difficult for a broadcast audience to understand. Look them up in a dictionary or thesaurus to find synonyms that would be more appropriate for broadcast copy.

Writing Compelling Leads

CONTENTS

INTRODUCTION

The *lead*, which is the opening sentence of a news story, is the most crucial element of any report. In a matter of seconds, the viewer (or, in radio, the listener) makes a decision whether to listen to the story actively or to merely "tune out" until something more interesting comes along. Even worse, the audience may simply move to another station with a more compelling story.

However, this vital part of the story, which passes by in less than 5 or 6 seconds, is the most difficult to write. It must set the tone for what follows, provide enough information to intrigue the audience, and offer enough news so it simply doesn't burn away precious seconds.

While there are few "perfect" leads, some are better than most. As you pursue a career in journalism, you'll encounter those leads that are memorable, those leads that are acceptable, and those that are simply not very good. And because all news stories are different from one another, you'll also learn that different methods can solve the challenges in writing good leads.

THE FIVE Ws AND H RULE

Unless the story is a feature, the lead must include an element of news. It must begin to address the traditional journalistic concept of discovering information. To guarantee that all of the important news elements are reported in a story, journalists have devised a rule that requires newswriters to answer six

131

basic questions: *who, what, where, when, why,* and *how.* This rule is referred to as the *five Ws and H rule.*

At one time, most newspaper editors expected every lead to answer all of these questions. But few newspaper editors still require this, and broadcasters never follow the rule. Still, at least one or more of the questions must be answered in the lead of the story for it to be news. By the end of the story, most—if not all—of the questions should be answered.

An opening sentence that contains no news is referred to as a *nonnews* lead, and such leads are unacceptable in a news story. Here's an example from sports:

Mayor Paul Savoy has met with reporters.

This lead could become news by answering some of the journalistic questions. *Why* did the mayor meet with reporters? *What* did he tell them? For example,

Wheatland Mayor Paul Savoy says the city council has two budget choices this month—either raise property taxes or close two of the fire stations.

This revised lead does not deal with all five Ws and the H, but it's a start. The *who* is the mayor. The *what* is the issue of budget woes. The *where* is Wheatland. The *when* is this month. Still unanswered are the *why* and the *how.* These questions would be answered in the balance of the story—if the answers are available.

FIGURE 8.1

An anchor and producer go over a script at WTVJ-TV, Miami (courtesy of WTVJ-TV, Miami).

This revised lead is an example of a *hard lead.* Such leads address the most important aspect of a story immediately. There are a variety of ways to lead your story, and all of them are examined in the following sections. The decision about which kind of lead to use depends on a number of factors, but the most important is the nature of the story. Is it a feature or breaking news? Is the story sad or upbeat? Is it about people or an event? Is the story about politics, a war, a medical development, or the kidnapping of a child? Is the story brand new or a continuing one? The lead is like the foundation of a house. How the foundation is built determines how the rest of the house will look. In news, the lead sentence determines how the rest of the story should be constructed.

THE "RIGHT" EMOTION

One challenge in writing a lead is deciding on the appropriate emotion, or tone, to express in the story. The tone depends mainly on the kind of story you are going to tell. For example, if the story is about something amusing, you would establish a lighthearted tone in the lead. Let's look at an example:

> A Center City schoolteacher got enough kisses today to last—well, maybe not a lifetime, but a few weeks, anyway. Mary Saint Clair kissed 110 men at the annual fund-raiser for the local zoo. At ten bucks a kiss, she raised eleven hundred dollars for the zoo. When she turned the money over to zoo officials, she joked that all the animals were not behind bars.

Even stories about accidents can sometimes be treated lightly:

> "I'll never drink hot coffee in the car again." That's what Carl Wade said when he left the Center City hospital. This morning, his car struck a fire hydrant, bounced off a tree and smashed into the window of a flower shop. Wade said he had bought a container of coffee at a McDonald's drive-through. When he tried to add sugar, he spilled the coffee in his lap and lost control of the car.

Stories about tragedies, as you would expect, require a more serious, straightforward approach:

- It's now believed that the death toll in the earthquake in Mexico has reached more than 50.
- At least three people are reported dead in the collision this morning of a half-dozen cars on the freeway.

For these leads, the writers chose to give just the facts; a decision that creates a quiet tone that underscores the loss of life described in the stories. While every story requires the writer to choose a certain tone, features and nonbreaking news stories allow more flexibility than breaking news. Some writers are very effective at evoking joy, pathos, and other emotions from an audience through the tone they create.

TYPES OF LEADS

If you hand the same news assignment to 50 different reporters, you may likely end up with 50 different lead sentences. Each story presents its own opportunity to craft a good lead, while each reporter brings a unique perspective to that story. While there may not be a lead sentence that every reporter agrees is the perfect starting sentence, a number of options are available to make a lead that is better (or worse) than another.

FIGURE 8.2

Hard and soft leads

In choosing a lead, decide first whether it will be hard or soft. As shown in the previous example, a hard lead tells the audience the vital details of the story immediately. Hard leads are usually used for breaking news:

- At least 30 people were injured in the collapse of the building.

- More than a dozen people were arrested in the drug bust.

- The government announced today that 150 thousand more Americans were employed in November.

A soft lead takes a more subtle approach; it alerts the audience to the news that is to follow. This approach is sometimes called "warming up" the audience. The following soft leads could be used for the aforementioned stories:

- A building collapses in Center City. At least 30 people have been injured.

- A major drug bust in New York City. More than a dozen people are under arrest.

- Improvement in the unemployment figures. The government announced that 150 thousand more Americans were employed in November.

Soft leads may not sound as exciting or dramatic as hard leads, but they do invite the audience to keep listening. Notice that two of the example soft leads are not full sentences but phrases that serve the same purpose as headlines in a print story. Soft leads can be helpful to listeners carrying out other tasks or fighting traffic on the way to the office by giving them time to shift their attention to the news.

Many editors discourage soft leads because they tend to slow down a newscast, particularly if used too often. But if used in moderation, soft leads add variety to broadcast copy. Experienced editors tend to be flexible in dealing with a writer's style, including the kinds of leads writers choose. Good editors recognize that there is not just one way to write a story. They might say, "Well, it's not the way I would have written it, but it's not bad."

Quote leads

Sometimes a *quote*, like the "hot coffee" example used earlier, can provide an excellent hook for a story:

> "It happened so fast, we didn't have time to take a picture. But we know what we saw." Those are the words of a hiker on the Appalachian Trail, who says there's something scary in the North Georgia mountains. Something that looks like Bigfoot.

Here is another example:

> "The first thing I'm going to do is quit my job and take a trip around the world." That's what lottery winner Lawrence Atling said when he redeemed his ten million dollar winning lottery ticket.

FIGURE 8.3
V-J Day Times Square, New York City, August 14, 1945, by Alfred Eisenstaedt (Alfred Eisenstaedt/Life Magazine © Time Inc.).

Quote leads should be used sparingly. Unless the quote is comparatively short, the listener may miss its connection with the rest of the story.

Shotgun leads

The *shotgun*, or *umbrella*, lead can be effective for combining two or more related stories:

> Forest fires continue to roar out of control in California, Oregon, and Washington State. The drought that has plagued the three states is now in its second month. Fires have scorched more than a million acres of timberland in California and another half million acres in Oregon and Washington.

The advantage of the shotgun lead is that it allows the writer to eliminate the boring alternative of reporting the fires in three separate, back-to-back stories. Here is another example:

Congress today is looking at three bills. One would make it easier for police to collect evidence, another would open up more trade with Canada, and the third would put a halt to government bailouts.

Delayed leads

Instead of loading the most important information into the top of the story, the *delayed lead* withholds the most important details for a few sentences.

The scene in the locker room of the Center City Rockets was quieter than usual last night although the team won by three goals. There also was a lot less swearing than usual and no nudity. Also new in the locker room last night was Julie Grice.

The sports reporter for the Center City Times is the first woman to be allowed in the team's locker room. Club officials broke the female ban after Grice threatened to go to court to win the right to enter the locker room after games.

If the delayed lead had not been used, the story probably would have started out this way:

For the first time, last night a woman reporter was allowed in the locker room of the Center City Rockets.

The delayed lead gives writers another option for adding variety to a script, but, like some other leads mentioned earlier, it should not be overused.

Negative leads

Negative leads, which include the word not, should be avoided. A positive lead can easily achieve the same result. There is always the chance someone in the audience might miss the word *not* and reach the wrong conclusion about what is happening. Here are some examples:

Avoid: Striking newspaper workers say they will not return to work.
Use: Striking newspaper workers say they will continue their walkout.
Avoid: The mayor says he will not raise the city sales tax.
Use: The mayor says he will keep the city sales tax at its present rate.

Trivia leads

An occasional bit of trivia in a lead can work well, but the payoff needs to be immediate. A story on the vendor who fills ice machines may be a good feature on a hot summer day, so let's see how a trivial lead can bulk up this feature story. Instead of the standard "As the temperature rises, the demand for ice increases—that's good news for ice vendor Roland DeMarse" lead, let's try this:

The American Beverage Institute says Americans use three-point-two ice cubes in every soda they drink. That number increases in the summer, and that's good news for ice vendor Roland DeMarse.

By this example, you see an immediate tie-in to the story. Although trivial leads should be used sparingly (you don't want the news to evolve into a game of *Trivial Pursuit*), they can be effective in hard news stories as well.

- The governor issued his fourth veto in five days—breaking a record for fast vetoes that had stood since 1868.

- During his career, the quarterback threw for more than 20-thousand yards. That's like throwing the football from City Hall to the state line with a thousand yards to spare.

- Each Wheatland school bus covers nearly 400 miles a week. At that rate, the bus driver would wind up in Alaska by Thursday.

Question leads

The question lead is the easiest lead of all to write. For this type of story, you simply ask the viewer a question such as

- Did you ever wonder how much money it takes to run a school bus?
- Want to know about the big events in the city parks this Easter weekend?
- With summer coming up, are you thinking that it's time to get in shape?

The problem with question leads is that it can lead to very lazy writing; why bother putting a statement in the lead when you can start off with a question? Also, the audience will rapidly tire of the interrogation. Since you are the news authority, you should not put the audience in the position of having the answers.

However, there is one overlooked benefit of having question leads. When you are stuck for any lead for a news story, simply make it a question lead. The second sentence will have the answer to the lead and then you can write the story from there. Once you are finished with the story, go back and remove the question lead! The story will flow from the "answer" you provided. It's a simple trick, yet it will motivate you to getting the story moving along.

UPDATING THE LEAD

News is everywhere. Constant updates from Web sites, streaming video on cell phones, and an endless 24-hour news cycle put pressure on journalists. Obviously, not all news happens at convenient times just before the newscast. Shootings occur overnight, civic events happen on the weekends, and trading on the stock exchange opens nearly 9 hours before the 6 p.m. newscast on the East Coast. How does a reporter provide fresh news to past events?

The answer is to consistently advance and update the story. If a murder occurred, where is the killer? If the civic event is over, are they still cleaning up? If a local business saw big gains in the stock market today, is it part of a trend?

While this chapter focuses on how to write a good lead, seasoned reporters consistently strive to update their stories. After all, the only word that should never be in a lead is "yesterday."

Updating and reworking the lead

One of the most effective ways to attract and hold listeners is to convince them that the news is fresh. There will be days when news is plentiful. But on slow days, newswriters need certain skills to make the news sound exciting and timely. One skill is the ability to update leads, which means finding something new to say in stories used in an earlier newscast. Another is the ability to *rework* the original lead to include new developments. For example, take a story about the arrest of a dozen men on narcotics charges. Police say the men were found in a cocaine "factory" where they were "cutting" more than one hundred million dollars' worth of cocaine.

Here's the first version of the lead:

> Police have arrested a dozen men during a raid on a cocaine factory in Center City. They say the men were cutting more than 100 million dollars' worth of cocaine.

An hour later, the lead might say:

> A dozen men are under arrest after police raided a building in Center City. Police say the men were cutting more than 100 million dollars in cocaine.

Still later, the lead might read:

> Police are guarding an estimated 100 million dollars in cocaine that they scooped up in a raid on a Center City building. A dozen men are behind bars in connection with the raid. Police say the men were cutting the cocaine when the raid took place.

Another possible updated lead might say:

> A dozen men are being held for arraignment on narcotics charges following a raid on a Center City building. Police say they found about 100 million dollars' worth of cocaine in the building. Police say the men were in the process of cutting the cocaine when the officers broke into the building.

As new developments occur in the story, there will be added opportunities to rework the lead. Within a few hours, detectives may reveal details about how they found out about the cocaine factory. They also may give more details about the raid. For example,

> Center City police now say that their raid on a cocaine factory that resulted in the arrest of a dozen men came after two months of surveillance by detectives.

A skilled writer will be able to tell the story many times without making it sound stale. News stories, particularly those that involve crime or breaking news, require regular updates for subsequent newscasts. If stories are not updated, the viewer would be left with never-ending manhunts, ongoing criminal trials, and stock market stories stuck in the Great Depression. Only by updating information do journalists contribute to delivering news.

Constructing the rest of the story

Once you have the lead of a story, its foundation, you are ready to construct the rest of the story by building on the lead. The audience has been prepared for what is to come. Now you must provide the details in a clear and logical manner.

In broadcast news, you can use more than just words to accomplish your goal. You can employ sound on radio and use both sound and pictures to help tell the story on television. Those techniques are examined later. For now, let's just deal with words, starting with a hard lead:

> The chairman of the Joint Chiefs of Staff says U.S. troops will stay in Iraq for a number of months.

The viewers now know part of the story. A military leader is telling them something important: that their sons, daughters, husbands, wives, and other relatives and friends—at least some of them—are not coming home right away. The audience will want to hear the more of the explanation:

> General Nelson Felts says American forces will stay in Iraq to enforce provisions of a pending U.N. cease-fire agreement. He says the troops would also prevent Iraq from developing chemical weapons in the future.

FIGURE 8.4

Now the audience knows why troops will remain in Iraq. What it does not know yet is how the troops are going to prevent Iraq from developing the chemical weapons. The next sentence addresses the question:

> General Felts did not explain how the U.S. forces would prevent Iraq from developing the weapons.

Once the general made reference to the chemical weapons, the statement had to be explained to the audience even if the general did not elaborate. Otherwise, the audience might have been asking the question and accusing the newscaster of withholding the information. Once the main thrust of the story has been covered, the reporter can add more:

FIGURE 8.5

Felts also says he is surprised by the strength of the resistance against the U.S. forces. But the general says that the longer the fighting continues, the more likely it is that the U.N. sanctions will ultimately be felt by the Iraqis.

The general had much more to say to reporters, and newspapers carried the story in greater detail. But the broadcast newswriter, who had eight other stories to cover in a 3-minute newscast, told the Felts story in just 20 seconds. The essential details were given; nothing vital was left out. This is key to broadcast newswriting: condense the important material and eliminate the unimportant without distorting the story or the facts.

SUMMARY

Writing good leads takes practice. Fortunately, this practice can be gained rather quickly as you write copy for ongoing newscasts. If you find yourself stuck on the first few words, try to rough out a question lead. No good? Maybe there's a quote in the story that can rise to the occasion or, if you look hard enough, there may be a bit of trivia to provide a starting point. Some leads may be more appropriate than others, depending on the nature of the story, but remember that there is always more than one way to lead your story.

While the previous two chapters placed emphasis on the mechanics and style of broadcast newswriting, this chapter targeted how to capture the audience in the first seconds of the story. Now that you know how to construct a news story and include all the important details in your story in a logical manner, you are ready to write readers and voiceovers for a newscast.

Broadcast journalism requires a great amount of fieldwork, interviewing, and news packages, which are self-contained stories delivered by a reporter. The following chapters in this text address those topics.

Test Your Knowledge

1. Many writers have problems writing the first sentence of a story. How can they overcome this block?
2. What is the most important part of a news story? Why?
3. Although the five Ws and H rule is basically a print journalism concept, it does have application for broadcast journalism. What are the five Ws and H, and what is the major difference in the way they apply to print and broadcast journalism?
4. What is the difference between hard and soft leads?
5. Do quote leads work for broadcast? Explain.
6. What is a shotgun lead?
7. What is a delayed lead?
8. What is a trivia lead?
9. How do you update a lead?

EXERCISES

1. Using the following information, write both hard and soft leads:
   A tanker registered to the Zabo Oil Company of Panama has run aground. This happened off the coast of Charleston, South Carolina. One half million gallons of oil already have spilled into the Atlantic. It is believed that another half million gallons are still on the ship.
2. Write a quote lead based on the following information:
   A man on welfare, Bill Nelson, found a purse on the street. When he opened it, there was $5000 inside. Nelson counted it a dozen times. After two hours, he went to the police station and turned over the money to the officer at the desk. When questioned about his honesty, Nelson said, "I may be poor but I am honest."
3. Using the information from Exercise 2, write a delayed lead.
4. Write a shotgun lead using the following information:
   Forest fires in Oregon have burned more than 10,000 acres of timberland and the flames are threatening thousands of additional acres. In California, firefighters are battling flames that already have destroyed 15,000 acres of woodland.
5. Use your imagination to figure out ways to update these leads:
   The president is scheduled to leave this afternoon for a vacation in Florida, where he will work on a new budget.
   The hurricane is off the coast of Jacksonville, Florida, and could hit the mainland within the next three hours.
   Striking autoworkers are meeting at this hour to decide whether to accept the auto industry's latest contract offer.
   The countdown has begun at Cape Canaveral for the launching of the space shuttle Atlantis.
6. Using any of the types of leads discussed in this chapter, write a story from the following information:
   Lori and Kevin were married today. It was exactly 30 years ago to the day that they met. When they were teenagers the two had dated for about a year after meeting on a blind date in 1963. "I remember the date, of course, because it was my birthday," said Lori Scott. Lori and Kevin Rowce broke up following a fight. They both married and had children and had not seen each other for 29 years. Kevin contacted Lori when he heard from a friend that her husband had died. Kevin had been divorced a number of years ago. They decided to marry after dating for the past year. They were married on New York's Staten Island ferry. "That's what we did on our first date," Kevin said.

PART 3

Reporting the News

Fieldwork

KEY WORDS

B-Roll
Batteries
Camera Body
Cover Footage
Earphones
Establishing Shot
Filter
Frame

Handheld Microphone
Lavaliere Microphone
Lens
Mixed Light
Nat Sound
Pass
Primary Sound

Room Tone
Sequence
Time Code
Tripod
Videotape
Viewfinder
White Balance

INTRODUCTION

Although we emphasize the need for journalists to develop writing and reporting skills, students also need to acquire some basic technical and production skills, such as how to use video cameras and editing software. These skills are necessary in the increasingly competitive world of broadcast journalism.

Some stations have always required reporters to shoot their own stories, interviews, and even standup reports and then bring that material back to the station where the video is edited for that evening's newscast. At some of these stations, the reporters sometimes even anchor the news and introduce the packages they have shot and edited. The advantage of working at small stations is that you get to do everything and, therefore, have an opportunity to learn how to do everything.

However, interacting with a professional videographer provides many benefits to the field reporter. The videographer is another set of eyes in the field, seeing images that the reporter may miss. They can also troubleshoot most technical problems, drive the news van while the reporter reviews footage, and even serve as a sounding board for story angles and possible interview questions.

145

This chapter introduces some of the technological tools used in broadcast news and the skills necessary to operate them. The first part of this chapter examines the equipment used in the field, while the second part concentrates on the techniques used to obtain the best video and audio possible. Finally, we'll examine the logistical differences when working with a videographer or when operating alone.

FIGURE 9.1

FIGURE 9.2

Microwave dishes outside CNN headquarters in Atlanta (©1992; all rights reserved).

EQUIPMENT

The gear available to news crews changes frequently. Previous newscasters shot on 16-millimeter film before videotape formats were developed. Even these videotapes have evolved, as the old ¾″ tapes have been replaced by new sizes with far superior quality. Because the equipment changes so frequently, this section provides an overview of the gear; the ever-changing specifics will be found in newsrooms across the country.

Make sure all the equipment is operating properly before leaving to do a story. Shoot some video and play it back to be sure that the camera and recorder are functioning. Also, test the microphone and the lights. Don't wait until you arrive at the scene to discover that something is not working. Also, double-check that you have ample videotapes and batteries with you before setting out; these items are so often overlooked that we'll begin our equipment discussion with them.

Videotapes

A critical yet often overlooked component of fieldwork is the actual videotape. Newsrooms use professional formats (such as DVC-Pro or Beta SP) as opposed to consumer formats like VHS. Some stations use "prosumer" formats, such as Mini-DV, which consist of small handheld camcorders.

Regardless of format, all videotape is subject to failure. Extremes in temperature can degrade tapes quickly and even render them useless. Shooting in dusty environments or storing tapes without their plastic cases can introduce debris onto the tapes. They are also more likely to fail over time, as older tapes lose their elasticity and usefulness as they age.

One poor habit that can prematurely ruin footage is consistently shooting from the start of the tape. In this scenario, a videographer puts a 60-minute tape into the video camera and shoots for 15 minutes. At the end of the day, suppose the videographer rewinds the tape to prepare for the next assignment. The videographer then shoots again on the same segment of videotape, making another *pass* on the same segment. By repeating this process for a week, part of the tape is subjected to multiple passes while a large section of the tape remains fresh and unused. Because too many passes will eventually degrade the tape (and thus the image), it is important to use as much of the tape as possible—a quick written log on the tape's label is an easy way to track usage.

Always take more tape than you think you'll need in the field. Even if all tapes work perfectly and don't require replacement, the news crew can be called into action to cover a breaking story. Heading into the field with just one working videotape is inexcusable.

New technology is removing videotapes from the field production as portable hard drives are entering the market. These have not gained acceptance in most newsrooms, as news directors wait for the price to drop before making the transition from tape. As these portable drives become more popular, the same rules apply for field production; make sure you have enough recording space on the hard drive before you shoot, plus protect the drive from extremes of heat and cold.

Batteries and AC power

Like videotapes, batteries require more care than one might assume. Be sure to have plenty of battery power and carry an extension cord and an AC adaptor. Some new batteries will power equipment for up to 8 hours. One good battery and a backup should be all you need to complete your story. Batteries are often the weak link in your equipment chain. It's hard to tell exactly how long batteries will last, especially under different temperature conditions.

A word of caution: Keep all types of batteries away from extreme temperatures. Always keep them as close to room temperature as possible. Batteries can lose their power quickly in below-freezing temperature. Many videographers keep their batteries in inside jacket pockets in winter. Never leave batteries in the trunk of a car or in direct sunlight when it's hot outside, as they will lose their stored energy.

FIGURE 9.3

If you are working indoors and doing interviews, using an AC power source helps conserve your batteries for shooting outdoors. It's also a good idea to carry a three- to two-prong adaptor (because many older buildings do not have three-prong outlets) and a four- or six-outlet power strip.

Tripods

Most videographers who have been in the business for a while have little trouble shooting video with the camera on their shoulders. But even the pros use a tripod for an interview if they have the time to set it up. For beginners, it is best to use a tripod as much as possible, particularly for interviews, because weaving and bobbing heads are not acceptable in professional newscasts.

Try shooting some of your cover footage (discussed later in this chapter) without a tripod when the video is not critical so you can start to feel comfortable with the camera on your shoulder. Unfortunately, many of the cameras used in colleges are difficult to use on the shoulder because they are lightweight models. It is easier to shoot from the shoulder with the heavier, more expensive professional cameras because the weight adds stability.

FIGURE 9.4

Some shakiness is expected when covering spot news. If you come upon a story where paramedics are removing an injured driver from a wrecked car, leave the tripod in the news van and shoot off the shoulder. News directors would much rather see bumpy footage of the actual extraction than a tripod-steady shot of the closed ambulance pulling away.

Video cameras

As mentioned earlier in this chapter, camera operators began with 16-milli-meter film stock, which was eventually replaced by videotape. Now, the shooting platform is again shifting, as digital hard drives are quietly making their way into field cameras.

The primary video formats used in newsrooms today are DVC-Pro and BetaSP; each of these offers exceptional quality. Fortunately, videographers trained on one format can easily adapt to the other, as the basics of video cameras are consistent regardless of manufacturer.

There are three standard components in every video camera: the lens, the body, and the viewfinder. The lens is frequently the most expensive part, as its layers of glass are calibrated to allow enough light in to see the visual image (the aperture), achieve optimum focus of the image (the focal ring), and change the image to appear either near or far (the zoom function).

The body of the camera processes the lens's electronic signals onto the videotape. It also serves as a portable video cassette recorder, allowing the field crew to view, rewind, or fast forward the tape as needed. External microphones and input jacks are affixed to the camera body for recording audio.

The viewfinder is the smallest part of the camera. It transfers the image from the lens to a small viewing screen so the videographer can see what he or she is shooting.

Every video camera used by a field crew will have these same attributes. Because the technology is evolving so rapidly, videographers frequently train themselves on new gear, attend conventions and seminars on digital technology, and read industry magazines about what equipment is being developed.

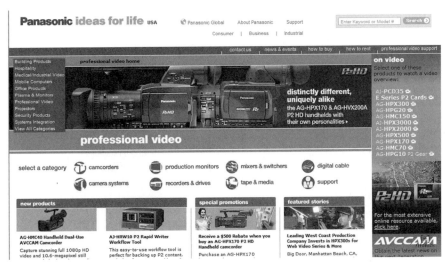

FIGURE 9.5

www.panasonic.com/business/provideo/home.asp.

FIGURE 9.6

VIDEO

Now that we've seen what a video camera can do, let's investigate it further to see how videographers can manipulate the images. Good shooting is well lit, the right color, and conveys the story well. Because poor shooting can ruin an otherwise compelling story, videographers must know the nuances of each camera they use.

Filters

Every camera has a built-in filter system to accommodate different lighting situations. If you shoot indoors with artificial light, you should use a different filter than you would outdoors in natural light. If you use the wrong filters, the colors on the tape will be badly distorted.

Light is measured by Kelvin temperatures, which measures the relative "redness" or "blueness" of white light. Indoor light from incandescent bulbs is 3800K (reddish-orange) and outdoor sunlight is at 5600K (blue). While these Kelvin temperature differences are invisible to the human eye, video cameras cannot shift between light sources of various colors. Thus, if you shoot outside and your camera filter is set for that Kelvin temperature, moving inside with the same filter will result in blue footage.

Cameras may also have additional filters for shooting outdoors in bright situations, such as after a snowfall or on the beach. The initials ND that appear on some 5600K filters stand for "neutral density." These filters produce the same colored video as the 5600K filter but reduce the amount of light entering the camera.

White balancing

Along with filters, a white balancing system is built into video cameras to provide accurate color. To white balance the camera, you must aim it at something white, such as a white wall or piece of white paper, while you push the white balance switch or button on the camera. You must repeat this process each time you shoot at a different location.

All modern ENG video cameras have preset and automatic white balance settings. In the preset mode, the video will look good if the color temperature of the light in which you're shooting is near 3200K indoors or 5600K outdoors. Many videographers use the preset white balance for most of their shooting.

The automatic white balance setting is for use when the light in which you're shooting is not near 3200K or 5600K. Fluorescent lights, for example, are not close to 3200K, so to make the video look right, flip the white balance selector to automatic, fill the screen of your viewfinder with a white object, and then toggle the white balance switch on the camera. This process prevents the video from having a sickly green fluorescent look.

Mixed light

Any light entering a room through a window can cause problems for news videographers. The best practice is to avoid shooting with windows anywhere in your background. Even a window with the blinds closed can create a distracting blue highlight in the background of an indoor interview shot. For a beginner, it is best to shoot the interview either with all artificial light or outside with natural light. If there is enough light coming through windows, the interview can sometimes be shot nicely with natural sunlight if either (a) the outdoor camera filter (5600K) is used or (b) the camera will take a white balance while set to the indoor filter (3200K). Just remember to keep windows out of your background. As you gain experience, you'll learn the various filter and white balancing combinations to use in mixed lighting.

FIGURE 9.7

A WAFB-TV microwave truck prepares to send a live signal to the Baton Bouge station's tower, seen in the distance (courtesy of James Terry).

Most professional news videographers use what are called *dichroic* or "dicro" filters that clip onto the front of their lights. Dicro filters simulate sunlight and allow you to use your artificial light during the day to augment the natural sunlight already present. Dicro filters on a light can be used to illuminate a head when shooting in a room already filled with natural sunlight from windows. Dicro filters are also handy during the day to brighten the face of your subject when you have a bright background, to light a reporter doing a daytime shot, or to brighten a head when shooting during the day in deep shade.

Meanwhile, professional news videographer Lennie Tierney provides these tips to help you avoid mistakes:

- Always check your filter first. It must be on 3200K for artificial light or on 5600K for sunlight.

- When in doubt about lighting color (temperature), check that you are using the appropriate filter and then switch to the automatic setting and white balance your camera on a white object.

- When in a hurry, use the preset setting and the appropriate filter.

Focusing

Poor focus can destroy a story. Tierney advises beginning videographers to focus every shot by zooming into every subject, focusing on it, and then pulling out to set the desired composition. "When shooting a large subject, such as a stadium," Tierney says, "I'd zoom in to the farthest part of the subject, like the backfield fence, focus on it, and then pull out to reveal the entire subject."

Tierney says shooting moving subjects is more difficult, especially in low-light situations such as at some high school basketball games. "It is second nature to an experienced videographer to roll the focus barrel on the camera lens in the right direction in order to keep the subject in focus as it gets closer or farther away," says Tierney. He suggests that beginning videographers practice this technique by shooting people as they walk around the newsroom.

When you are shooting a head, zoom in and focus on the eyes. Most lenses have a "macro" function that allows you to shoot small things at close range, but caution should be used. If your lens is in "macro" function when you are trying to shoot normally, everything will be out of focus no matter if zoomed in or out. In most cases, the macro function is a ring on the barrel of the lens near the aperture (iris) ring. You can feel it click into place when it is secured in the disabled mode.

Shooting techniques

Let's look now at a few fundamental shooting techniques that beginners should learn immediately. First, avoid zooms and pans. Unless there is some important reason to zoom in or pan on to something, avoid those movements. It is better to cut from one shot to another. Consider composition carefully. Shoot heads slightly off center, not right in the middle. Shoot the head over the reporter's shoulder or at a slight angle. Profiles do not work well because they lose the viewer's attention; you can easily determine if a shot is "too profile" if you cannot see the subject's second eye over the bridge of the nose. Once you see the subject's second eye and far cheekbone, the shot is fine. The head should be looking at the reporter and, if the camera is positioned correctly—just behind or slightly to the side of the reporter—the audience at home will see the whole face of the interviewee.

Videographers working for a regular newscast must get some medium shots that will leave enough room for "supers." Some news directors discourage tight head shots because most sound bytes are short and it is difficult to super them. Tight shots are sometimes effective if the interview is dramatic or emotional or if the head is interesting because of age, beauty, or some other reason.

Some videographers like to get a variety of headshots, but it is important to remember not to change shots while someone is speaking unless there is a good reason. If, for example, the person on camera begins to cry, you would probably want to slowly zoom in for a close-up.

Remember that the reporter will not appear on camera most of the time, so all of the shots should concentrate on the head. The reporter is brought into the picture after the interview is completed when the videographer shoots the cutaways and reversals used as a part of the editing process to avoid jump cuts. As discussed earlier, editing interviews presents a problem because sound bytes cannot be juxtaposed without creating a jump cut. Without something in between the two sound bytes, the head appears to jerk when the sound bytes are edited together.

Cover footage

The best way to avoid jump cuts is to use appropriate *cover footage*—video illustrating what the newsmaker is discussing. Good pictures usually are more interesting than heads, anyway, and cover footage allows editors to connect as many sound bytes as they like without jump cuts.

Cover footage is also called b-roll, which is a series of visual images used to illustrate the story. B-roll received its name because it typically consists of video and natural sound. This natural sound is traditionally recorded on the second, or "B," audio channel.

Establishing shots

Some of the first pictures a videographer takes at the scene are establishing shots. These are wide shots of the activity at the scene of a fire or an accident, of floodwaters pounding against seawalls, or of baseball fans lined up outside the stadium before a World Series game. Establishing shots set the stage for what is to follow, and they often provide the opening video for the story.

One technique that draws viewer interest is to begin with establishing shots

FIGURE 9.8

that are interesting. A novice mistake is to start a visual report with an "official" shot, such as the exterior of a building. As an example, picture a story about a class of schoolchildren who've excelled on a state-mandated test. The stodgy opening shot would be a wide shot of the exterior of the building, followed by the obligatory medium shot of the school's name on an outside sign. Not only is this dry video, it shows the viewer nothing they can't see by driving down the street. As a rule of thumb, if a viewer can see the exact same image by simply looking out the window, you're not doing your job as a videographer.

Instead, try the same story with a more compelling image as the establishing shot; how about some video of the schoolchildren? A close-up of a pencil solving a math problem on a piece of paper? A medium shot of a student hunched over a pile of homework? Remember, an establishing shot need not be a wide shot—it should, however, be a compelling image that will invite viewers to watch the story. A tepid shot of a building or sign is not an effective strategy to hook someone to stay for another 90 seconds.

FIGURE 9.9

Better footage can be obtained by getting a variety of close-ups, medium shots, and wide establishing shots. Too many novice videographers hesitate in shooting close-ups, leaving a bland array of wide shots for editing. To combat this, an easy strategy is for students to watch an hour of dramatic programming on television. Narrative stories are conveyed through the power of close-ups, which attract and maintain a viewer's attention. News stories without close-ups will not have the power of those that do.

Sequences

Good videographers shoot their footage in groups called *sequences*, which are a collection of shots concentrated in a single visual setting. A sequence need not tell a story in a sequential manner; it simply covers the images in a setting so the editor has ample editing options.

Let's take a visually dull story about taxes being prepared just before the annual April 15th deadline. To simplify this example, picture a taxpayer typing a spreadsheet on a computer program. A quick suggestion of shots would include

- WS of the taxpayer and the computer
- MS of the taxpayer

- CU of the taxpayer's face
- CU of the taxpayer's hands typing on the computer keyboard
- MS of the computer screen
- CU of the tax forms on the desk

Now, imagine editing with these six shots and each shot will average about 5 seconds on the air. The editor now has the ability to easily cover 30 seconds of audio narration. Of course, discretion must be used. This type of shooting requires you to direct your subjects a bit—something that can be inappropriate and even unethical in some circumstances. As you get better at using this technique, you'll find ways to shoot sequentially on most assignments.

Shooting enough footage

Reporters, especially inexperienced ones, often wonder whether they've asked enough questions. Videographers often feel the same way. With experience, they learn when they've shot enough pictures, but initially they all tend to overshoot, fearing that they might miss something. Eventually, a videographer and a reporter who work together come to know when they have enough video. Until that time, shooting too much video is better than returning to the newsroom with too little.

Time coding

As you shoot, the video camera is prelogging your footage with time code. Videotapes record images on individual frames. A *frame* is a frozen picture that lasts 1/30th of a second. To see what a frame looks like, just pause a videotape; the image you see is one frame. Since there are 30 frames per second, finding the exact footage you want for editing can become a daunting task.

Fortunately, there is time code, which marks each individual frame with a unique address. Time codes appear as hour:minute:second:frame. Thus, if you see a code reading 01:52:03:13, you know your footage is just over 1 hour and 52 minutes into the tape.

When you review existing videotape, you will log the time code of the desired footage. For example, if the desired shot is found at 01:15:02:19, you can jot that number down for future reference. Since the time code is a permanent address on the videotape, it will remain the same even if you move the videotape to a different machine.

AUDIO

Comparatively speaking, video is much simpler to manage in the field than audio. Most video cameras have two audio tracks (Channel 1 and Channel 2). The easiest way to manage audio recording is to record the primary sound, such as field interviews and stand-ups, on Channel 1. This leaves Channel 2 free for recording natural sound and room tone.

In addition to microphones and earphones, field crews will carry a small arsenal of wind screens and pop filters to deaden background noise. These are placed on microphones to reduce ambient sounds and wind noise when recording.

Recording primary sound

Primary sound is the audio recorded as the reporter's narration, sound bytes, and stand-ups. To obtain a good audio level, the videographer should have the subject talk into the microphone before the tape is rolling; this will allow the audio levels to be set accurately. The truest audio checks come naturally, when the subject is simply speaking into the microphone. Having the person count "1...2...3..." may confirm that the microphone is indeed hooked up, but the counting is so stilted that the videographer will likely need to adjust the level once normal speech begins. As a rule of thumb, don't settle for counting.

Aside from setting the proper audio level, the videographer must decide what type of microphone to use. The two most common are the lavaliere mic and the handheld mic. The lavaliere is a clip-on microphone that affixes to a jacket, shirt, or tie; the advantages are that it allows for both hands to be free and provides a solid audio level. The second type of microphone, the handheld, also gives a quality signal. It tends to be more durable than the lavaliere and can be used without bothering to clip on a microphone, plus it works well when interviewing multiple subjects on a breaking news story. As an added advantage, the news director will purchase mic flags to be placed on the hand-held microphones; these are the square or triangular mini-signs that display the news channel's logo prominently on the mic.

Recording natural sound

Good pictures are essential for good television, but pictures are not nearly as effective without their natural (or nat) sound. In television, seeing traffic, a heavy downpour, or a construction site without the benefit of audio in the background gives an antiseptic feeling for the viewer. For radio, nat sound is important because the sound provides many of the "pictures" for the radio audience.

Video cameras offer several audio inputs, one of which is a small microphone mounted atop the camera body. This is the nat sound microphone. There are two reasons why it should always remain in the "on" position. First, it will capture the ambient sound whenever the camera is recording; thus the nat sound is simple for the videographer to obtain. Second, if the lavaliere microphone fails (due to a dead battery) or the handheld microphone is not working, the nat sound mic will serve as an emergency back-up for primary audio. It should not be relied on to provide quality audio for interviews and stand-ups, but it will work in an emergency.

At the end of shooting at a given location, it is customary for the videographer to ask for quiet while recording. This is when the videographer is recording ambient noise, also known as *room tone*. This audio will then be used as "filler" audio if there are unusable sounds that must be covered elsewhere on the videotape. When these shots are being taken, it is important that the reporter simply walk away from the camera. Fewer things are more irritating to a videographer than a reporter who uses this occasion to stand near the camera to discuss lunch plans—not only does this make the ambient noise unusable, it forces the videographer to stand behind the camera for a few more minutes for no good reason.

FIGURE 9.10
Ed Elkins, control board operator at WAFB, Baton Rouge, Louisiana.

Earphones

A common problem for young people just starting to work with equipment is recording good sound. A particular problem is the set of switches on the camcorder that directs the signal from the two microphone inputs to the two (or four) audio channels on the tape.

A set of earphones is critical in ensuring that you are getting the signal from the handheld microphone to the tape. If you aren't listening, you could end up with both audio tracks containing a signal from the shotgun microphone mounted on the camera. If you are responsible for recording good sound, wear earphones during the interview. You cannot depend on the camera's sound meter reading or the tiny monitor speaker because they just tell you that sound is being picked up. They do not guarantee that the sound quality is good. The only way to hear if there is radio interference or microphone problems is to listen to the sound through earphones.

Earphones range from small iPod-style sets to over-the-ear headphones that cover both ears in their entirety. Either way, the small investment needed for a pair of earphones is a worthwhile purchase for any field videographer.

FIGURE 9.11

It is important to establish a good relationship between a reporter and a videographer.

Establishing rapport with the videographer

The beginning of the chapter mentioned that a good relationship between a reporter and a videographer is essential. Here are some suggestions and observations on how to establish that relationship.

NBC News correspondent Bob Dotson tells reporters to look for help and advice from the videographer. "They should have a shorthand, kind of like what a married couple would have," he says. "If you have this sort of camaraderie, the videographer is going to think, maybe for the first time in his life, that somebody thinks what he's doing is important."

Dotson credited Tom Zannes, a freelance cameraman for NBC, for the outstanding video used in Dotson's excellent package about a woman trapped in a cavern in Carlsbad, New Mexico. Zannes was in the cavern with the team that was exploring it for the *Encyclopaedia Britannica* when a member of the team slipped and broke her leg. When Dotson arrived at the scene to cover the story, Zannes was still in the cave. Dotson said Zannes was allowed to remain there during the rescue because he is a world-class caver and because "he knew when to take pictures and when to put the camera down and help with the rescue."

Reporter Morton Dean says it is always a good idea "to discuss with the videographer what you are looking for, what your expectations are, and what you plan to do with the story."

Former *CBS News* correspondent Ben Silver says that if there is not a close working relationship between the reporter and the videographer, each may go off in a different direction, and they won't end up with a good product. "If you want videographers to get good video for your story," he says, "they have to know where you're going with the story."

Silver, now professor emeritus at Arizona State University, says reporters should remember that videographers often have journalism backgrounds and have good ideas too. "Two sets of eyes are better than one," he says, "and three sets of eyes are even better." Silver notes that when reporters are working on a story, strangers sometimes approach them with information. "Listen to them," Silver advises. "They may have seen something you and the videographer missed because you were busy doing something else. You always have to keep an open mind."

One-man band

If you start out in a small market, which is where most young people right out of college begin their careers, you may not only be reporting the news. You may be shooting it as well. To save money, many small stations—and even some bigger ones—are hiring people who can "do it all."

Due to lighter cameras, digital technology, and tighter budgets, some stations are employing people who know how to write, report, and handle a camera in the field. At some stations, those same people edit the stories when they return to the station. Many of the people who are working alone seem to enjoy the freedom of doing everything by themselves. Does the quality of the product suffer? Probably, but those writing the checks often are willing to accept less quality if it costs fewer dollars. On the positive side, it means that there may be more opportunities for young people who have learned the basic skills—writing, reporting, and videography.

Michelle Kosinski, the bureau chief in Salisbury–Piedmont for WSOC–TV in Charlotte, says working alone helps her get better stories. "It's just me and my camera," she says, "so people tend to tell me more. They feel closer to me." Kosinski says she writes her story while she shoots. "There's a beauty in seeing something and making it look the way you want it to look."

Lisa Goddard, who worked on her own in Myrtle Beach, South Carolina, before moving on to another reporting job, agrees. She liked having control over her packages. "You can shoot based on how you want to write," she says. But Goddard admitted that being alone was difficult when she had to do stand-ups. She said that for the first 2 weeks on the job she kept cutting off her forehead.

Peter Landis, news director at NY1, the 24-hour cable news operation, has 23 people who both shoot and report. He says economics force newsrooms to do more with less. He asks: "Why pay for two people to do the job one person can be trained to do?"

Quality suffers

James Rosen, a former one-person shooter–reporter, sometimes referred to as a video journalist, says, "I loved shooting but hated the *schlepping*." He recalls that, when he was working for News 12 in the Bronx, he once covered a college graduation speech by Bill Cosby and had to park 10 blocks away. He says he left the tripod behind and blew his stand-up. "The quality of the piece suffers," he added, "when you work alone." Rosen says he was grateful for the challenge and opportunity to learn the skills. Rosen is now a Washington correspondent for Fox News Channel and has a videographer, editor, producer, and makeup person.

Steve Sweitzer, news operations manager at WISG–TV in Indianapolis, doesn't think that news videographers should be worried about losing their jobs. He says the videographer's job may be redefined somewhat, but there is still plenty for two people to do when out on a story. "Two minds are still better than one," he adds. Sweitzer says news operations that value quality will hire pros to operate the cameras and get the most out of the equipment. That feeling is shared by Jim Disch, director of news and programming for CLTV in suburban Chicago. "We prize our photography," he says. "We use tripods unless we're running after something." And he adds that he believes the station will best serve its viewers by hiring both videographers and reporters.

Jack La Duke, New York state bureau reporter for WCAX–TV in Burlington, Vermont, has been going solo for 35 years and loves it. But he admits it is not a perfect way to cover the news. He says you are shooting the interview and thinking about the questions, listening, and asking follow-up questions while worrying about the focus and the batteries. He says he enjoys working alone, but it's not for everybody.

Some critics also raise safety issues about working alone. In breaking news, the reporter often watches the videographer's back and helps protect that person from danger. Sweitzer notes that good reporters stand right next to the videographer. Other news directors worry about theft of equipment when only one person is doing the job. Still another news director was concerned about stand-up shots, which he described as "often god-awful when only one person is trying to shoot and talk at the same time."

Despite the criticism of "one-man bands," Michael Rosenblum, a former producer at *CBS News*, is busy training them. He said his consulting firm has trained more than 1000 people to be shooter–reporters in the past 10 years.

For students interested in broadcast journalism, we advise you to learn how to do it all as well as you can, not necessarily because you may have to do everything in your first job but because if you know how to write, shoot, and report, you will be able to cover all of the bases. That background will make you better at your job, whatever that job may be.

SUMMARY

The gear available to field crews has improved dramatically in the past decades as digital technology has made steady gains for video recording. But even as the gear becomes lighter and more foolproof, there are still fundamental techniques that must be followed when working as either a one-man-band or with a videographer.

First, television relies on great video. Viewers will quickly lose patience with a newscast that offers out-of-focus footage that is shaky and has an unusual bluish tint. Anyone working with field gear must instinctively use a mental checklist (white balance, filter, focus, fresh tape, etc.) before recording.

Second, even though excellent audio is expected in radio newscasts, it is equally vital in television news. The correct microphones are needed, mic levels must be monitored, and earphones should be standard in all shooting situations.

Finally, reporters and videographers must work together to create the best images and sound possible. While one-man bands are common in smaller television markets, the benefits of having a videographer cannot be understated. Not only do they provide technical expertise for a news story, they also enable the reporter to offer the best package possible.

Test Your Knowledge

1. What are some of the basic rules to remember to take care of videotapes in the field?
2. What are the three standard components of a video camera?
3. Why is it important to use camera filters?
4. What does white balance do?
5. How can you easily tell if an interview subject is being shot too far to the side, revealing too much profile?
6. What is a sequence?
7. How long does a frame last?
8. What are the basic types of field microphones?
9. What are the two different types of audio?
10. What are some of the advantages and disadvantages of working as a one-man band?

EXERCISES

1. Describe a scenario in which you would deliberately leave a tripod in the news van during a field shoot.
2. List a sequence of six shots that could be used in a typical classroom setting in which a teacher lectures to a room full of students.
3. Describe what time code is and how it can help an editor.
4. Watch a field report on a newscast. Identify the sequences used in the story.
5. In the same report, identify primary and nat sounds.

Interviewing

CONTENTS

INTRODUCTION

One basic method used by reporters to gather information is the interview. Newspaper, radio, and TV journalists use different techniques, but they generally all try to achieve the same end: to find out as much newsmaking information as they can from the person they are interviewing. In broadcast jargon, the interviewee usually is referred to as the *talking head*, or simply the "head." Quotes that are used from the interviewee are called *sound bytes*, but are usually referred to as simply *bytes*.

Newspaper reporters have the luxury of going into depth in their interviews. Because radio and TV reporters have limited time on the air, they have less time to conduct their interviews. Therefore, they must be selective in their questioning and must be well prepared; spending a full hour on an interview to retrieve a mere 15-second byte is a colossal waste of everyone's time.

This chapter is segmented into the three different time frames of interviewing. First, it reviews how reporters perform background research before the interview takes place. Second, the dynamics of how to conduct a successful interview are explored. Finally, we'll examine what steps the reporter must take after the interview is over.

PREPARATION

Reporters should always research the subject and find out as much as possible about the person to be interviewed. In addition to sources around the

(continued)

newsroom, some news organizations also have access to computer database services such as LexisNexis, which indexes national and some regional newspapers, the wire services, and more than 100 magazines and journals. There are also a number of other information-providing services on the Internet (Google, Yahoo, searchable wire services, etc.), but journalists must choose their sources carefully. Far too many "news sources" on the Internet are merely blogs and personal opinion.

Reporters also must decide before the interview what kind of information they want. Interviews are not always expected to produce news. Some are designed to solicit emotional responses, such as those conducted for a human-interest story. Other interviews are attempts to find out more about the newsmaker or, perhaps, his or her family. Reporters might seek such information if, for example, the interviewee had been appointed to some public post or as head of the local hospital.

If a reporter is interviewing the winner of a congressional seat, she is going to be looking for information that is different from what she sought the day before when she interviewed the mother of quadruplets. The reporter will want to ask the congresswoman-elect about her priorities when she gets to Washington, why she thinks her campaign was a success, and, perhaps, whether she believes her victory indicates some sort of national trend. When the reporter spoke to the mother of quadruplets, she asked questions about the problems of taking care of four babies, about whether the house is big enough to accommodate the family, and so on.

WARMING UP

Reporters differ on just how much they should disclose to the interviewee about the line of questioning before the interview starts. The advantage of *warming up* the head is that it gives the person time to collect his or her thoughts, usually ensuring a smoother interview. Without a warm-up, the interviewee might be caught by surprise. The person might say, "I had no idea you would ask that; I really don't know the answer" or try unsuccessfully to fake an answer. Warming up an interviewee also tends to put the person more at ease. A relaxed head usually provides a better interview.

Reporters sometimes do not want the interviewee to know the questions in advance because they plan to ask questions about a controversial topic designed to catch the person by surprise. There is no rule against warming up the interviewee, but some reporters are opposed to it. Almost all agree that it should be restricted to those situations in which the reporter is looking for noncontroversial information. For example, a reporter would not warm up the head if the questions dealt with charges the person misappropriated funds during an election campaign.

SETTING THE STAGE

Informational

In a noninvestigative situation, the main reason for interviewing people is to get information that is generally not known to the reporter and the public. Once the cameras and audio recorders are rolling, reporters shouldn't spend time asking people how long they have been employed, where they were educated, whether they are married, or whether they have any children. If that sort of information is important, it should be learned informally before the actual interview begins. You might want to include such information in the introductory sentence of your story, but you would rarely waste valuable air time with video- or audiotaped responses on these subjects. The recorded questions and answers should be restricted to those that gather information about what the newsmaker knows or thinks about an idea or issue or, perhaps, to those that capture emotions.

One simple trick for reporters is to ask the interviewee to say and then spell their name just as the camera begins to record. This allows the videographer to double-check the audio level, plus it captures the spelling of the name that can be transcribed for the graphics operator during the newscast. Also, if the name is difficult to pronounce, having the subject say it on camera is the best way to learn the correct pronunciation.

Technical

As the reporter is asking background information prior to the interview, the videographer should set up the camera, audio, and any needed lights. Basic considerations can be broken down into the following categories.

- Video—Is there enough physical space for the subject, the reporter, and the videographer with gear? Is the space aesthetically pleasing or is it so sloppy that it will detract from the interview? Is there a computer or video screen in the background that may show a distracting screen as the subject is speaking?

- Audio—Will a handheld mic be sufficient or is a lavaliere mic needed? Is there too much background noise from a fan or passing traffic? Is a television or radio playing that needs to be shut off before recording?

- Lighting—If outside, are lights or a bounce card needed? If inside, are there mixed light sources that will make the image appear to be blue or orange? If the subject is against a window, will only a silhouette be visible?

One hurdle for novice videographers is they may hesitate to ask for a radio to be silenced or a distracting pile of papers to be slid over a few inches. The rule of thumb is to simply ask politely; most requests will be eagerly accommodated, especially if the interviewee understands you are trying to make them look and sound as good as possible.

Finally, it is often easier to ask the subject to move to another location. An interview with a fire chief behind his desk is boring. Instead, why not ask if he can stand outside in front of the fire truck?

PHRASING QUESTIONS CAREFULLY

Many people interviewed by reporters are shy by nature or intimidated by microphones and cameras. Some others just seem to measure their words carefully. In order to prevent one- and two-word responses, reporters must phrase their questions so they are impossible to answer with a "yes" or "no" or by just a shake of the head.

If you ask a person, "Do you like farming?" you are bound to get a "yes" or "no" answer, but if you ask "What do you like about farming?" you should get a sound byte. If you ask a witness to an auto accident "Did you see what happened?" you might, again, end up with a one-word response. If you ask "What did you see?" you'll most likely get a longer response. Children are particularly likely to give "yes" or "no" answers so ask them open-ended questions and be patient.

AVOIDING LEADING QUESTIONS

Do not lead the interviewee toward giving a particular response—some of the best reporters are sometimes guilty of this bad habit. During the Gulf War, a nationally known TV reporter asked a Bush administration official if he was "upset" after viewing pictures of an air raid that showed heavy destruction to a civilian target. The reporter herself clearly *was* upset by the pictures, and phrasing the question in that manner was a disservice for two reasons: (1) it probably influenced many viewers' feelings about the video and (2) it put the administration official in an uncomfortable situation. If the official had said he was *not* upset, he would have appeared callous; if he had said he was upset, he might have sounded critical of the military, which may or may not have been fair or accurate. The reporter allowed her personal feelings about the air raid to influence the question. It was a leading question. She should have asked the administration official, "What did you think about those pictures?"

LISTENING CAREFULLY

Reporters should arrive at an interview with a list of questions that they intend to ask the newsmaker. They also must develop a keen habit of listening carefully to the answers and asking follow-up questions. Many inexperienced reporters are so intent on asking their prepared questions that they fail to listen to the answers. They often do not realize that their previous question was not answered fully, or at all. Sometimes, to the embarrassment of all, the reporter asks a question that already has been answered. The astute newsmaker—often anticipating the reporter's next question—sometimes adds additional information to an earlier response. The rude awakening comes when the reporter asks another question on the list and the newsmaker says, "I just answered that."

Another effective technique is to establish direct eye contact with the person being interviewed. It's easier for reporters to concentrate on what people are saying if they look them right in the eye. This habit also establishes good rapport. Maintaining eye contact with newsmakers lets them know that the reporter is listening and interested. If the reporter's eyes drift toward the list of questions or to the cameraperson, the newsmaker might take that as a signal that he or she has said enough and wait for another question even though he or she might not have finished answering the previous question.

THE TOUGH QUESTIONS

One of the more difficult traits to overcome as a novice reporter is the reluctance to ask tough questions. It often goes against instinct to directly ask someone a question that might prompt discomfort or hostility. However, the reporter's job sometimes requires asking questions that the subject may perceive as irritating or even confrontational. These instances may happen when asking an engineer about flooding in a new subdivision, questioning a football coach about a poorly called game, or interviewing a jaywalker about crossing the street without looking both ways. Seasoned interviewees, like veteran politicians, may not be riled easily. Others may pass you off to their attorney or, in the case of celebrities, to their manager.

Although there are no good ways to ask tough questions, some techniques work better than others. First, unless the interview is going to be brief, avoid asking a tough question at the start; this only creates a confrontational atmosphere for all subsequent questions. Second, if the question may be attributed to a third party, you can phrase the question neutrally. For example,

> "Senator, your challenger in the upcoming election says fraud is
> rampant in your campaign. How do you respond?"

This will still elicit an answer without putting you in a direct confrontation with the subject. Use this technique if there are indeed charges from another source. It is poor journalism to use a "straw man" question to an unnamed source, such as

"Senator, a lot of people say fraud is rampant in your campaign. How do you respond?"

There are also some instances where reporters are expected to ask direct questions. One painful example of a missed opportunity occurred at a White House press conference during the first months of the Barack Obama administration. As the other reporters focused on the economy, the war in Iraq, and the housing crisis, one reporter asked the president what he thought about baseball players using steroids. The question was not only inappropriate for the setting, but there's only one way to answer it—does anyone expect the president to say he favors illegal steroid use?

Most interviews will not require a tough question. However, the reporter's job is to ask such a question if the occasion warrants. Remember that politicians, police chiefs, and football coaches are accustomed to direct questions that require direct answers. The worst possible outcome is that they refuse to answer. Still, you need to ask.

FIGURE 10.1

Reporter Jeff Duhé, anchor, public affairs director, LPB, Baton Rouge, Louisiana, interviews Louisiana State Senator Allen Bares.

KEEPING CONTROL

Sometimes reporters inadvertently allow newsmakers to take control of an interview. Politicians are particularly skilled at manipulating interviews. For example, some politicians take a couple of minutes to answer a question, whereas others ask reporters how long a response they want and then give an answer of exactly that length. Because politicians and others accustomed to working with broadcast journalists know that reporters think in terms of sound bytes, they usually try to express their views in about 12 seconds to make sure their answers are not edited.

A problem arises when the newsmaker takes too long to respond. The choice then is either to interrupt or to allow the head to finish the answer and then reask the question, saying, "That was great, but could you cover that same ground again in about half the time?" Most often the individual is happy to comply, which simplifies the editing process and results in a more natural-sounding response. Editing a sound byte down from a minute to 20 seconds sometimes alters the speaker's inflections.

FIGURE 10.2

Reversal shot of reporter Jeff Duhé, anchor, public affairs director, LPB, Baton Rouge, Louisiana, interviewing Louisiana State Senator Allen Bares.

Some newsmakers try to mislead reporters. They avoid answering some questions and skirt around others. Unless challenged, newsmakers often dominate interview situations. If the head doesn't answer the question or gives only a partial answer, the reporter should try to follow up. The newsmaker often then gives largely the same answer phrased differently. The reporter then needs to decide whether to ask the question a third time or perhaps to say to the newsmaker, "I'm sorry, but you still have not answered my question." When the response is "That's all I'm going to say on the subject," that in itself makes a statement. The reporter might then note in the story, "When pressed to answer the question several times, he refused to elaborate on the original answer."

CURBING NODS AND SMILES

Television reporters must be concerned about their facial expressions and head movements during an interview, particularly in a studio situation when two or more cameras are being used. Limiting this natural tendency is also important in field situations when listening shots of the reporter (called *reversals*)

FIGURE 10.3

Reporters should be concerned about their facial expressions. A smile, frown, or nod could send the wrong signal.

are being taken for editing purposes. It's permissible for reporters to smile or to nod their heads in agreement during an interview about a noncontroversial subject. To the contrary, when the issue is controversial and involves a subject with more than one point of view, a reporter cannot be shown expressing agreement or disagreement. A smile or frown or nod could send a wrong signal to an audience. The question of credibility and objectivity immediately comes into question.

IDENTIFYING SOUND BYTES

Successful reporters who have researched the topic and the newsmaker know when they have just the right amount of material on tape. Because they have an idea of what information they hoped to hear, they know which sound bytes they will probably end up using, plus they also have a fairly accurate idea of how long those bytes will run.

Most usable sound bytes from an interviewee will last between 8 and 12 seconds. Less than that is tricky, as the subject appears on camera for only a few seconds, which is barely enough time for their name to be superimposed. Further, it doesn't give the viewer enough time to connect with the subject. Longer bytes pose their own problems, however, as the reporter effectively cedes the story to the subject to make a prolonged speech.

The balance remains in a two- or three-sentence sound byte, which allows the subject to appear on camera and make a cohesive statement without monopolizing the story. Veteran reporters conduct interviews while listening for sound bytes; even though they don't mentally count how many seconds a sound byte lasts, they develop a sense of what will work in the story.

Finally, it is vital to not talk over the interviewee. Instead of quickly rushing in with a follow-up question, allow a brief second between the subject's voice and your own. This will make editing easier back at the station.

CHECKING FACTS

Some responses during an interview may not sound right. If that happens, reporters should tell the newsmaker that something is puzzling them or that they do not quite understand the answer. If the answers still do not sound true or are confusing, the reporters should check the information as soon as possible. Reporters could try contacting other sources who might have the same information or be doing some research in the newsroom files, the library, or computer databases. If the information cannot be verified, reporters should explain that in the story. For example,

> The head of the Newtown Power Company said there had never been an accident at the plant in the two years since it opened until today, when four people were seriously injured. We were unable to reach a union representative to verify the statement.

ASKING ENOUGH QUESTIONS

It takes time to develop the skill of knowing when you have asked enough questions during an interview. Reporters just entering the field tend to ask too many questions, usually because they are understandably insecure. As reporters gain experience, they develop a feel for when they have collected enough information.

Because time is precious to a broadcast reporter, asking too many questions means that the reporter spends more time than necessary at the scene or on the phone. That leaves less time for working on other stories and complicates the editing process.

The pressure of conducting interviews quickly can sometimes cause reporters to miss important information. It is often a good idea for the reporter to ask the interviewee if he or she would like to add anything or to ask candidly if the reporter might have missed anything important. It is surprising how often the response is "Well, as a matter of fact, I probably should tell you...."

FINISHING THE INTERVIEW

As the interview winds down, there are a few basic strategies to gather the last information as well as to signal the subject that you're wrapping up; you will find some interviewees can ramble on all day.

Some reporters ask an open-ended question such as "As we're wrapping up, do you have any final

FIGURE 10.4

thoughts on the subject?" Others prefer to ask for how to cover the story, such as "We're heading out to the location right now. Can you suggest anything we might want to get on videotape?"

One effective technique is to ask for a Web site or e-mail address that you can release on the newscast. For example, if the Red Cross Disaster Services is having a fundraiser and its Web site has the details, asking for the Internet address wraps up the interview while giving you a tidbit to pass along to viewers as well.

Once the interview is over, thank the interviewee for their time. Grab a business card (or double-check the contact information) so that you can follow up with them later. Also, take a moment to help the videographer break down the equipment; you need to get out as quickly as possible so the interviewee can get on with their day.

Finally, never promise that the interview will be on a particular newscast. Stories are frequently dropped, plus there's always the chance that the story may air but the interview will not make the final cut. To avoid frustrating interviewees, let them know you hope to get it on that evening, but make no promises in the field. If they are insistent on knowing if they'll be on or not, you can always call them later from the newsroom once the rundown is finished.

RETURNING TO THE STATION

Too much time is lost in the driving period between an interview location and the newsroom. If the videographer is driving, the reporter has an opportunity to review the sound bytes through either an audio recorder or a portable video player.

When building a news package (as detailed in the next chapter), it is important to identify the usable sound bytes as quickly as possible. This can be done just as easily in a moving news van as in the station's editing room. Your memory of the interview is fresher directly after it occurs, so it's more effective to scan the interview's bytes while en route to the newsroom.

SPECIAL CONSIDERATIONS

While interviews may follow a predictable pattern, no two interviews are the same. Some of them are spur-of-the-moment questions of a passing politician, whereas others have the luxury of more planning. Still, no discussion of interviewing would be complete without acknowledging a handful of special considerations: interviewees who want to talk off the record, interviews conducted on the phone, and man-on-the-street interviews.

OFF THE RECORD

One frustration of being a reporter is being told: "I'll discuss that with you only if you promise not to use it." When the tape recorders and cameras are turned off, the newsmaker sometimes reveals what turns out to be the best part of the interview. That information—even if it is *off the record*—is often useful to reporters because it can put them on a trail that might lead to other people who will reveal the same information for the record.

Reporters must honor any off-the-record agreement. A reporter who breaks that promise is guilty of a serious breach of ethics. It should be noted that any off-the-record agreement must be acknowledged in advance by both parties. Imagine the chaos that would result if an elected official said the following during a press conference:

> Obviously, we're hoping to settle the employee's lawsuit out of court. But our attorneys have informed us that we have a solid case against him and we're looking forward to proving his guilt. I think he is a terrible, terrible man who has no business living in our city. Of course, since this is a pending case, all of this is off the record.

Wrong. The interviewee and reporter must both agree to go "off the record" before the information is released; the agreement must be accepted by both in advance to be binding. Once agreed, the reporter puts down the pen and shuts off the camera. After the off-the-record conversation has finished, both parties then acknowledge to go back "on the record."

MAN-ON-THE-STREET INTERVIEWS

Although these do not occur as frequently as in years past, reporters can still expect to conduct the occasional man-on-the-street interview. The premise is simple: Take a question that the ordinary citizen might like to give a comment on, put a camera up at a busy location, and quickly pose the question to those happening by.

These interviews either succeed or fail by the quality of the question. Again, like any good interviewing question, avoid a query that will result in a "yes" or "no" answer. Asking people if they like the local football team is a waste of time. But asking them to predict what it will take for the team to win the championship will pull in better answers.

Man-on-the-street interviews usually do not require the subjects' names to be superimposed as they speak. Instead, these are edited back to back with no reversal or cover video to hide the edits.

When shooting a succession of interviews, it's important to vary both your background and the direction the interviewee is facing. If you're limited to

FIGURE 10.5

For man-on-the-street interviews, make sure to vary the background and the direction the interviewee is facing.

one location, this means to spin the camera in a different direction so that the background will change between shots. Otherwise, you'll leave your editor with various heads popping into and out of the frame while the background remains static.

THE PHONE INTERVIEW

Radio reporters have the option of conducting many of their interviews on the phone. Current audio technology, which is available in most radio newsrooms, allows the radio reporter to dial a number, press a button on a computer input, and digitally record an interview with superb quality. The recording may suffer if the interviewee is on a cell phone with spotty reception, but radio reporters frequently rely on nothing more than a phone line for their news. Of course, TV reporters use the phone only as a last resort because interviews without pictures are weak.

FIGURE 10.6

http://newstalk1059.valdostatoday.com/.

One disadvantage of the phone interview is that it's sometimes difficult to know when the newsmaker has finished giving an answer. Unless reporters listen carefully, they might interrupt the answer before it is complete, which sometimes makes editing sound bytes difficult. When you realize you might have missed something, apologize and ask the interviewee to repeat the answer.

Phone interviews should only be used when it is impossible to interview the individual in person. It sounds unprofessional to conduct an interview on the phone with the mayor or someone else in your city or town when you could hop in a car and go to the person's office. Phone interviews are most effective when used to reach newsmakers in another part of the country or overseas. Such interviews demonstrate to the audience that the station is making a special effort to cover the news.

AN INTERVIEW CHECKLIST

Finally, while there are literally bookshelves filled with suggestions about how to conduct interviews, Susan Morris of the University of Pittsburgh boils them down to these suggestions—think of them as a quick reminder of how an interview should be handled.

- Develop a technique of asking short questions that get right to the point.

- Phrase the questions without apologies and in a matter-of-fact manner. Avoid beginning a question with "I hate to ask you this, but...."

- Pause between questions even when dealing with less volatile subjects. You are likely to get more thoughtful answers.

- If a person is hedging, take time to explain what the information is being used for. Explain that you do not have an editorial position.

FIGURE 10.7

Investigative reporters and editors can find a great resource at www. ire.org, a site where journalists can share story ideas, techniques, and sources.

SUMMARY

To conduct a good interview, you must prepare for it. Do some research to find out as much as you can about the person you will be interviewing. Decide on the kind of information you want and choose your questions accordingly.

Remember to listen carefully during an interview. Make sure your questions are answered to your satisfaction. If they aren't, say so, and follow up on your questions. Don't be used. Try to maintain control of the interview. If you permit it, the interviewee will often take over. Keep to your objectives; don't let the head go off on tangents.

Finally, interviews are not necessarily a reliable source of accurate information because those being interviewed want to be perceived in the best light. Do not hesitate to ask to double-check facts or ask a tough question. After all, that's the heart of what reporters do.

Test Your Knowledge

1. Why must radio and TV reporters be more selective than their newspaper colleagues in choosing questions to ask in their interviews?
2. How should you prepare for an interview before you leave the station? Give some examples.
3. It's always a good idea to prepare a list of questions for an interview, but there also are dangers. Explain.
4. How should you phrase questions to make sure you get complete answers?
5. What kind of trouble can reporters fall into if they do not listen intently to the person they're interviewing?
6. Discuss the pros and cons of warming up the person you're interviewing.
7. Discuss tough and surprise questions.
8. What are the advantages and disadvantages of off-the-record comments?

EXERCISES

1. Interview a faculty member in a department other than your own. Before doing so, find out as much as you can about the individual and turn in those notes, along with a story based on your interview.
2. Conduct a man-on-the-street interview with a dozen students on campus. Edit the sound bytes together as they would appear on-air.
3. Interview someone in the community who is in the news. Produce a wraparound report or package.

Covering Planned Events

CONTENTS

INTRODUCTION

There are literally thousands of corporations, politicians, special-interest groups, nonprofit organizations, government agencies, and other individuals and groups looking for exposure on network and local newscasts. Assignment desks are inundated with news releases and telephone calls from public-relations firms and publicists working for these various groups. And, of course, most of these organizations have Web pages on the Internet where newsrooms can reach them and vice versa.

Every one of these publicists tries to persuade the assignment staff that there is something special or important about the product, company, issue, or individual they represent. The assignment desk rejects most of these news releases and telephone calls for a variety of reasons—usually because they are too commercial or have little or no news value or because there just is not enough airtime available to go around. However, some of these releases and telephone calls alert the assignment staff to events that are important and warrant coverage.

Gathering a crowd of journalists with tape recorders and cameras in one room is a triumph for anyone working in public relations. The number of journalists who attend such news conferences depends on what is being "sold." Make no mistake about it, that is what we are talking about—"selling."

The coverage of planned events can bring out the best among competing news crews. It is common for news teams to loan batteries or share electrical cords with one another. Because covering a planned event can occupy a news crew for several hours, it is acceptable for news crews to share footage. After all, the footage recorded will look similar no matter who shoots it, plus no station will scoop the story from the others. In cases like these, camaraderie among the news stations is to be admired.

This chapter discusses these events and describes why some of the events are newsworthy whereas others are not. City council meetings, which are planned events, may be tedious, yet have nuggets of information for the audience. However, a showy press conference may have more visual impact but not the newsworthiness of the council meeting. Learning to gauge *why* to cover these stories and *how* to cover them well are key elements of this chapter.

PRESS CONFERENCES

It makes no difference whether the news conference is called by a government official, a Broadway producer, a major corporation, or the Red Cross; each news conference has a message to sell to the American people. For example, the local district attorney may call a meeting with the news media to announce the arrest of several organized-crime bosses. The arrest is news, of course, but the district attorney also wants to let everyone know what a good job she and the department are doing.

Not all news conferences are that hard-hitting. If there is a local theater company, the producer may believe that the media will turn out to hear about a new show. To make it even more visual, the news release just happens to mention that the chorus line will be there in full costume.

Some news conferences are not visual at all, but they are important to the viewing audience. The local Red Cross chapter will hope for the best but knows that it may have difficulty getting reporters to show up at its news conference to discuss a blood shortage—simply put, it's not likely to provide good pictures for television or exciting sound bytes for radio. The news conference may just earn a 20-second read story on the 6 o'clock news. You might wonder why a blood shortage is not considered an important story. It is, but it probably will get more attention from newspapers than from radio and television. It just isn't a "good" broadcast story.

The underlying current of covering any press conference is to understand why you are there as a reporter. Press releases (issued by public relations personnel) are inherently slanted by *subjectivity*; they want you to portray the event favorably in your story. As a broadcast journalist, your goal is to present stories with a large degree of *objectivity*, meaning you approach the subject matter as neutrally as you can.

This is not to say that a reporter should dismiss all press conferences as mere opportunities to be a cheerleading mouthpiece for the organization. Instead, if the reporter acknowledges that he or she is at an event that is heavily slanted to one point of view, they can achieve a more balanced story with a bit of effort.

COVERING THE PRESS CONFERENCE

How do reporters get ready for news conferences? Let's look at a reporter preparing for a press announcement being held by the local district attorney. Depending on the sophistication of the newsroom, the reporter starts with the clips and video morgue, which may be computerized, to see what's available on the arrested organized-

FIGURE 11.1
Setting up for a news conference (photo by James Terry).

crime figures. If there is video of them, she asks for it to be pulled. She reads carefully any clips on the arrested men and checks the Internet and Web sites for local newspapers. Before she leaves for the news conference, she also might make a quick check with other reporters in the newsroom to see if they have any additional information they gathered while covering other stories involving the men.

The reporter and her videographer arrive at the news conference early because it will be crowded and she wants to get a good position for her and the camera. When the conference begins, the DA reads a prepared statement. The cameras and tape recorders will be rolling, although little of the statement—and maybe none of it—will get on the air. The question-and-answer period following the opening statement usually produces the best sound bytes.

The reporter keeps notes on the opening statement, in any case, so she will know where the best bytes are if she decides to use any of them. She does the same when the question-and-answer period begins, keeping track of the time when the best comments are made. While she was reading the clips in the newsroom, the reporter noticed that the organized-crime leaders were arrested 5 years before. The DA—the same one—got a conviction, and the men were sentenced to 5 to 10 years in prison. The reporter hopes that no one else beats her to the question she is ready to fire at the DA: "How come these guys aren't still in prison? It's only 5 years since you grabbed them and put them away the last time." The question would surely be provocative; perhaps the answer would be one of the highlights of the news conference. In all likelihood, the DA would respond with something such as "I just convict them; ask the judge and the parole board why they are back on the

FIGURE 11.2

street so quickly." The DA, who had been critical of the judiciary on several other occasions, provided anchors with the headline, "DA Criticizes Judges and Parole Board."

Sometimes it is important to ask tough questions. News conferences should not be just a forum for those calling them. It's also important to ask follow-up questions, particularly when the individual holding the news conference is evasive or unclear. Techniques for asking good questions were discussed in Chapter 10, *Interviewing*. Remember, just because you received an invitation to a news conference does not mean you are restricted to asking softball questions; watching the White House Press Corps ask questions of the president at a press conference will reveal that some reporters are more timid whereas others are much more direct.

INTERVIEWING AROUND THE PRESS CONFERENCE

Many broadcast reporters like to interview individually the person holding the news conference when the conference is over. Former *ABC News* correspondent Morton Dean said he did this if he didn't hear what he wanted during the news conference or if he wanted to go in a different direction. "Otherwise," he says, "I would pull a byte from the news conference."

Reporters often call in advance to arrange an interview with the person before the news conference. Some people agree; others refuse because they know it sometimes irritates other members of the media. This is particularly true when the reporter is still conducting the interview when the rest of the news corps arrives in the room. Other broadcast reporters, seeing what's going on, tell their camera people to set up and start shooting. Suddenly, there's a mininews conference going on before the regular one starts. Such occurrences are particularly offensive to print reporters, who must then wait for the scheduled news conference to begin. Once the broadcast people have their interviews, it is not unusual for them to pack their gear and be on their way, leaving the person holding the news conference with just the newspaper people. Many broadcast reporters cover news conferences this way because their assignment editors tell them to be in and out of the news conference quickly so they can move on to other stories.

Doing an interview before a news conference has its risks. Another reporter may know something important that the early reporter missed in the one-on-one or a confrontation may occur when one of the print reporters asks an embarrassing question that catches the news conference host by surprise. The early reporter who came and went will not have this confrontation on tape.

FINDING WORKABLE VIDEO

Press conferences present their own problems for news coverage. In smaller markets, there may only be a handful

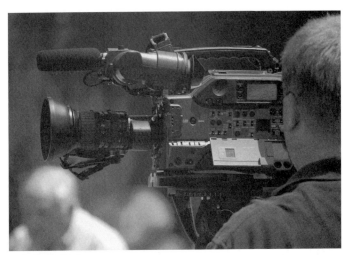

FIGURE 11.3

of people in the room; in fact, a camera crew may find itself at a press conference with only the person who sent over the press release! Conversely, major stories in larger markets will attract a flock of news crews and spectators, thus limiting the physical space around the video cameras.

As mentioned earlier, finding a suitable spot to set up the camera is key. Your location should be with your back to any dominant exterior windows to prevent returning with shadowy footage. Ideally, you also want to set up near an exit; there is no joy in being pinned against a far wall when your newsroom pages you to cover a breaking story. Being near an exterior door also allows you to position yourself between a potential interview subject and the exit, allowing you to ask a question should they try to make a hasty retreat.

Veteran videographers will position themselves at the side of the room or at least not in the center. By shooting from the side, you have access to not only the lectern in the front, but also to shooting reaction shots of those in the audience. When the room is full of people, a simple strategy is to shoot reverse shots of various audience members as the speaker prepares; a quick handful of close-ups can be a lifesaver when editing later. Should the room be nearly vacant, it is not uncommon for one television crew to get reaction shots by videotaping the competition's cameraperson.

MEETINGS

Because of sunshine laws, it is easy for reporters to find out where meetings are happening, what items are on the agenda, and when the meetings will begin. City and county governments, local advisory boards, university planning sessions, and a host of other councils and groups routinely post their agendas on their Web sites. In fact, government meetings must be announced well in advance to prevent secret votes.

But while the work of city and town government is extremely important, it can also be one of the dullest assignments that radio and TV reporters cover. The problem for broadcast reporters is that deliberations of the city council, the board of supervisors, and other local officials often take hours. Still, the debated issues often affect many people. An increase in local taxes, a curfew for teenagers, or a company's effort to locate a waste disposal plant in a community brings out a big crowd and lots of journalists. Because such meetings can go on for hours and days, what do radio and TV reporters do?

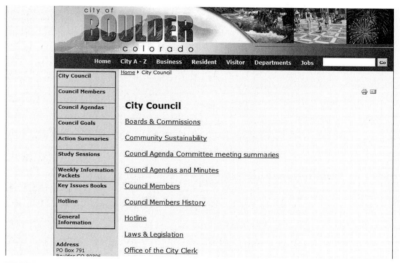

FIGURE 11.4

City Web sites post information on council meetings and committees on their Web sites. For an example, see http://www.bouldercolorado.gov/index.php?option=com_content&task=view&id=68&Item id=130.

As an example, let's suppose that the Wheatland city council members are considering an out-of-town company's offer to build a waste-burning incinerator in the town. The company claims that the facility will employ 100 people and that it will be completely safe. Wheatland could use another 100 jobs. Basically, Wheatland, a dairy-farm community of about 5000 people without much industry, is hurting financially. These people are farmers because they appreciate the pristine environment and are suspicious of anyone or anything that might damage their area. A local newspaper has already reported that the company wants to burn medical waste.

More than 100 people show up at the high-school auditorium to hear exactly what the company has in mind. There is a radio station in town but no TV station. A TV reporter from a nearby city shows up along with a local radio reporter and several print journalists. TV cameras and tape recorders are rolling as town officials introduce a spokesperson and an engineer from the waste-disposal company. After some lengthy statements by the two representatives—complete with charts and statistics—a heated debate begins. The broadcast reporters take detailed notes, keeping a record of who is speaking and when. A local real estate agent says the plant would hurt property sales. "People escape the city to get away from pollution. They won't buy here if you build the plant," the agent says.

A parent questions the effect of toxic fumes on the town's children. The company official tries to reassure the crowd, which clearly is reacting negatively to the idea of building this plant in town. "There is absolutely nothing dangerous about anything we will be burning," the spokesperson says.

A man stands up holding a newspaper clipping. "Wasn't your company cited for not burning things in Nebraska?" he asks. "This story says your company left a real mess around and you were burning all sorts of dangerous things improperly."

The company official tries to explain away the story, saying, "We had a few workers who weren't doing their jobs the way they should have, but they've been replaced and things are all squared away now."

The man with the paper is still standing. "And this story says that you only employ about a dozen workers at that Nebraska plant. You claim the plant here would mean 100 jobs for our town."

The debate went on for 2 hours, but the story prepared by the TV reporter would probably last no more than 90 seconds, maybe a little longer if the meeting took place on a slow news day. The local radio reporter would devote more time to the story because the issue is big news in Wheatland. The radio reporter might do a special in-depth wrap-up of the meeting in addition to some 1-minute wraparounds during newscasts throughout the day. There is no local daily newspaper, only a weekly, so the townspeople are anxious to hear as much as they can on the debate.

The cameraperson with the TV reporter picked up the heated debate and stopped shooting during the dull periods. After a while, a cameraperson develops a sense for knowing when to start and stop shooting a story like this one. Because the cameraperson knows that less than a minute of sound bytes will make the news, it is unnecessary to shoot continuously.

After shooting the highlights of the debate, the reporter and cameraperson moved outside and interviewed some people as they left the building. Everyone they spoke with was opposed to the incinerator. In an effort to be as fair as possible, the reporter continued interviewing until she finally found a man who said he was "keeping an open mind on the matter" until he heard more. "If there really would be an extra 100 jobs," he said, "I'd want to think about it."

The reporter decided they had enough material. She would have liked to do a separate interview with one of the company representatives, but there was no time. The debate had continued for almost 2 hours, and the ride back to the station would take 40 minutes. She decided to use part of the official's remarks for balance and to include some of the debate along with the interviews she conducted outside the building. She also decided to use some of the crowd shots to go along with the sound bytes. The company had provided her with a video of the Nebraska plant.

The reporter opened her package with a sound byte. This is known as a *cold open*, as the first image seen must have audio up full and the graphics operator ready to drop in a quick identifying graphic if needed. The package appeared as follows:

SOT Woman yelling at meeting	SOT runs :04
	"I'm not going to let you put anything in my backyard that's going to poison my children!"
V/O Crowd debating	V/O
NAT SOUND UNDER	This woman was one of almost 100 people who showed up at a meeting in Wheatland tonight to listen to a proposal. The plan would establish a waste-burning incinerator in this predominantly dairy farm community of five thousand people.
SOT Man talking in crowd and waving a newspaper	SOT :12
	"I don't trust your company. This story says your company left a real mess around and you were burning all sorts of dangerous things improperly …"
V/O shots MEDVAC plant	The company that this man is referring to is the Quadrocare Medvac Waste Disposal Corporation out of Omaha, Nebraska. And there have been published reports that Medvac was fined for not properly disposing of medical waste at its plant outside of Omaha.
SOT	SOT :06
FONT: Bob Smith	"We did have some trouble for awhile, but we've corrected all those problems." (protest from crowd)
CEO, MEDVAC	
Waste Disposal	
V/O angry crowd	(V/O)
	There was no doubt about the sentiments of most of the people assembled here tonight. These are farm people and the environment—the land they work and the air they and their cows breathe—is precious to them. But many young people have left the farms and are desperate for work in Wheatland. Medvac claims it would hire 100 people at the incinerator it wants to build.
Video of farms and rolling hills	

SOT Angry man	SOT :08
	"And what about these 100 jobs you're talking about? This story says that you only employ about a dozen workers at that Nebraska plant."
V/O Crowd leaving hall	V/O
	The debate lasted almost two hours and we only found one man who had anything positive to say about the proposed plant.
SOT O/C two-shot	SOT :05
	"Well, if it's true that the plant would bring 100 jobs to town, I'd want to think about it."
V/O Town officials and others talking outside the meeting hall	V/O
	Town supervisors told Medvac that they would have a decision for them within 30 days. But from the tone of tonight's meeting, it seems unlikely that the project will be approved. This is Janet Baker reporting from Wheatland.

This package is a good example of the proper way to cover a local government meeting. Unfortunately, many local reporters cover such stories from the back of the meeting room or on the steps of city hall. In such stories, the opening shot shows the reporter and then the camera moves from the reporter to the members of the city council or other governing body. In dull fashion, the camera pans from one member to another while the reporter voices the report. There usually are no sound bytes in the story, just the voice of the reporter and the nameless faces and voices of the town officials. Former *CBS News* correspondent Ben Silver calls such reports "video clichés."

To avoid such uninteresting stories, the reporter covering local government meetings should find out in advance what is going to be discussed and select the most interesting subject and, if possible, one that lends itself to video footage. For example, let's consider a story about the extension of sewers to a certain part of town. Before the debate, the reporter and cameraperson should go to the location, take pictures of the area, and speak with some of the residents. Some might like the sewer idea, but others might oppose it because it would mean higher taxes.

Now when the reporter attends that public meeting and reports that the town supervisors voted to extend the sewer system, she can say, "Earlier in the day we spoke to some residents of that area, and here's what they had to say." The taped comments and video of the area make better news than pictures of the reporter announcing the supervisors' decision and shots of the members voting.

POLITICAL CAMPAIGNS

People are running for some political office just about everywhere. Most reporters find themselves covering a political campaign early in their career.

Even relatively small communities hold elections—for mayor, sheriff, town supervisor, and numerous other positions. Reporters also cover the campaigns of candidates for the state legislature, for Congress, and for the presidency when those candidates visit the area.

Covering politics can be one of the more interesting stories that reporters cover, although sometimes the politicians themselves are less than inspiring and the issues sometimes not very stimulating. Also, covering politicians can be frustrating because the candidates often skirt the real issues and get into name-calling and personality assassination. Compounding the problem is that the public is often indifferent to politics, ranking the subject fairly low, below topics such as education, crime, and the environment.

A group at Harvard University measured voter interest in the 2000 presidential campaign and found that two-thirds of the public were paying little or no attention. This apparent indifference of the public to such an important subject that impacts so keenly on their lives presents a real challenge for journalists—to make their coverage of politics as interesting and stimulating as possible. And covering politics is not just an assignment for top journalists covering the race for the presidency.

The most important requirement for reporting on politics is remaining neutral. Regardless of how reporters feel personally about the candidates, they must maintain their objectivity. Assignment editors and news directors are not going to ask reporters what their politics are when they're assigned to cover the campaign of a state assemblyperson. The reporters are expected to report fairly, without any bias, even if they think poorly of the candidate.

However, it is not unusual for reporters to find that they like some candidates after they have been on the road with them; reporters need to watch that this admiration doesn't creep into their scripts. When it does, the reporter might not even be aware of it, but sometimes it is painfully visible to the audience and other journalists.

When covering a candidate during a campaign, a political reporter should not just parrot the candidate's speeches. If the candidate says the same things every place he or she goes, it would be appropriate for the reporter to point that out. It would be equally important for the reporter to note when candidates change their positions on the issues depending on the kind of group they're addressing.

The reporter should also tell the audience things about the location of the speech and the crowd. Was the candidate speaking in a predominantly Republican or Democratic area? Was the crowd mostly white-collar or blue-collar? Obviously, if the candidate was Republican and she was addressing a crowd in an affluent area of the city, her reception could be expected to be warmer than in the inner city. Likewise, the opposite could be expected if the candidate was a Democrat.

The crowd's reaction is important. Was it enthusiastic or relatively quiet? Was the crowd large or small? If the weather affected the turnout, that should be noted. Did people challenge the candidate's remarks? Did they seek out the candidate to shake his or her hand?

Former *CNN News* correspondent and anchor Bernard Shaw suggested that broadcast media should be doing more to put political statements and claims into perspective. He questioned

FIGURE 11.5

When covering a political event, it is important to gauge the crowd's reaction.

whether radio and TV stations really want to stop "attack ads." He noted that millions of dollars in ad revenue are at stake and that sales departments "are loaded with people who have never seen an ad they didn't like. But isn't there a higher calling? A higher need?" asked Shaw. He added that attack ads have become news stories, and it is the responsibility of news directors to point out the distortions and to expose candidates who "work harder at ducking than discussing issues."

Shaw also suggested that the news media should let candidates know that the voters are not more interested in a "staged picture than a thousand words of discussion of issues on their minds." He spoke of the "arrogance of the candidates and their managers and their media manipulators who fly into an airport, speak for 5 minutes, pose for pictures for 10 minutes, and get back in the plane and move on to another location."

Shaw said that when a candidate does that, there is nothing wrong with leading the newscast that night by saying, "Democratic candidate Gus Harmin thought enough of San Jose voters to spend 22 minutes at the airport today before going on to a Los Angeles fundraiser tonight. The senator said nothing he did not say before, but he did note that our weather was the best he had seen in days."

Shaw cited another way to put a political story into perspective:

> The president took his election campaign to the Springfield nursing home for the elderly today, promising that he would not allow Congress to tamper with Social Security. But when he left, the president used a side door and his motorcade went the wrong way on a one-way street, apparently to avoid some two thousand unemployed workers whose benefits had run out.

Shaw said audiences are "keen for those kind of reporting distinctions. They need them for perspective on the sleights of hand that they are subjected to by politicians lusting for votes but lacking in so many ways."

Additionally, Shaw attacked some "sins" committed by politicians, citing as an example the arrogant refusal to answer reporters' questions on the issues. "But worse than the candidate's refusal to answer the question," he said, "is the news media's complicity by generally failing to point out and underscore that the politician did not answer the question."

Shaw said that every time this happens it reinforces "the politician's misguided belief that he can get away with it and voters don't care." The former *CNN News* anchor said he believes it's time to stop the exploitation of the news media by politicians. "If what politicians are saying and doing is not news, why put it on the air?" he asked. Some reporters privately agreed with Shaw's criticisms and suggestions, but others doubted most political reporters would change. One political reporter said his boss wouldn't be very happy if he told him he wasn't going to do a package that evening because the candidate didn't say anything new.

Some stations are to be commended for examining politicians' paid campaign spots, analyzing them for content and inaccuracies, and pointing out flaws in them when appropriate. During the 2004 and 2008 presidential campaigns, several television networks offered so-called "fact-checking" segments on a regular basis to correct inaccurate statements made by the candidates.

GRAND OPENINGS

Invariably, reporters will be called upon to cover the ribbon-cutting, groundbreaking, or grand opening of a new store or manufacturing facility. The decision to cover these often depends on how big a facility it is. A tiny ice cream shop may not justify coverage, but the earth-breaking of a major manufacturing plant that will employ 3500 people is a story that will leap into the A block.

While these events are planned, it is crucial to remember that the focal point of the event will only happen once. The ceremonial cutting of the ribbon must be captured on video; thus the videographer must be positioned and the camera rolling before scissors meet ribbon. Similarly, the tape must be recording before the ceremonial groundbreaking (which, bizarrely, will feature a slew of business folks in suits wearing hard hats in an open field). When events like these happen, it is often best to schedule the interviews immediately *after* the ribbon-cutting/earth-opening moment. If the interview is scheduled just before the big moment, you risk either missing the video or slowing down the entire event as everyone awaits you to release the subject from the interview. Grab them afterward.

Feature events

Covering hard news—whether spot news or planned events—is the "meat and potatoes" of broadcast journalism, whereas feature stories are the "dessert." Those are the stories that often bring a smile and sometimes a tear to our faces.

Feature stories invariably end up near the bottom of the newscast, as coverage of the county fair or high-school dance do not contain much hard-hitting journalism. But no matter where a story may land in the rundown, reporters should still treat the subject matter and their interviewees with respect. It is far too easy for a "hard news" reporter to scoff at the accomplishments of a Cub Scout ceremony or a watermelon-eating contest. Just because a story may be on the lighter side is no reason to treat it with disdain; if nothing else, it gives the reporter and videographer the opportunity to be a bit more creative with their story.

SUMMARY

Reporters spend much of their time covering planned events. Unlike spot news, which is unpredictable, most planned events are known about by the assignment editors days and weeks in advance. These events fill part of the newscast almost every night. A good percentage of planned events are news conferences. Because news conferences are called by people trying to "sell" something, reporters must be prepared to ask tough questions; they cannot allow themselves to be used.

Other common planned events are those provided by the workings of government—town and city council meetings and, in state capitals, meetings of

FIGURE 11.6
The moment when the ribbon is cut must be on video.

FIGURE 11.7

FIGURE 11.8.

the legislature. Research is important. Reporters must be familiar with the issues under discussion and be ready to ask intelligent questions about them. Planned events are not always exciting; they often have few or no picture opportunities. They are, however, an important part of covering the news, even if they wind up as a 20-second voiceover.

Political events are solid additions to newscasts, even though they are limited to those months before an election is held. It is vital that reporters do not become either cheerleaders or attack dogs against a particular candidate or party; remember that objectivity is the cornerstone of broadcast journalism.

Grand openings are also planned events that are announced well in advance, yet coverage of these is determined by the size of the business. The most important lesson in reporting these stories is that the pivotal moment occurs but once; thus advance setup and position are crucial for the field crew.

The final category of nonbreaking stories is the feature event. These stories give reporters more opportunity to display their creative talents. Every reporter has his or her favorite type of story, but you must remember that you have to learn how to cover them all, regardless of where they will appear in the newscast.

Test Your Knowledge

1. Name some of the planned events that broadcast reporters cover.
2. How do assignment editors determine which planned events they will cover?
3. What are the chief reasons that people and organizations call news conferences?
4. How does a reporter prepare for a news conference?

5. What is the best way for broadcast reporters to cover a town or city council meeting?

6. What is the worst way to cover such a meeting?

7. What are the most important things to remember when covering a political campaign?

EXERCISES

1. Cover a city council or town meeting with a tape recorder or video camera. Prepare a wrap or package.

2. Attend a news conference and prepare a wrap or package.

3. Read a newspaper account of a planned event and then watch a television news report of the same story. In what ways are the stories similar and different?

4. Track down the agenda for an upcoming city council meeting on the city's Web site. Estimate how long you think the meeting will last based on the number of agenda items.

CHAPTER 12

Reporting Live

KEY WORDS

Ad-Libbing

Communication
  Chain

Dining Table
  Solution

Immediacy

Interrupted
  Feedback

Reporter's
  Notebook

Voiceover

CONTENTS

INTRODUCTION

The immediacy of broadcast journalism is the greatest advantage it possesses over print media. This chapter discusses how radio and television newsrooms may exploit that advantage by using reporters in the field to deliver live reports. Further, this chapter offers some suggestions for handling the special pressures and responsibilities that live reporting places on broadcast journalists.

Reporting live from a mobile unit has always been routine for a radio reporter; since its inception, immediacy has been radio's big advantage. Since the early days of radio, Americans have been accustomed to getting the first news of an important story from that medium. Often, the breaking news has come from a radio reporter at the scene.

Radio has lost some of its advantage as new technology has made it possible for television to put a live signal into homes almost as quickly and easily as radio does. However, radio continues to be first in reaching a large portion of the listening audience—those traveling on the highways.

Unfortunately, the ability to dispatch a crew to a field location for a live report has led to some newsrooms producing live shots without compelling reasons. If there is a massive traffic accident during the newscast and a live report can be filed to provide up-to-the-minute information, that's good use of a live shot. Of course, not all stories conveniently happen during news broadcasts. The most egregious examples are when early morning newscasts feature a live

FIGURE 12.1

WTVJ-TV reporter Ed O'Dell and cameraman Pedro Cancio rush to the scene of a story in Miami (courtesy of WTVJ-TV, Miami).

shot at 6:00 a.m. Often, these have the field reporter shivering before a dark courthouse, delivering forgettable lines such as "In a matter of just 8 hours, jury selection will begin for the upcoming trial." As a rule of thumb, if the location is dark and empty, all of the newsmakers have gone home, and the only people around are mopping up and locking the doors, the producer should provide a compelling reason for putting everyone through the effort and expense of a live shot.

ORGANIZING THOUGHTS

Because they broadcast live so often, radio reporters learn early in their careers how to organize their thoughts quickly. They also develop the skill of *ad-libbing*, which means they can improvise an impromptu speech without preparation. Radio reporters are often expected to report from the scene of a breaking story for much longer periods than their TV counterparts—this is because radio is normally not under the same time limitations as television. It is much easier to interrupt a music format on radio with a breaking story, for example, than it is to interrupt a soap opera on television. Lost advertising revenue is far less expensive for a radio station than for television, and it is much easier for a radio station to make up those lost commercials.

The best way to organize material for a live report is to use a *reporter's notebook*. Its slim design is particularly handy because it fits into a handbag or jacket pocket. Also, reporters should always take more than one pen or pencil. (In freezing weather or pouring rain, a pencil works much better than a pen.)

In anticipation of going live from the scene, broadcast reporters must keep notes on a variety of happenings. First, they must keep track of important comments that are made, whether during a news conference or a one-on-one interview. They must note exactly when the remarks were made so they can be located quickly on the videotape or audiotape. Some reporters take courses in speedwriting. Others develop a shorthand system of their own; thus their notes are illegible to anyone who happens to look at the page.

Experienced reporters learn that they cannot get so involved in taking notes that they lose control of the interview. They make entries only when comments are important enough to be used as a sound byte or in the narration that will surround it. Television reporters who synchronize their video camera with a time code recording system that shows the actual time of day that each scene is recorded only have to note the time when they record something important.

Reporting live presents different problems for radio and TV reporters. For starters, radio reporters work alone, whereas TV reporters have at least one and sometimes two people with them in the microwave truck.

The production of the live report also is handled differently by a TV reporter than by a radio reporter. Sometimes the news conference or individual interview is microwaved back to the station while it is in progress. An associate producer or a writer at the station may monitor the feed and make notes. When the feed is over, producers can quickly confer with the reporter on which sound bytes he or she wishes to use and then instruct the tape editor to cue them up. The reporter then does a live open from the scene, and the sound bytes are played from the station. The reporter returns after the bytes to do a live close.

It is also possible to do everything from the mobile unit. New technology allows TV crews to record and edit video in the truck, add the reporter's narration, and actually play the story from the truck without using any of the support equipment at the station. This type of sophisticated equipment was once found only in larger markets, although it is becoming more accessible to smaller markets as the technology becomes more affordable.

Another major difference between reporting live for radio and TV is obvious— the audience does not see the radio reporter. It does see the TV reporter, which adds some complications. The radio reporter can get comfortable in the front seat of the mobile unit, cue up her tape, spread her notes out, and concentrate on delivering her narration without worrying about anyone seeing her. Meanwhile, her TV colleague may be memorizing his script so that he is not looking at his notebook constantly during his time on camera.

Let's examine a typical live report filed by a radio reporter from the scene of a fire:

> Two people are known dead in a fire that swept through an apartment house on Rose Avenue in the suburban West End community of Center City. Fire Chief Kenneth Daw says he doesn't know if everyone else in the building escaped.
>
> (sound byte)
>
> "We think everyone but the one couple got out of there, but it's too early to tell. So far no one has reported anyone missing, so we are hopeful."
>
> (reporter)

The dead have been identified as Barbara Swift and her husband Robert. It's believed the fire started in their apartment shortly after midnight and spread to the rest of the building. So far, there's no information on what caused the fire, which was brought under control about an hour after it started. More than two dozen people were in the building. One woman who escaped, Val Hills, said she is happy to be alive:

(sound byte)

"There was so much smoke, that's what scared me the most. When I heard some shouting, I got up and I knew there must be a fire. Fortunately, I was able to get to the stairs and get out."

(reporter)

Some 50 firefighters and 10 pieces of equipment are still at the scene. Some of the firefighters are still hosing down the building and others are going through the debris just to make sure no one else is in there. Once again, two people are dead in this Rose Avenue fire in the West End. It's believed that everyone else escaped from the building. This is Cynthia Nells. Back to you in the studio, Bill.

Meanwhile, a TV station was carrying this story from its reporter at the scene via microwave. The story opens up with the reporter on camera and the fire scene behind her:

O/C Heather	Two bodies have been removed from this burned-out apartment building on Rose Avenue, and it's not yet known if there were any other fatalities. The fire started around midnight in one of the apartments and spread quickly through the rest of the building. Earlier, we spoke with a couple who escaped from the burning building.
SOT Font: Frank Lewis	SOT "We were asleep when we heard shouting and jumped out of bed. I could smell smoke. I grabbed some trousers and my wife tossed on a robe and we got the hell out of there."
Font: Laura Lewis	"I was scared stiff. I'm just happy to be alive." (Heather)
O/C two shot	With me now is Fire Chief Kenneth Daw. Chief, do you think everyone is out of there? (Chief) "Well, we're hopeful. So far no one has reported anyone missing so that's a good sign. But you never can be sure." (Heather) Do you know how the fire started? (Chief)

"Well, we think it started in the apartment of the couple who died in the fire and then spread to the other apartments, but so far we aren't sure how it started."

(Heather)

Thank you, Chief.

O/C tight shot of Heather	The couple who died in the fire have been identified as Barbara and Robert Swift. There was no other information available about them.
V/O	V/O
Shots of building and firefighters wetting it down	As you can see, this building is completely gutted, and if everyone else got out alive it would be amazing. Apparently some two dozen other people were in the building. About 50 firefighters have been battling the blaze. They brought it under control around one o'clock—
Shots of smoky building	about an hour after it began. Some of the firefighters have been moving slowly through parts of the burned-out building in an effort to determine if anyone could have been trapped inside. Meanwhile, other firefighters continue to hose down the smoldering remains of the building.
O/C Heather	O/C
	Once again, two people dead and apparently everyone else escaped from this apartment complex on Rose Avenue in the West End section of the City. This is Heather Nelson, KTHU News.

After the radio and TV reporters finished their live reports, they would probably be asked a few questions by the anchors. In a perfect scenario, the anchors and reporters confer in advance on what questions the anchors will ask. Not only does this allow the reporter to prepare to deliver an answer, it lets the anchor ask a solid question that will receive a knowledgeable answer.

Of course, such advance communication between the studio and the field is not always possible (or, on occasion, the anchor might just throw out a curveball question the reporter can't answer). If this is the case, the reporters must try to field whatever questions come their way without any advance preparation. That's when ad-libbing ability is important.

AD-LIBBING

Certain methods can help reporters improve their ad-libbing ability, or speaking without a script. Word association is one common method used by reporters to make sure they do not run out of things to say during a live

FIGURE 12.2

FIGURE 12.3

remote. Many reporters write down a list of key words or phrases in the order in which they want to cover their material. When they exhaust all the information dealing with a key word, they move to the next one on the list until they have covered everything. Good ad-libbing reporters need only that one word or phrase to keep them going, which is important because reporters are often forced into remote situations that require a considerable amount of ad-libbing.

ABC News correspondent Barry Serafin says the best way to learn how to ad-lib is by doing it. He says he never thinks about reporting to an audience of 20 million people but concentrates on the idea that he is conversing with a single person in a "natural and human manner." Serafin adds that "the main thing about ad-libbing is not to sound perfect. … Don't try to tell what you don't know. Don't speculate."

THE CHALLENGES OF ELECTRONIC NEWS GATHERING

A great way to prepare for the world of electronic news gathering is to do radio remotes. It is easier for TV reporters to handle the challenges of live television if they have a radio background, but not as many reporters are making the transition from radio to television as in the past.

Most TV reporters now start their careers in television, and they have to learn how to do remotes from the start. During the transition from film to videotape and microwave in the mid-1970s, many TV reporters found it difficult to make the adjustment. They were accustomed to having 45 minutes or more to write their scripts while the film was being developed. The only time TV reporters went live was when the station or network bought a telephone line, and that was reserved for important occasions. Many TV reporters were unable to handle the pressures of going live and thus changed jobs.

Former *ABC News* correspondent Morton Dean notes that it is "scary" when you have to go live and you are not quite sure what is going on. "I think that is the most difficult part of this business—covering a breaking story live," Dean says. "You are often out there 'naked' and you have to resist the pressure to give information that you're not certain of and to give your own personal thoughts as opposed to what's really going on." Dean says he's often asked to give his opinion about "what is going to happen" at the scene when he really does not know.

Dean recalled his reporting experience in the Gulf War when he was going live. At the time, Iraqi Scud missiles were zooming overhead, people were putting on their chemical outfits, and troops were running around with guns and taking their positions. "It's really very difficult to keep your wits about you," he said.

When asked if he was ever uncomfortable about his live reporting during the Gulf War, Dean said only to the extent that he developed a habit that may be considered bad in television: saying "I don't know" when he really doesn't know. "I think there's a terrible temptation to be glib," said Dean, "and just talk nonstop and maybe not say anything. You must have the courage to say 'I don't know,' and some people think that's a sin when you are on television."

Dean said there are times "when your mind is not working that quickly … and you have to feel secure enough to say 'I'm not sure about that' or 'I have to think about that.' " He also said there have been times when he refused to go live, telling his producer he really had nothing to say.

Similar concerns about technology were expressed in the mid-1990s by the late veteran newswoman Pauline Frederick of NBC. She noted that technology has "given our profession marvelous tools with which to work. But the question that should forever confront us is whether in our eagerness to use these instruments, the import of the message may become confused with the messenger, who could be perceived as trying to make and shape the news."

Former *CNN News* anchor and correspondent Bernard Shaw also raised some questions about the new technology. "We can fire up, and fly in or roll in portable satellite earth stations, slap on a wireless mike, report live, and not wait for tape at 11. We have digital this and digital that, telephones that connect to a satellite, fiber optics in the wings, and technology that will provide even smaller satellite dishes and antennas that will fit in an oversize briefcase. But," asked Shaw, "how are we using this stuff?"

Shaw went on to suggest several situations that raise the question of whether broadcast news technology offers balanced and fair reporting. "If

FIGURE 12.4

in covering a nation at war, a correspondent shows pictures of devastation without pointing out that the host government is severely restricting the movement of reporters and showing only what that government wants shown, is the crucial element of perspective for the viewer or listener well served?" asked Shaw. "If there are no pictures to videotape and no sounds to record but only shreds of information gained from listening and observing, is expensive live capability that impressive?" he asked. "If you are a reporter covering a protest around a nuclear power plant and you have the cameraperson shoot, say, 50 demonstrators tight so that it looks like 500 demonstrators, and if the reporter decides not to interview a plant spokesman because it's too close to satellite feed time, has that technology yielded better balance and a fair report?"

All the correspondents agree that electronic news gathering has increased the risk of inaccuracy. As stressed in earlier chapters, nothing is more important for journalists than accuracy. Reporting live to a community, to the nation, and often to the world carries with it a tremendous responsibility. As with any story, but particularly when covering a story live, reporters must check and double-check their information and must rely heavily on attribution when the slightest possibility exists that the information may not be accurate.

KEEPING COOL

All of us have seen a TV reporter in trouble during a live remote. The scene usually goes something like this: The reporter is standing in front of a camera getting ready to report live and something goes wrong with the ear piece system that allows the producer or cameraperson to speak with the reporter. The reporter ends up looking mystified because she does not know whether she is on the air. A cameraperson may be trying to signal what's going on, but sometimes this person is also in the dark. A worst-case scenario is when the reporter actually says, "Are we on?," when in fact she is.

Sometimes these mishaps can be avoided if a TV monitor is available for the reporter. That way, the reporter would know if she is on the air without having to wait for verbal instructions. These situations are trying for reporters, who understandably do not like to appear foolish in the eyes of the audience, but the TV audience has become so sophisticated that it tends to ignore such mishaps or, at worst, to chuckle a little over the breakdown in communications. It's best for reporters to accept the fact that mistakes are going to happen and equipment is going to malfunction.

The most common reason why a reporter might lose composure on camera is when a technical problem might prevent the reporter from being seen or heard. Technical problems are often the cause of reporters losing their cool during less dramatic live reports.

MEMORIZING AND DELIVERING LIVE REPORTS

Some reporters have an amazing ability to memorize scripts. Others cannot memorize more than a few lines of copy at a time. Overall, it's unfair to ask reporters to try to recall more than 20 seconds of a script. Because all TV reporters are eventually asked to do live reports, they must either develop the ability to memorize their material or use some tricks to help them. Most stations and networks have no problem with reporters glancing down at their notes during live reports, particularly during a breaking story. It's less acceptable, especially in a routine live report outside a city-council meeting or the mayor's office, to see a reporter's head bobbing up and down every few seconds to read notes.

Former *CBS News* correspondent Ben Silver says it sometimes helps "to just throw the script away." Silver recalls: "I was having trouble memorizing the close to a story and I must have done it 10 times when the cameraman finally said, 'Give me the script.' He took the clipboard from me and I did the close without any problem."

This thinking mirrors the *dining table solution*. Here, the reporter literally tosses the script down and pretends he's telling his family the story around the dining table. The advantage is that the report will usually hit the salient facts and ignore the minutiae that are merely cluttering up the story.

VOICEOVERS FROM THE FIELD

A *voiceover*, which is described in much greater detail in the following chapter, is a story in which you hear the anchor talking while video footage is aired; the voice is aired over the visual images, thus the term voiceover.

A growing trend when crafting live reports is for video to be rolled in while the reporter is narrating. To accomplish this, the field videographer will beam footage to the newsroom prior to the live shot. This footage may either be raw, which is unedited field footage, or be cut into a voiceover. When the live shot is then under way, the newsroom will roll the footage over the reporter's narration. While this is a bit trickier than a standard live shot, it gives the

FIGURE 12.5

CNN's Bill Hemmer reports from Florida during Hurricane Frances.

viewing audience more to look at than the reporter merely presenting from the field.

Adding a layer of video requires more preproduction than a regular live shot, plus there must be precise communication between the field and the newsroom during the actual report so the video rolls at the right time. These technical considerations can be managed with a clear communication chain, which is addressed in the next section.

TECHNICAL CHALLENGES

In no other aspect of broadcast journalism is the reporter more at the mercy of technical difficulties than during a live field report. There is a *communication chain* that must be followed during the report. This chain ensures several elements will flow in both directions between the newsroom and the field reporter.

The most obvious elements are the video and audio that emanate from the field report. The video is the simplest to define; it's a clear visual image from the remote location that's beamed back to the studio's engineering center. The on-air audio is usually limited to one handheld microphone that is handled by the reporter, although there may be a second microphone for either ambient audio (such as at a political rally) or an interviewee who has a dedicated lavaliere microphone.

But these are only two of the four parts of the communications chain. The third element is an open phone line, usually between the field videographer's cell phone and a studio engineer, who coordinates the technical aspects of the feed. Because getting a clear signal often requires the reaiming of portable antennae, calibrating the audio and video feeds, and general tweaking to eliminate noise and enhance the image, a phone line must be reserved for the engineer to send commands to the field.

The final element is the *interrupted feedback* (IFB) line. An IFB is the return audio from the studio that allows the reporter to hear the anchor's questions from the set. This is accomplished through a simple audio line, although it feeds audio backward—from the newsroom and back to the field. Of course, it must reach the field reporter through an

FIGURE 12.6

(Foreground) Photographer Rick Portier and (background) photography editor Patrick Perry checking video at WBRZ, Baton Rouge, Louisiana.

earpiece and not a field speaker; if the anchor's question was transmitted to the field by a speaker, it would loop back into the reporter's field microphone, causing feedback.

Each of the four lines in a communication chain (field audio, field video, engineering phone line, and reporter IFB) must be operational well before the reporter appears on the newscast. Reporting live entails a great deal of coordination with ample advance time for setting up. Additionally, the field crew must make sure that the reporter can deliver the news without any background distractions. Far too many field reports have been ruined by uncooperative people in the background mugging for the camera or making fun of the reporter.

SUMMARY

The biggest challenge that most broadcast reporters face is reporting live. Radio reporters have always faced that challenge because they could report from the scene of a breaking story in minutes with the use of a two-way radio. TV reporters relied on film for their coverage until the 1970s, when two tech-

FIGURE 12.7

nologies were developed: small, portable videotape cameras (minicams) and microwave. Reporters suddenly lost the luxury of preparing their reports while they were traveling back from the scene of a story and while the film was being developed. Suddenly, reporters found that with microwave technology, they were often asked to go on the air immediately, while their videotape was being edited or cued up within minutes of being shot. They discovered that most of their thinking time had disappeared.

These developments brought about not only new challenges but also new risks. When thinking time is reduced, the chance of inaccuracy is increased. As a result, TV reporters have two concerns: (1) to collect information and sort it out quickly and (2) to ensure that it is accurate. The immediacy of the new technology also requires that reporters learn to ad-lib, making their improvised speech look easy and comfortable.

Test Your Knowledge

1. New technology permits broadcast news reporters to go live from almost any part of the globe with short notice. But these technological advances also place new burdens and responsibilities on journalists. Explain.

2. Good organization and note taking are important when a reporter covers a story live. How can these skills be developed?

3. What is ad-libbing and why is it essential that field reporters master it?

4. What is the dining table solution?

5. What are the four elements of the communications chain? Why is each needed for a successful live shot?

EXERCISES

1. Cover some event in the community and then arrange for another student in the school's broadcast lab to videotape your stand-up report. After you have given your report, have the other student question you on tape. Return to the lab and watch the tape.

2. Cover a news conference with either an audiocassette player or video equipment. If you are using an audiocassette player, pick a sound byte and cue it up so that you can play it over the phone in the middle of a wraparound. If you are using a video camera, do an open and close at the scene without preparing a script. Return to the lab and insert a sound byte between the open and the close that you recorded at the scene.

3. Have another student read a lengthy story to you from a newspaper. Make notes as he or she reads the story. Study your notes for 2 minutes and then record a report either on audiotape or on video. Play it back for other students and your professor, and ask for an evaluation.

4. Watch several local newscasts until you see two or three live shots. Discuss if these live shots are justified by whether the stories are "current" or if the live shots are being done in front of a "closed" location.

CHAPTER 13

Voiceovers, Packages, and Story Formats

KEY WORDS

Advancing Stories	Reader	Stand-up Open
Assignment Board	Sound Byte	Touch and Go
Font	Split Page	The Tricycle
Natural Sound	Stand-up Bridge	Principle
Package	Stand-up Close	Voiceover

CONTENTS

INTRODUCTION

The major difference between radio and TV news is, of course, pictures. When you write for television, pictures are always crucial to a story. In radio, you must create pictures in your mind and then find the words to paint those pictures for your audience. In television, you can show the actual pictures.

In television, as in radio, a writer's duties depend on the size of the newsroom. In a small market—and even in some medium-sized markets—no one is assigned solely to writing. The anchors, reporters, producers, and perhaps an intern from a local college write the news. Television newsrooms in big markets and at the networks usually have several writers and, perhaps, associate producers who also write. There are also *packages*, which are self-contained video stories that come from reporters in the field.

This chapter introduces a variety of terms used in television news, such as *split page*, *voiceover*, and *font*, and describes a television writer's most common writing assignments.

In carrying out these assignments, you need to learn to work with both words and pictures; broadcast news professionals have strong views on which is more important—words or pictures. The truth, of course, is that *both* words and pictures are critical to a successful TV news script. Television is a visual medium, and the pictures must be effective, but if the words that go with those pictures

205

FIGURE 13.1

Readers *are stories read by anchors without the use of pictures.*

are unclear, confusing, or contradictory, the story will fail because no true communication will take place.

Choose your pictures carefully and do the same with your words. We'll start with readers, the most basic form of story on an evening newscast.

READERS

Readers are stories that are read by the anchors without the use of pictures. Visually, readers are the least interesting in TV news; they are virtually the same as radio copy. They are, however, a necessary part of the TV newscast because they give the anchors exposure to the audience. Anchors are paid well, and the audience expects to see their faces on camera at least part of the time.

Sometimes, readers are used because no video is available. They might even lead the newscast if it is a breaking story. But readers are often stories that are not important enough to require video or whose video would be dull. At the same time, readers play a major role in the TV newscast—they break up the other types of material. Because too much of anything tends to be boring, the readers provide a change of pace.

Another option for readers is to air them with a full-page graphic. This is more visually interesting for the viewer, plus it allows the newsroom's graphic artist the opportunity to put bullet points, contact information, or a map over the talking anchor. A reader on a simple story such as a blood drive could be supplemented with full-page graphics, such as the location and operating hours of the donation center. For a traffic accident or other breaking news for which there is no video yet, a quick map of where the incident is happening is useful to the viewing audience.

Finally, readers are easiest to work with in a newscast because they are flexible. They are the putty that fills in the holes of the newscast. Readers often play the same role as radio pad copy; they provide an opportunity to make adjustments that guarantee that the newscast gets off the air on time. If the TV newscast is long, the readers are the likely stories to be dropped. If the newscast is short, more readers will probably be added. While readers are straightforward stories of just written text, television news depends on video images; let's examine the interaction between the visual pictures and the spoken narration.

COMBINING WORDS AND PICTURES

The battle over which are more important in television news—words or pictures—is endless. There is no doubt that words are vital and that some broadcast writers use them more effectively than others. *Great* pictures and *great* words make great television news.

The beauty of good pictures is that they do not need a lot of words—just some good ones. The challenge for TV writers is to avoid clashes with the video. Do not tell viewers what they are seeing. Instead, support the video by saying what the video does not or cannot reveal. Fill in the blanks, but do not overpower the video. Give your viewers time to savor the pictures.

This is best explained via the *touch and go* principle. Assume you have a series of five shots for a voiceover; they show a family festival in the park. The shots are a wide shot (WS) of dozens of people milling about a park playground, a WS of two kids on a seesaw, a medium shot (MS) of one of the kids bouncing up and down, a close-up (CU) of one of the kids' smiling faces, and a final WS of adoring parents watching the kids. One example of poor narration would be:

> Saturday in the park brought out dozens of people. Two kids played on the seesaw, going up and down. Judging by their smiles, they both seemed to be having a good time. Even their parents were happy to be there.

Awful. Not only is it lousy writing, you are simply telling the viewers what they're already seeing. Instead, the touch and go principle allows you to tie the establishing video and narration together and then lets the narration advance the story while the video maintains the story line. For example,

> Saturday in the park brought out dozens of people. But moments like this are in jeopardy with state budget cuts. The latest figures would remove 15 percent of the money from parks and recreation. First to go? Local parks.

See the difference? By merely touching the first video in the sequence and then proceeding into solid narration, you can expand the storytelling beyond mere recitation of what the viewer sees. Of course, such advice assumes that you have good pictures to work with. If you don't, then the words become more crucial because they are needed to prop up the video. But because TV news is not about using poor video, stories with bad pictures are likely to be dropped for more appealing ones unless the messages they convey are too vital to be eliminated completely.

If the pictures are poor, you can be sure you'll be asked to tell the story quickly. A common criticism of television news is that it relies on the pictures too much, but right or wrong the formula is not likely to change: poor pictures, short stories; good pictures, long stories.

VOICEOVERS

The simplest type of video story is the *voiceover* (VO). The structure is similar to that of a reader, but the anchor reads the copy while video or other visuals are shown. The video can either be silent or have a soundtrack that is kept low for natural effect, a technique referred to as *sound under* or *natural sound*.

Remember that the copy must complement the video; it should not duplicate what is obvious to viewers. Avoid phrases such as "what you are seeing here" unless the video is difficult to understand. For example, if you are showing video of a train derailment, rather than tell your viewers "What you are seeing is the derailment of a Conrail freight train that left its tracks last night," you would say "A Conrail freight train left its tracks last night" and let the pictures show the derailed train.

FIGURE 13.2

Great stories come from a combination of great pictures and great words.

To write voiceover copy intelligently, you need to look at the video and take notes. When viewing the video, use a stopwatch to time each scene. The cameraperson sometimes shoots a series of short shots that may require little editing, but individual shots are often too long to use without editing. To illustrate, let's assume a field crew returned to the newsroom with video of a train wreck.

The cameraperson shot a long, continuous pan of the wrecked cars that lasts about 30 seconds. There's another shot of a derrick hovering over the scene for 20 seconds and a third 20-second shot of railroad workers huddled around a hastily made trashcan fire to ward off the frigid weather.

FIGURE 13.3

Voiceover copy must complement the video footage.

Finally, there's an additional 30 seconds of video that show some of the train's wrecked cargo—an assortment of steel rods and girders and lumber. The total running time of the video is 1 minute and 40 seconds. The producer asks the writer for a 20-second voiceover. The writer then must lift an assortment of brief shots from the video that can be strung together in some logical order that will make sense when narration is added. In a small newsroom, reporters often write the script and edit the videotape. In a large operation, a tape editor follows the writer's or reporter's instructions.

Now that the writer has notes on the length of each scene, she must decide how to *edit*, or *cut*, the video. (*Cut* is a film term that has carried over to video. All editing is done electronically; the videotape is not physically cut.) The writer decides to use part of the long pan of the wreck scene first. The cameraperson held steady on the scene at the end of the pan, knowing that the writer might wish to use part of it. It is poor technique to cut into a pan, but it is acceptable to use part of it as long as it comes to a stop before the next shot. The writer uses 8 seconds of the pan. Then the writer selects 5 seconds of the wreckage video that shows the steel girders and the lumber spread over the tracks and terrain. Four seconds of the derrick at work follow, and the voiceover closes with 3 seconds of the railroad workers around the trashcan fire.

The writer gives her instructions to the tape editor and then returns to her desk to type out the script from her notes and wire copy. In preparing the script, the writer uses a format different from that used in radio.

SCRIPTING THE VOICEOVER

In a VO, the newscaster or reporter reads copy as the video appears on the screen. Normally, voiceovers are not long because they are usually used to break up a series of packages or to give the anchors some exposure. The following is the script for three short voiceovers used in a newscast produced by WBRZ-TV in Baton Rouge, Louisiana:

Two shot O/C Jayne and Andrea	(Jayne) Updating some of the other stories making news across the nation...authorities in Newport News, Virginia, are investigating an accident involving a Conrail train.
Roll VO—Train Video of derailed train	(Jayne VO) A dump truck collided with this train at a railroad crossing. The force of the collision sent the engine and all five passenger cars off the tracks.
Video of injured people	The driver of the truck died in the accident...about 50 people on the train were hurt, but not seriously.

Wipe to VO—Plane	(Andrea VO)
Video of plane wreckage	And divers in North Carolina are searching for the
Font: Blevelt Falls	bodies of nine people who died when a military
	transport plane crashed into this lake in North
	Carolina.
Lake Lilesville, NC	
More video of wreckage	The victims were stationed at Fort Polk. They were
	on a training mission. So far, the cause of the
	crash is unknown.
Wipe to VO—Kennedy	(Jayne VO)
Kennedy and wife shaking hands	And a citizens' group called Public Citizen is
with people in Dallas	demanding the National Archives release nearly
Kennedy motorcade in Dallas	200 autopsy photos and X-rays of President
	Kennedy.
Video of people on lawn as	A bill in Congress would require the release of
Kennedy motorcade goes by	documents pertaining to the assassination, but
	excludes the autopsy material to protect the
	Kennedy family's privacy.
ON CAMERA TAG	(Andrea O/C)
	A spokesman for this citizens' group says the
	materials should be public record.

Most newscasts use voiceovers along with readers to fill in the time around packages; voiceovers seldom run longer than 20 or 30 seconds. The first VO in the example ran 24 seconds, the second ran 16 seconds, and the third ran 27 seconds. They were separated by *wipes*, an electronic technique that slides one video picture off the screen and replaces it with another—in this case with the opening video of the next story.

INCORPORATING SOUND BYTES

As in radio, *sound bytes*, the words of newsmakers, are key to telling a good TV news story. An advantage for TV writers is that TV sound bytes feature the faces of the newsmakers as well as their voices. A byte is also referred to as sound on tape (SOT).

From a technical standpoint, there are certain elements a reporter wants from a SOT. First, it needs to contain relevant information; plastering in a SOT that conveys no usable words is a waste of air time. Second, production skills such as good lighting and audio are expected, as poor production values will eliminate the effectiveness of the interview. Finally, an ideal SOT lasts 8 to 14 seconds. If it's much longer, it becomes a speech. If it's too short, the technical director will not have enough time to key in the graphics font of the interviewee's name.

The next layer of news beyond a voiceover adds a sound byte to the video. This is known as a VOSOT, V-SOT, or VO-BYTE—the terminology differs from newsroom to newsroom. Essentially, it's a VO with a sound byte woven into it.

Let's go back to the train wreck story and suppose that there is some sound on tape of one of the workers trying to keep warm around the trashcan fire. The writer decides to add that sound on tape to the script at the end of the VO before the anchor comes back on camera. The script would look like this:

SOT :15   TRACK UP
FONT: Mark Florman   OUTCUE "... get any railroad
                                 worker warmer."
                                 Time :15
ON CAMERA TAG   (Andrea O/C)
                                 Railroad officials say that while
                                 the wreckage is being removed
                                 and repairs made to the
                                 tracks, Conrail passenger
                                 trains will be detoured. This
                                 probably will cause delays for
                                 at least 48 hours.

The sound-on-tape symbol and the time appear in the left-hand column to indicate that sound on tape will be used at this point in the script. The director now knows that when the anchor reads the last words of the voiceover, it is time to bring in the sound on tape.

FIGURE 13.4

The terms "Track Up" and "Time 15" also appear in the right-hand column along with the outcue, the final words of the sound byte. This lets the anchor know that a 15-second sound byte comes up before he returns on camera to read the last sentence in the story. The abbreviation *FONT* in the left column means that the name and identification of the railroad worker are to be super-imposed over the lower portion of the screen while the railroad worker is speaking. The director will signal the font operator to punch up the informa-tion approximately 3 seconds into the sound byte.

After the sound byte instructions, the anchor returns on camera to wrap up or "tag" the story or to begin a new story.

Here's an example of a V-SOT script, but this time there is more video available to the director; the editor has placed video before and after the SOT, thus giving the director the option of returning to the anchor after the SOT or staying with the field footage.

VO	(Jayne VO)
Video of police officers at graduation Video of female graduates Video of Black and family Video of Black holding daughter	Wheatland's fight against crime got a boost today with the graduation of 45 new officers from the police academy. Among the officers—eleven women. One of them is Ann Black, and she had her own cheering section: her mother and father, her husband, and her three-year-old daughter, Janet. Black's father also is a police officer.
SOT: 05	(SOT/Ann Black)
	"It's just a wonderful time … to finally be on the force, like my dad, and to have everyone I love here to cheer me on … it's just great."

At this point, the anchor could return on camera to do a tag to the story or go back to a voiceover, as is the case here:

VO	(Jayne VO)
Video of graduates tossing hats in air	The 45 new officers will not have too much time to celebrate. They report for duty in the morning.

VOSOT stories are usually used when the producer decided that the material was not strong enough, or of enough interest to the audience, to warrant the time necessary for a package. Because there is no on-camera reporter, VOSOTs are usually shot by the field videographer alone.

There have been countless newsroom battles between reporters and producers over VOSOTs, particularly when a reporter returns from the field only to learn the story had been "downgraded" to a VOSOT. This is frustrating if the reporter had already outlined the package and even shot a stand-up, but the finite time in a local newscast often means packages may be turned into VOSOTs to save time on the rundown.

THE SPLIT PAGE

Audio

As you'll notice from the aforementioned examples, scripts are written in a split-page format—television scripts differ from radio scripts because they contain both the newscaster's words and an explanation of how the video is to be used. The format for a TV script is known as the *split page*. On a standard-sized sheet of paper, the split page is divided vertically so that about 60 percent of the page is in the right column and about 40 percent is in the left. Although their product is often sent electronically to the teleprompters, backup scripts are also printed out in case the computers malfunction.

The right side of the split page is reserved for the copy that will be read by the anchors, the running times (which also appear on the left), and the outcues (final words) of any videotape that has sound. The anchors—and this is important to remember—will be able to see only the right side of the script on their teleprompters. It is also important that you write only in the column on the right side. If you write outside the column, the words will not appear on the teleprompter screens.

Video

The left side of the split-page script is set aside for the slug, video and audio instructions, and tape times for the director. Because of the limited space on the left side of the script, abbreviations are used for the various technical instructions. Here are some common ones:

- O/C, "on camera," tells the director that at this point in the script the anchor will be on camera.

- VO, "voiceover," means the anchor is reading copy while the audience is seeing something else, such as silent videotape or graphics.

- SIL indicates "silent" videotape and is used in combination with the VO symbol.

- SOT lets the director know that there is "sound on tape." It could be a sound byte with a newsmaker or a report from the field that was taped earlier.

- ENG, "electronic news gathering," tells the director that the video is on a videotape.

- FONT, an abbreviation for the manufacturer Videfont, indicates that names, titles, and other information are superimposed over videotape or graphics to identify newsmakers, locations, and various other pictures appearing on TV screens. Many stations use the term *super* or the abbreviation VG (video graphic) instead of FONT.

- SL, ESS, or ADDA indicates that pictures or graphics of some sort will be shown next to the anchor. SL stands for "slide"; ESS refers to Electronic Still Storage, an electronic graphics and video computer system; and ADDA is the name of a computer system that also provides electronic storage. If the word box appears next to any of these abbreviations, the graphic will be enclosed in a box next to the anchor rather than fill the entire screen.

The following split-page script is used for the train wreck story discussed earlier. Unlike the previous version that showed how the video was put together shot by shot, the on-air director doesn't care which individual shots were used. Instead, the concern now is for the finished video to be incorporated into the newscast, complete with the anchor, graphics, and technical cues.

TRAIN WRECK 3/15 6pm	(Jayne O/C)
O/C Jayne Box ADDA	A Conrail freight train today left the tracks near Wheatland, causing some major problems for passenger service trains that also use the tracks.
VO SIL (TRT: 40 sec.)	VO
	Railroad officials say the locomotive and eight of the train's 14 cars were derailed. They blamed a broken rail. Remarkably, there were only two injuries—to the engineer and his assistant—and they were not serious.
	The train was on its way to southern California with a load of steel and lumber when the accident took place shortly before midnight.
	The wreckage was scattered over a wide area. Within hours a derrick was sent to the scene to help clean up the mess. Officials say the job will take days.
	Freezing temperatures—dipping into the teens—will make the cleanup difficult and unpleasant.
Jayne O/C Tag	(Jayne O/C)
	Railroad officials say that while the wreckage is being removed and repairs made to the tracks, Conrail passenger trains will be detoured. This probably will cause delays for at least 48 hours.

If you examine this script, you will see that the slug *TRAIN WRECK* is in the upper left-hand corner along with the date and the time of the newscast.

On the next line in the right column is *Jayne*, the name of the anchor. Because most newscasts have two or more anchors, the name of the anchor reading the copy must always be displayed at the top of the right-hand column.

On the next line at the left is *O/C Jayne*, which lets the director know which anchor is on camera. Underneath that are the words *Box ADDA*, which tell the director that a picture will be displayed in a box next to the anchor's head. In this case, it could be a generic train wreck graphic that TV newsrooms keep on hand along with scores of other such graphics. It also could be a freeze frame of part of the video that would be shown with the voiceover. But if that were the case, the writer would have to indicate it by typing *SIL/FF* (silent/freeze frame) next to *Box ADDA*.

The anchor's script continues on the right side. Below the first sentence, you see the VO symbol, which means that at this point in the script the video will be shown. The anchor continues reading, but the audience no longer sees her face.

The VO symbol is also displayed in the left-hand column with the abbreviation for silent videotape, *SIL*, for the benefit of the director. In parentheses is the total running time of the videotape (TRT: 40 seconds), which tells the director that there are actually 40 seconds of wreckage footage on the videocassette. Because the VO copy should take only about 30 seconds to read, the director has a 10-second cushion to avoid going to black, which is a nightmare for directors and their bosses. To avoid that problem, tape editors always "pad the tape"—cut more tape than the writer requests.

When the anchor has finished reading the VO copy, she returns on camera (which is why we show O/C in both columns) to read a final sentence about delays in rail service brought on by the wreck. That final sentence is called a *tag*, and the writer of this script has added the word *tag* after O/C in the left column just to remind the busy director that this is the end of the story.

THE PACKAGE

The foundation of any TV newscast is its packages. That's because, if they are done well, packages have all the elements that bring a story alive: good pictures, interesting sound bytes, and a well-written script. If any of these elements is weak, the story may be downgraded (to a VOSOT or even a VO) or kept short. In other words, the quality of the video and the sound bytes often determines the length of a package. But even great video and excellent sound bytes do not always guarantee a long package; it depends on what else is going on in the news that day. Even on slow days, packages rarely run longer than 90 seconds.

For this example, let's walk through a package on how a drought is affecting local crops. Before leaving the newsroom, reporter Emily Goodwin has scheduled interviews with two subjects. The county extension agent, Jay Price, can meet for an interview at his office at 9 a.m. to provide statistics about crop failures and how farmers are coping. At 10 a.m., she is slated to interview Mark Stewart, a local blueberry and peach grower. That interview will take place at his farm, where her videographer expects to record footage of irrigation sprinklers, farm machinery, and shriveled crops.

Good organization is essential in putting together a successful package. In fact, most reporters understand the fundamentals of their stories before they actually produce the package. They may not have every detail pinned down, but in this example, Goodwin knows there will be two interviews, footage from the farm, and the opportunity for a *stand-up*; this is part of the story where the reporter appears on camera and addresses the camera directly. A discussion of how to create a good stand-up follows, but for now, know that the reporter plans to be on-camera during the package.

The first interview is a snap; most county extension agents are familiar with reporters and have been on-camera a number of times so the interview is relaxed yet informative. Goodwin jots down notes, listening for a good sound byte. Halfway through the interview, Price mentions that federal aid may not be coming this year, saying "The federal aid program is out of money, and even if there's any money at all, it won't get here for a good six months. We're looking at bankruptcy for a lot of really good people."

Although the interview continues, Goodwin had mentally flagged that quote. It's good, informative, and lasts about 12 seconds (perfect for a sound byte). Note that she doesn't immediately halt the interview once she has her workable byte, as there may be more to come.

When finished, she thanks the extension agent, the videographer gets a few quick shots of her talking to the agent (to use as cutaway footage if needed), and they head to the farm. On the way there, Goodwin may review the footage in the news vehicle or, if she brought a small audio recorder, will listen to the interview to time any potential sound bytes.

The next location, Mr. Stewart's farm, reveals a number of shooting possibilities: idle farm equipment, irrigation sprinklers spraying the crops with water, and fruit that may not be saved despite the farmer's best efforts. Goodwin talks to Stewart for a few minutes while the videographer shoots some cover footage. Included in this footage are several shots of Goodwin and Stewart walking among the crops.

The interview is shot beneath the peach trees. Stewart is passionate, near tears, at the thought of losing this year's crop. Again, Goodwin listens intently, silently counting the number of workable sound bytes. She identifies four, all of which are between 10 and 15 seconds, that bring a human emotion to the story.

As the interview ends, they thank Stewart and then Goodwin turns the videographer loose to finish shooting. Goodwin sits in the news vehicle for a minute, writes a few notes for a stand-up, and rejoins the videographer. They shoot several takes of the stand-up; this is standard as the videographer never knows when a part of the tape will be wrinkled or "drop out." Goodwin presents the stand-up as a bridge, which will occur in the middle of the story.

Back in the newsroom, Goodwin confirms that the producer still wants 90 seconds for the package. She then times the sound bytes: one from Price (12 seconds), two from Stewart (10 seconds each), and her stand-up (13 seconds). Note that her stand-up is logged as a sound byte, as she will incorporate it into her package just like any other SOT from the field. Her list is:

> Price—"The federal aid program is out of money, and even if there's any money at all, it won't get here for a good six months. We're looking at bankruptcy for a lot of really good people."—12 seconds
> Stewart (1)—"The way the crops have been affected, I've had to lay off half of my field crew. They're gone. I don't know when I'll get them back."—10 seconds

Stewart (2)—"I don't understand why we can't get help. That's why we
pay taxes into the government, to help us out. Ain't they got any
money for us?"—10 seconds
Goodwin—"The workers are gone because the crops may be a total loss.
Right now, the only movement in the fields comes from the automated
sprinklers. But even these sprinklers can't make up for lack of rain.
"—13 seconds

As a visual medium, television allows flexibility in building news packages.
One way is to emphasize the best video images first, thus hooking the viewer
into watching the story. A number of news directors advocate putting the
strongest video within the first 5 seconds. This plays to the strength of television, as compelling images are unmatched in other media.

Another strategy is counterintuitive; instead of concentrating on the pictures,
the reporter builds the audio track first. This is useful for novice reporters
who have difficulty hitting their allotted time. With the preceding four bytes,
let's arrange them as follows: Stewart (1), Goodwin, Stewart (2), and Price.
Adding the bytes together gives us a running time of 45 seconds out of the
90 seconds possible. This leaves 45 seconds of airtime for Goodwin to tell
the story.

The next step is to link the bytes together with bits of narration, which
Goodwin will record onto an audio track. During editing, the bytes (and their
accompanying video) will be interspersed with the audio segments. For this
example, Goodwin writes her narration like this:

Narration (1)—"Usually, the peaches and blueberries at this farm are
ready to pick by now. But there's not enough rain. And it's killing the
crop."—10 seconds
Stewart (1)—"The way the crops have been affected, I've had to lay off
half of my field crew. They're gone. I don't know when I'll get them
back."—10 seconds
Goodwin—"The workers are gone because the crops may be a total loss.
Right now, the only movement in the fields comes from the automated
sprinklers. But even these sprinklers can't make up for lack of rain.
"—13 seconds
Narration (2)—"The drought started three months ago, sending farmers
scrambling to find either water or money. Right now, they can't find
either."—10 seconds
Stewart (2)—"I don't understand why we can't get help. That's why we
pay taxes into the government, to help us out. Ain't they got any
money for us?"—10 seconds
Narration (3)—"But unlike past years, the agriculture department's relief
funds are already gone."—7 seconds

Price—"The federal aid program is out of money, and even if there's any money at all, it won't get here for a good six months. We're looking at bankruptcy for a lot of really good people."—12 seconds

Narration (4)—"While the outlook for federal funds is bad, the extended weather forecast is even worse. No rain is expected for at least two more weeks. And as the drought continues, farmers like Mark Stewart say the irrigation may only save a fraction of their crops. For News 20, I'm Emily Goodwin."—18 seconds

Once the audio track is laid down, the editor lays video and natural sound on top of the narration segments. The end result is a 90-second package, complete with field footage, interviews, and a reporter's stand-up.

Most reporters use a hybrid of these two strategies. They are aware of their best video, plus they position their audio clips to tell a cohesive story. With practice, broadcast journalists create the package's narrative structure as a holistic combination of video and audio.

STAND-UPS AND REPORTER INVOLVEMENT

Many news directors want to see their reporters' faces in their stories. They encourage reporters to appear on camera either at the end or in the middle of their packages. The theory is that the audience should think of the reporters and anchors as "family," and the more on-air exposure these family members get, the better management likes it.

The best reason for a reporter to appear in a story is to help explain it. Some reporters would argue that should be the only time a reporter is seen on air. Whenever a reporter appears on the camera and continues the narrative by speaking directly to the viewers, it's called a *stand-up*. These are broken into three categories: *opens*, *bridges*, and *closes*. Closes are the most common, as the reporter gives a final sentence, followed by their name and station.

A stand-up open takes place at the start of the reporter's package. It looks much like a live shot from the reporter in the field, as the first frame of video shows the reporter addressing the camera. CNN Newsource and other news services even distribute such packages as "look lives" where the reporter begins the story with a stand-up open. This allows the news anchors to toss directly to the prerecorded tape as if the reporter is live in the field.

If there is a lack of video, the story is late-breaking, and the producer wants to give the appearance of urgency, stand-up opens can offer options for those in the field. But stand-up opens are often clumsy and lead to poor story structure. Far too often, a stand-up open offers nothing but time-killing sentences as the reporter talks on camera. For example,

> I'm standing here outside of the nightclub that's the focus of a
> number of noise violations. I decided to talk to the owner of the club
> to see what's going on.

Not only is that a poor stand-up, but it shifts the attention of the story to the reporter. You're standing there? You decided to talk to the owner? That's called being a reporter; the audience isn't necessarily enthralled with you actually doing your job that day.

Another challenge with stand-up opens is that it's hard to write good leads in the field. Unless you've screened the sound bytes, written the copy, and committed yourself to the final product, you take a risk in recording your lead sentence on the videotape. As noted in the chapter on writing leads, the first few seconds are the most important in the story. By locking in the lead in the field, you lose the option of crafting something better before you edit.

Finally, some news directors frown on stand-up opens that are used consistently. The implication is that the reporter is more important than the story. Use the stand-up open sparingly if you're a veteran. If you're a student journalist, don't use them at all; it sends the message to prospective employers that you want the viewer to see your face before the actual news.

On occasion, a reporter can help the viewer better understand a situation by appearing on camera in the middle of the story. This is called a stand-up bridge, which can be useful in tying together two parts of a complicated story.

Let's say the football team must practice for a big game, but a deluge makes the practice field a soupy mess. The coach calls for practice inside the gym. This scenario lends itself to a stand-up bridge, as there will be two physical locations in the same story. The package can begin with video of the soggy field and then cut to a stand-up bridge inside the gym:

> But the coach said there was just too much rain and too much risk
> that a player would be injured while sliding around. The solution?
> Bring the team inside and run some plays inside the old gym.

In this way, the stand-up bridge can tie together two physical locations. It may also bridge the gap between two different sides of an issue (hunters versus vegans, Democrats versus Republicans) or two competing aspects of an individual's life (day care teacher by day, kickboxing champion by night). Consider using bridges when there are two sides of a story, but remember they can disrupt a story when a reporter suddenly appears for no practical reason.

Some of the worst examples of reporter involvement occur when the reporters become a part of the story. Unfortunately, many news directors have no problem with reporters sledding down hills during a snowstorm, eating a hot

FIGURE 13.5

The late CBS News *correspondent Charles Kuralt and his camera crew work on one of his* On the Road *reports (courtesy of CBS News).*

dog at a street festival, or lifting weights at the opening of a new health spa. The late Charles Kuralt, in his book *A Life on the Road*, wrote this about reporter involvement:

With respect to my own appearances on camera, we have adopted the Tricycle Principle. We were somewhere in the Midwest, watching the local news on the TV set in the bus before going out to supper. There was a feature about a children's tricycle race, cute little toddlers pedaling away and bumping into one another, an appealing story pretty well-filmed and edited.

Izzy said, "You know what? Before this is over, the reporter is going to ride a tricycle."

"Oh, no," I said. "That would ruin the whole thing."

Sure enough, the reporter signed off in a close-up with a silly grin, the camera pulled back to show that he was perched on a tricycle, and he turned and pedaled clumsily away, making inane what had, until then, been charming. The anchor people came on laughing to sign off the show.

The Tricycle Principle is simple: "When doing a tricycle story, don't ride a tricycle." The story is about CHILDREN, dummy, not about you. Keep yourself out of it. Try to control your immodesty.

Some TV audience members and news producers think such reporter involvement is cute. However, many news directors agree with Kuralt. They will tell you that they discourage such behavior and want reporters involved in their stories only when there is a legitimate reason. For example, it would not be inappropriate for a reporter to demonstrate how to use a new at-home device that measures blood pressure. Doing so could be the best way for the reporter to explain how the new device works.

POSTING STORIES

Once a story is finished and on the air, broadcast journalists do not simply go home for the day. Due to convergence and the audience's never-ending demand for updated news, reporters are now expected to post their finished stories on the television station's Web site. The time commitment varies from newsroom to newsroom; some merely have an assistant post the entire newscast onto the Web site, whereas others require reporters to put their individual stories online into different files and folders.

Fortunately, the days of reporters using the cumbersome HTML computer programming code have ended. Posting digitized news packages is often a simple matter of transferring a video file into the Web site and adding a few

FIGURE 13.6

lines of explanatory text. Although posting video stories may seem daunting, it usually takes just a few moments to move the files over. The greatest concern is keeping the files current. This requires the newsroom to update its video files every few hours.

SUMMARY

As you can see, writing television news is more complicated than writing radio news. Although one individual writes the television story and may even edit the videotape used in the story, the final product involves other people in the newsroom.

In radio, writers usually pick the stories they wish to tell their audience. In television, those who write the stories are told what to write and how long the stories should be. In radio, one person may do it all—record interviews on the phone, cover a news conference, and include in the newscast some of the tape he or she has edited. There are no one-person newsrooms in television, although at small stations you may be expected to play more than one role.

As in radio, television affords opportunities to learn how to do several different jobs. Writers often go on to other positions as reporters, anchors, and producers. Some move over to the assignment desk, where the people "find the news," a subject discussed in Chapter 1.

When reporters leave the newsroom on assignments, they never know how their stories will turn out. The producers and assignment editors may be looking for a package—a story that includes one or more sound bytes, the reporter's narration, and video. Sometimes they must settle for less because the story itself turns out to be less important than they originally thought or because the interviews are not strong or the video is weak. When that happens, the story becomes a VOSOT or perhaps even a VO.

No matter what the final format of a story is, one thing reporters find exciting about their job is that they rarely know what's going to happen when they get to work. Once a story is handed to them, they may be reassigned to a breaking news story while they're in the field, learn that the story has been shortened from a PKG to a VOSOT, or even find out that their story has been "upgraded" to the lead slot (complete with an on-set appearance next to the anchor). If reporters have enough flexibility to accommodate the needs of their newsroom in generating stories, they'll find themselves a valuable part of the news team.

Test Your Knowledge

1. What is the major difference between writing for radio and writing for television?
2. How will poor pictures affect TV news stories?
3. How important are sound bytes to a TV news script? Why?
4. What is a reader?
5. Why are readers important to a TV newscast? List the different ways they are used.
6. What is a voiceover? Describe what the audience sees and hears during a voiceover.
7. Describe some of the things to remember when writing for pictures in a voiceover script.
8. Explain the steps that a writer takes in selecting videotape to be used in a voiceover.
9. Explain the term *split page*, indicating the dimensions and how the page is used.
10. What factors determine how long a package runs?

EXERCISES

1. Take a story from the wire or a newspaper and rewrite it on a split page as a reader. It should be 20 seconds long.
2. Using the same story, describe what footage you would use to turn the reader into a VO.
3. Now, using the same piece of copy, prepare a VOSOT. Suppose that you have a sound byte from someone who is involved in the story. Using the split page, indicate the proper symbols and time for a 10-second sound byte. You have 30 seconds for the entire story.
4. Prepare a package about a feature story. Limit it to 1 minute and 30 seconds and include two talking heads. If your school has the equipment, produce the package.
5. Discuss the differences among readers, voiceovers, voiceover sound on tape, and packages.

Producing the News

PART 4

Producing the Television Newscast

KEY WORDS

Ad-Libs

Associate Producer

Back Timing

Balancing the
  Anchors

Blocks

Bumps

Clusters

Executive Producer

Field Producer

Gatekeeper

Kicker

Leads

Line Producer

Live Shots

News Hole

Peaks and Valleys

Teases

Toss

INTRODUCTION

By following this text, we've acquired the news, written the copy, and reported the story. However, even those who only want to report, shoot, edit, or anchor must be keenly aware of the producing process. A reporter may shape an individual story, but it is the producer who frames the entire newscast.

Producing is an exceptionally difficult art. The time constraints are brutal; a 30-minute newscast contains 8 minutes of commercials, leaving only 22 minutes for news. Subtract 3 minutes for your weather report (19 minutes remain), another 4 for sports (now 15 minutes are left for news), and then another minute for bumps, opens, and closes. Your half-hour of news lasts a mere 14 minutes.

Another problem facing producers is they serve as the final *gatekeeper*, which is a person who allows or denies a news story to get on the air. The gatekeeping process starts with the assignment editor, who may or may not bother sending a crew to cover a story. Gatekeeping continues in the field with the videographer—remember, any time you point a camera at one subject, you effectively point it away from all others. A reporter filters the news as well, picking one interview over another. The person editing the story then truncates

225

FIGURE 14.1

the footage into a manageable running time, excluding excess footage. By the time the story is finished, it still must be approved by the producer.

An interrelated problem for producers is dealing with the personalities of those in the newsroom. The sports reporter may want more time for a compelling local event, whereas the investigative reporter may demand an extra 30 seconds for a lead story. Anchors want to be on the air; this is not merely their egos talking, but if the station's management is paying an above-average salary, they want to see their anchors frequently. Finally, television news reporters expect to see themselves on the air, crave the occasional live shot, and appreciate being called onto the set for a "live toss" to their news report. Producers must deal with these factors constantly, juggling times, deadlines, the competition, and a score of easily bruised egos. Facing these challenges is daunting enough, but for television producers, their success or failure is witnessed on the air every day.

PRODUCERS—DEFINITIONS AND SKILLS

Most TV news producers will tell you that they are the creative force that makes the difference between a good newscast and a poor one. It's hard to argue with them. Producers lay out the newscast, decide what stories will lead the newscast, and determine the flow of the rest of the stories so that they best hold the attention of the viewers. Producers also play an important role in deciding how to use the video and sound bytes that are available to them and their reporters and how to best work them into the newscast to maintain a maximum of interest. Each producer brings his or her own particular skills and abilities to the process and at the end of the day each newscast has a different look. The battle for viewers is intense.

The success of television news programs—regardless of whether they are at the network or local level—depends not only on the quality of the news gatherers, reporters, and videographers, but also on the ability of the producer, the executive producer, and the line producer. Producers determine not only what goes into the nightly news, but also how much time is devoted to each story and in what order the stories will appear.

No two producers would create exactly the same newscast, just as no two writers or reporters would write or report a story the same way. However, there are certain rules and philosophies about the production of a newscast. You have read about the differences and similarities in style and philosophy in writing and reporting in various parts of this book. This chapter discusses the thinking of producers on news and how they put their newscasts together. We'll begin by illustrating how producers are used differently in various stations.

Executive producer

The executive producer is responsible for the long-term look of the newscasts. He or she determines, in consultation with the news director and the station's general manager, the set, the style of the opening and close, the choice of anchors, the philosophy, and other details. The executive producer reports directly to the news director. If there are problems with the newscast, the executive producer will have to do some explaining after the show. Of course, the executive producer will review the problem with the line producer before the news director calls. If the ratings slip, the executive producer must explain why and try to fix the problem. Otherwise, he or she may be looking for another job.

Line producer (show producer)

On a day-to-day basis, the line (or show) producer is mostly responsible for deciding what goes into the news broadcast and making sure it's ready to air. The executive producer and news director will be watching in the wings, but most of the responsibility for preparing the individual newscasts is given to the line producer. He or she prepares the *rundown* (*lineup*), which outlines which packages, voiceovers, and readers will appear in the show, in what order they'll appear, and how much time will be devoted to each story. If there is any doubt about which story should lead the newscast, the line producer consults the executive producer and often the news director. This consultation also applies to any problem that cannot be resolved simply.

The line producer works closely with the assignment editor and reporters. They talk about the rundown, reporter assignments, the angle the producer wishes the stories to take, story times, and whether the story is used as a package or a voiceover. As the day progresses, the line producer updates the rundown to reflect any breaking stories. If the producer has a special liking for a story, he or she tells the assignment editor and a reporter is assigned to the story. Sometimes the producer and assignment editor decide which reporter covers a particular story.

Line producers also work with each other to ensure that their newscasts are not repetitious. Because viewers expect updated news throughout the day, line producers coordinate their efforts among the 5, 6, and 11 p.m. newscasts. For example, the 5 p.m. producer may inform the 6 p.m. producer that the 5 p.m. program will lead with a package on traffic fatalities. The 6 p.m. producer won't want to duplicate that lead, even if it is a hard-hitting story. Instead, that second newscast may have the reporter begin the newscast with a live shot in the field, followed by a voiceover (which was cut from the 5 p.m. package's footage). This allows the news to be updated for each program, offering viewers something new to watch on the next show.

Associate producer

In large cities and network newsrooms, the line producer sometimes has assistants to help carry the load. These associate producers help reporters put together packages when they are in a rush or have been assigned to a second story. They cut sound bytes and pick video for the packages. When a package is reduced to a voiceover, the associate producer usually handles all the details, including writing the script. They also produce VOSOTs.

The associate producer also takes in the microwave or satellite feed from reporters in the field. Working closely with the line producer, the associate producer informs him or her if the feed has any problems. The associate producer often selects and edits parts of the feed to be used as voiceovers. Again, depending on the size of the news operation, there may not be any associate producers—writers are assigned the same duties. In many smaller markets, reporters are responsible for editing the package together with little or no help.

Field producer

Usually found in larger markets and at networks, field producers help reporters with research, plus the detail work, setting up interviews, locating people at the scene of the story (often in advance), directing the cameraperson, and making travel arrangements. The field producer is often described as the "advance" person or "facilitator." He or she speaks with the newsmakers in advance of the reporter's arrival, briefs the reporter on what the interviewees know about the story, and suggests questions to ask in interviews.

Producers and writing skills

The executive producer for *Fox 5* in New York, Luke Funk, is concerned that producers do not get enough writing training before they start producing and then get too little help in that area when they get a producer's job. He said he had to learn to write on his own. Funk noted that the emphasis in training producers is on formatting

FIGURE 14.2

a show, placement of stories, and timing—all of which are important—but that there's not enough help in writing. He said young producers are "left to fake their way through some vos and vo/sots and copy stories."

Here's some other advice from Funk: "Don't be afraid to let an anchor change your copy if it doesn't change the facts. We all like to think we are the best writers out there," he said, "but anchors have to read the copy and may want to change it to suit their style of delivery."

Funk also suggested that producers learn to respect and work with field crews. He said producers should try to work out a schedule with the news director to get out into the field with a crew once in awhile to see news gathering from their perspective. Here are some other tips that Funk says he's passed along to young producers over the years.

- Check your facts, AP wire copy is not "the truth"; you need to independently confirm information.

- Think simple thoughts, simply expressed. If your writing is confusing, complicated, poorly written, or misunderstood, the viewer has an excuse to leave.

- Have another person read your copy. If you don't have an executive producer or copy editor, make sure your anchor reads copy before it hits air, which should be a must in any case, even if you do have a copy editor.

Finally, Funk recommended that producers "read, read, read—not only the local paper every day, but a variety of periodicals, most of which are available on the Internet, free of charge."

Producers and enthusiasm

Al Tompkins, who has 24 years of professional experience in major markets, says good producers manage things and lead people, they learn the skills of communication, and they remember to use active listening. Tompkins—now with the Poynter Institute in St. Petersburg—says successful producers come to work with "first-day enthusiasm." Tompkins offers the following list of things that news directors want from producers.

- *Be an adviser to your boss.* Be strong enough to give him or her the good news as well as the bad. Help your boss know what is really happening out in the trenches.

- *Value the judgments and contributions of others.* Listen to reporters, directors, and photojournalists; respect their ideas and expertise; and allow them to help you discover that there is not one truth, but many truths.

```
PAGE  ANC  SLUG                 FORM              PB TAPE#  WTR ?  TTIME TRT   BKTIME
=====================================================================================
S-3B  GARY VA BOMB SCARE        ENG#  VO  OS      -- ------ ---  R  :30  0:51 JE- 1:58
*****  **** 5:00PM*************  ************ ***  XX ****** ***  R  0:00 0:00  -  1:07
*****  **** DATE: 04/20/95      P: BUNTON                        R        0:00  -  1:07
            HEADLINES                                            R        0:00 DB- 1:07
            $$                   ††                              R        0:00  -  1:07
            $$                   ††                              R        0:00  -  1:07
            $$                   ††                              R        0:00  -  1:07
00000 ----                       OPEN CART                       R  :20  0:20  -  1:07
S-1   G/S  VIDEO OPEN            ENG#   SOT      X  R 00:05 0:25 DB- 0:47
                                 W/BANNER         B2 ------ ---  R        0:00  -  0:22
                                 2SHOT                           R        0:00  -  0:22
S-1A  SGC  WEATHER UPDATE        WX STUFF         X.             R  0:30 0:39 DB- 0:22
                                                                 R        0:00     0:17
S-2   S/G  OKC TODAY             INTRO/ESS/OS     X              R  0:00 0:35 DB  0:17
00    ---- ROEDEMEIER CART       ENG#  PKG        B3 95-54 ---  R  0:31 1:11 KD  0:52
                                 ESS BANNER                      R        0:00     2:03
NEW2A GARY OKC TAG               COPY             X              R  0:00 0:13 KD  2:03
S-3   SWAN GENERAL SECURITY      ENG#  VO  OS     B4 ------ X--  R  0:00 0:25 SC  2:16
                                 WIPE TO                         R        0:00     2:41
S-3A  SWAN SECURITY SOUND        ENG#  SOT/VO     B2 ------ X--  R  0:11 0:17 SC  2:41
                                                                 R        0:00     2:58
S-3B  GARY MISSING WOMAN         ENG#  VO         B3 ------ X--  R  0:00 0:28 AJ  2:58
                                                                 R        0:00     3:24
S-4   SWAN TOSS TO JTURNER       IN/OS/DBLBOX     X              R  0:00 0:21 JE  3:24
S-5   JTUR BOMB FACTS            CAM 7            X              R  0:00 0:15 JE  3:45
00    ---- JTURNER CART          ENG#  PKG        B4 ------ ---  R  0:48 1:30 JE  4:00
                                 ESS BANNER                      R        0:00     5:30
S-5A  S/J  BOMB TAG              DOUBLE BOX       X              R  0:00 0:17 JE  5:30
                                                                 R        0:00     5:47
S-6   GARY PEOPLE REACTION       INTRO/OS         X              R  0:00 0:08 PC  5:47
00    ---- CTURNER CART          ENG#  PKG        B2 ------ ---  R  1:15 1:38 PC  5:55
                                 ESS BANNER                      R        0:00     7:33
S-7   SWAN CHURCH SERVICE        ENG#  VO         B3 ------ X--  R  :05  0:21 DB  7:33
                                                                 R        0:00     7:54
S-9   G/S  TEASE#1(CRIME         ENG#             B4 _____ X    R  0:08 0:22 AD  7:54
           WEATHER RADAR                                         R        0:00     8:16
*****  **** ===== BREAK #1 ***   ************ ***  XX ****** ***  R 02:20 2:20     8:16
S-10  SWAN THUNDER PREPS         INTRO/OS         X              R  0:00 0:13 LS 10:36
00    ---- LASMITH CART          ENG#  PKG        B2 ------ ---  R  0:32 1:30    10:49
S-10A SWAN THUNDER TAG           COPY             X              R  0:00 0:12 LS 12:19
                                                                 R        0:00    12:31
S-12  GARY TOSS TO DOYLE         INTRO            X              R  0:00 0:00 AD 12:31
S-13  DOYL KIDS & CRIME          INTRO/OSONSET    X              R  0:00 0:13 AD 12:31
00    ---- DOYLE CART            ENG#  PKG        B3 ------ ---  R  0:49 1:28 AD 12:57
S-13A DOYL CRIME TAG             ESS              X              R  0:00 0:24 AD 14:25
      GSD  WRAP UP               THREE SHOT                      R        0:00    14:49
S-14  S/G  TEASE#2(WEATHER)S RADAR                X              R  0:00 0:15 DB 14:49
*****  **** ===== BREAK #2 ***   ************ ***  XX ****** ***  R 02:10 2:10    15:04
           WX OPEN/TAYLOR                                        R 00:10 0:10    17:14
S-15  TAYL WEATHER               ENG#  VO&KEY     B4 _____ X    R 02:15 2:15 KD 17:24
                                                                 R        0:00    19:39
S-16       WXR WRAP              2SHOT            X              R  :10  0:10 KD 19:39
                                                                 R        0:00    19:49
S-17  S/G  TEASE#3(SPORTS)       COPY             X              R  0:00 0:15 DB 13:49
```

```
           RADAR                 RADAR                           R  0:00 0:00    20:04
*****  **** ===== BREAK #3 ***   ************ ***  XX ****** ***  R 02:10 2:10    20:04
           SPORTSOPEN/GUPTON                                     R 00:10 0:10    22:14
S-18       1ST SPORTS            ENG #   /VO      B3 _____      R 00:03 0:05    22:24
                                                                 R        0:00    22:29
SP-1  GUPR ROYAL DONATION        ENG #   /VO      B4 _____      R  0:00 0:21 DB 22:29
                                 WIPE TO                         R        0:00    22:50
SP-2  GUPR ROYAL BITE            ENG#  SOT        B2 _____      R        0:10    22:50
SP-5  GUPR ELTISH                COPY                            R        0:15    23:00
SP-6  GUPR HUBBARD LEWIS         ENG#  VO         B2 _____      R        0:20    23:15
                                 WIPE TO                         R        0:00    23:35
SP-7  GUPR RYDER REAX            ENG#  SOT        B3 _____      R        0:15    23:35
SP-8  GUPR HOLE IN ONE           ENG   VO            S-___       R        0:00    23:50
S-19  GSD  SPORTS WRAP           3SHOT                           R        0:00    23:50
                                                  X              R  :10  0:10 KD 23:50
S-20  G/S  TEASE #4(BOMB  )      ESS FULL         _____      X  R  0:00 0:15 DB 24:00
*****  **** ===== BREAK #4 ***   ************ ***  XX ****** ***  R 02:55 2:55    24:15
S-21  SWAN NIGHTTEAM TEASE       ENG#  VO  OS B4  _____      R 00:20 0:20    27:10
                                                                 R        0:00    27:30
S-22  GSC  WXR WRAP              3SHOT/GRAPHX     X              R  :20  0:20 KD 27:30
                                                                 R        0:00    27:50
S-23  G/S  BOMB ESSAY            INTRO            X              R  0:00 0:22 DB 27:50
00    ---- SAMLER CART           ENG#  PKG        B2 ------ ---  R  1:46 1:46    28:12
                                 AUDIO CART                      R        0:00    29:58
*****  **** **** END BREAK ***   ************ ***  XX ****** ***  R  :02  0:02    29:58
                                                                 R        0:00 0:00 30:00
```

FIGURE 14.3

It's a good idea to avoid leaving viewers with a sense that "there's nothing good in the news tonight" by working some "uplifting" stories into the show.

- *Discover all you can about your audience and seek to serve them.* Draw from personal experience, research, and a wide network of diverse contacts; recognize that viewers are usually not all like journalists in the way they live, think, or view the content and execution of newscasts.

- *Be a writing example.* Teach, delegate, coach, and resist the tendency "to do it all yourself." Help develop associate producers. Ask open-ended questions. Listen more than you speak.

- *Anticipate major events.* Tompkins says effective producers know what graphics are needed to cover the big story and what special decisions about spending or staffing or equipment need to be made in advance.

- *Recognize that lead-in programming is important.* Tompkins advises producers to know their lead-in programming because it will help them step back from the show, consider the lead-in, and write preshow teases to the ear of the audience. He says the best place to capture the viewers is the show before your own program.

- *Step back from the show.* Tompkins says producers should take a good look at the broadcast they are about to present and ask if it truly reflects what happened in the community that day. Does it portray the community as it really is or as the producer narrowly defined it?

- *Producing is the glue that holds the newsroom together.* Producers set the tone, they regulate style, and they shape content. Effective producers nurture, value, and defend the principle of an individual's right to express ideas even if they are unpopular.

Producers and energy

Veteran producer Ted Kavanau says energy is the key to success for a TV producer. He says a casual person rarely makes a good producer. "An energetic producer always does a more exciting program … a fast-moving and interesting-looking newscast," said Kavanau. He also stressed that flow is important. Kavanau added that producers should find the most important reason a story should follow the previous one. Here is some other advice from Kavanau.

- Bridge your stories by using those that help bring you from one category to another.

- Write short leads to tape. Don't punish people with talk when you have good video.

- If you have good pictures, make them last by writing enough copy.

- End segments with strength. Never use a weak story at the top of a segment.

- Like packages, never put features back to back.

THE LOGISTICS AND STRATEGIES OF PRODUCING

Much like some other elements of news (anchoring, reporting, and editing), producing is best learned via real-life experiences. Through experience, newscast producers learn that they face the same challenges regardless of the size of their viewing audience, the number of reporters they lead, or whether their newscast is a 5-minute update at 7:25 a.m. or an evening report at 11 p.m. There is seldom enough time or manpower to make all of the stories fit.

There are basic steps that are universal in newsrooms. The newscasts begin with staff meetings, continue throughout the day as stories either thrive or die, and then finally go on-air at their appointed hour. While no two days are ever alike, there are steps that make the producing job much more manageable.

Staff meetings

The producers hold staff meetings as many as three times a day—in the morning, the late afternoon, and after the early evening newscast—to discuss that day's news coverage. That's where initial newscast decisions are made: What will the lead story be? Which stories will be covered? Which reporter and cameraperson will cover them? Keep in mind that these decisions are subject to change, depending on the day's events. The last meeting of the day is a debriefing to discuss what went right and wrong with the early evening newscasts and to plan coverage for the late evening news.

The meeting is a place to discuss story ideas—it's not unlike a war room where the battle plan is set for that day's action. All staff members are expected to contribute and share information. A good producer is a good listener who realizes that ideas are not limited to the assignment editor.

During the meeting, the staff goes over each story available for the day's news-casts. Decisions are made, and the line (show) producers of the early evening newscasts create a rundown (lineup), which is a list of stories planned for those newscasts. Reporters and camera-people are then assigned to stories.

As stated earlier, the early rundown is subject to change as the day's news events unfold. Sometimes the pre- and final rundowns look alike. On other days, there are so many new developments and breaking news stories that the final rundown lineup barely resembles the pre-rundown.

The rundown

The rundown is what comes out of the staff meetings. Decisions reached at the morning meeting determine what goes into the rundown for the evening news, and discussions at the afternoon meeting establish what the late-night news looks like. But all this, as noted, is subject to change depending on breaking news stories, because the rundown is a living document. At

FIGURE 14.4

times, the rundown looks exactly like the newscast, whereas at other times it looks nothing like it because of unpredictable developments.

A rundown is a blueprint of what stories will be presented in a newscast, which anchor reads them, how long the story lasts, and what type of story it is (such as a reader or package). Rundowns also contain detailed information for the technical crew, including which camera is to be used on the anchor, which tape machine has the footage for playback, and how many graphics are needed for a particular story.

Some nights, producers wish they could just toss everything in the air and put it in the show the way it falls down. Unfortunately, it doesn't work that way. A lot of thought must go into the arrangement of stories in the newscast to make it clear and interesting. As mentioned earlier, no two producers are likely to agree on the exact order of the stories in a newscast. If you examined the newscasts produced at stations in the same market on the same night, even the lead stories are often different unless some story completely dominates the news.

Assembling a newscast so that it flows naturally from story to story, engages the viewer, and includes all of the day's news is no easy feat; a sample exercise at the end of this chapter illustrates the juggling act faced by producers every day. There are, fortunately, some basic strategies that assist in fleshing out the rundown.

Leads, clusters, and kickers

As in Chapter 2, let's assume there are four blocks in a local newscast. The blocks are separated by commercial breaks; thus the newscast flows as A block, break, B block, break, C block (usually sports), break, and then D block. Most producers aren't terribly concerned with the content of C block, as the sports anchor will manage that for them. Of course, the producer is interested in the total running time of C block so it will fit cleanly with the rest of the newscast. Also, if there is a "news" story hidden in sports, that may be of interest. A referendum on building a new football stadium may be placed in C block, although the news angle may warrant that report being moved to A block.

By leaving C block to sports, we're left with A, B, and D. The first block, A, begins with the lead story of the newscast. The format of this news story may be a package, a live shot, or even a reader. Yet the mere placement of it above all others suggests that it is the lead story; thus it is more important to the viewers than anything that follows. Deciding which story is the most critical to the audience is not simple; there are sometimes shouting matches over which story deserves the top slot.

After the lead is decided, many producers cluster their stories into the remaining slots. All health stories may be bundled in B block, while three short statewide readers at the bottom of A block may constitute a "State Round-up." The life or death of stories is decided at this stage, as a precious 20 seconds spent on a traffic jam may erase the 20 seconds needed for a school board update. Also, the weather report may be attached to the end of B block, thus the producer must be very careful about what story to insert before the forecast. A light story on a farming success would be good, but tragic numbers on an increase in child abuse would not.

Unlike A and B blocks, D block does not have the same hard news implication. Instead, D block is home to entertainment news, feel-good pieces on cute kids, and community announcements of upcoming festivals. D block is designed as a kicker block for two simple reasons: first, if the newscast is running over time, it is easy to drop the feature stories from D block without losing the newscast's impact. Second, no anchor wants to end the newscast on a depressing story, only to then abruptly shift gears to saying "Good night, stay tuned for *Wheel of Fortune!*"

Peaks and valleys

One popular approach to producing a newscast is known as the *peak-and-valley* format. Although the phrase has been around for decades, many producers use the format without using that name. This format treats every segment, or block, in the newscast as a sort of mini-newscast that can stand on its own. That doesn't mean that each section has weather, sports, and financial news, but there is a good, strong story at the top of each segment, along with some

FIGURE 14.5

Lead stories for the day at WSBTV (http://www.wsbtv.com/index.html).

less important stories and, in some segments, perhaps a feature or special report. Each segment ends with a strong story before the commercial.

The concept behind peaks and valleys is that if you sprinkle your most interesting and important stories throughout the newscast, you'll hold your audience. If you place all your top stories in the early part of the newscast, you'll lose the audience because the newscast—and your audience—will fizz out by the middle. Worse yet, the audience will switch to your competition. Instead, you should spread your most interesting and important stories throughout the newscast.

It's also important to remember that weather is the most promotable element in a newscast. Many viewers say that weather is the main reason they watch local news, which is why producers tease it throughout the newscast.

For those producers who make use of the "peak-and-valley" theory, it is extremely important before going to a commercial break to tease not only with the weather, but also with a strong story that has special appeal. The idea is that if you do not hook listeners on the first tease, you may get them on the second. If you do, it will help keep the audience around through the commercial, which is the valley of the newscast. After the commercial, the audience expects another good story at the top of the next segment, and the process begins all over again: a peak and then a valley and another peak and another valley, throughout each section of the newscast.

This theory of producing is different from the traditional approach (which started in radio), which gives the audience the best stories at the top of the newscast and follows them with stories of less and less interest until it's time to say goodbye. This format made sense for radio and for early TV newscasts, which lasted a mere 15 minutes, including commercials.

The inverted pyramid approach continues in many small markets because it often is difficult even to find just one strong story each night. Too many producers still try to hold an audience by teasing sports and weather. In many communities, of course, sports and the weather are important news, as are college and high-school sports scores. In farming communities, the weather may be the best story of the day, night, and week. But creative producers, even in small markets, should experiment with the peak-and-valley theory that teases other important stories or good features.

Rhythm and flow

Although packages appeal most to the audience, producers shouldn't play one off another. You should place them effectively throughout the newscast, inserting readers or voiceovers between them. The package also serves another important purpose; it gives the anchors a breather and a chance for them, the producers, and the director to get organized for the rest of the show.

The line producer, who sits near the director in the control room, often needs time to reshuffle parts of the rundown and script because of late-breaking news and because packages are often still being edited during the newscast. Problems also develop when videotapes, or the decks that play them, malfunction.

FIGURE 14.6
WCBS-TV senior vice president and news director Diane Doctor (right) reviews news copy with executive producer Maura McHugh (left) (courtesy of WCBS–TV, New York, NY).

Ad-libs, bumps, teases, and tosses

In the 1980s, the "happy talk" phenomenon invaded a number of local television stations. This occurred when banter among the anchors became less about the news and more about themselves. Although it was an attempt to humanize the news anchors and make them more accessible to viewers, the fad seemed forced onto the news sets.

Today, most banter is limited to *ad-libs*, *bumps*, *teases*, and *tosses*. These terms may be used interchangeably in newsrooms, although there are some slight differences. Ad-libs are used when the newscast runs short by perhaps 20 seconds. Instead of cramming in a final reader, the producer will alert the news team to ad-lib.

Bumps and teases are similar to one another, but there is a subtle difference. Say the anchors are ending the A block and are heading to a commercial break. A bump is generic, such as "We'll be back with more. Stay with us." These are handy if the anchor doesn't know what's coming in the next block or, as is sometimes the case, the producer isn't sure if a late-breaking story or last-minute live shot will come through. In these cases, bumps are perfectly appropriate.

Teases are far stronger. They promote a story in the next block, give a peek at the weather forecast, or maybe tease viewers into staying for something much later in the program. Here are examples of possible teases at the end of an A block:

"You may think it's just cold weather around the corner, but Mike has a bone-chilling prediction when we return with his weather forecast."

"If you thought traffic was bad today, wait until you hear what streets will be closed for construction starting tomorrow. We'll have the details in a moment."

"Looking ahead to sports, a blockbuster basketball trade has made one local player very happy, but his teammates are crying foul."

Any of the above is better than the typical "Stay with us." A well-crafted tease is essential for keeping the audience over the commercial break. They are often the last tidbits inserted into the script (the rundown must be done first so the producer knows what story to tease), but are vital in holding the newscast together.

A toss is simple. This occurs when the sports or weather anchor is introduced to give their segment. These are unscripted; the teleprompter just reads TOSS TO SPORTS. The anchor finishes the news copy, sees the TOSS order on the teleprompter, pivots to the sports anchor, and quickly tosses the reins over. During the commercial break, the sports and weather anchors give the news anchors an idea of what would make a good toss. Although it's similar to an ad-lib, a toss is an internal transition among the anchors. An ad-lib is more likely used to just fill time.

An acknowledgment should also be made for local sports and weather anchors everywhere. Both deliver segments of several minutes per newscast, but each is aware that their respective time allotments can expand or contract dramatically depending on the news of the day. On a busy news day, sports and weather may each lose 30 or 45 seconds to accommodate an onslaught of news stories. On a slow day, the producer may ask them who would like more time to fill. This is when you'll see the weather anchor spend more time discussing the pollen count or the sports anchor may insert a "Play of the Day" segment that usually isn't aired.

Finally, both weather and sports anchors are expected to be on the set at the end of the newscast. If an ad-lib is needed, a quick weather update or a reminder about a local sports event is always good for 20 seconds.

Producing tips

Television news consultant and former producer Mary Cox provides her "baker's dozen" suggestions for news producers:

- Ask: What's the viewers' benefit?

- Win the lead.

- Put news in every section.

- Make the show video-driven—go from video to video to video. (Most producers disagree on this one.)

- Write tight, to the point.

- Look for live opportunities without going live for the sake of going live.

- Give stories the time they need.

- Don't "force" a package, even if a reporter worked all day on it. If it doesn't work, dump it.

- Tease news at the end of every section.

- Include some of the newscast's best writing and video in the teases.

- Go out strong, with a big finish (generally a package) to keep the audience with you.

- Create a "magic moment" consisting of something memorable, such as great photography.

- Avoid getting locked into local, local, local, national, national, national. People don't think that way and they don't tell stories that way.

TECHNICAL ASPECTS OF PRODUCING

Balancing the anchors

Visualize two anchors relaying the news on an evening newscast. Except for the weather and sports anchors, the two news anchors are the foundation of the program; the viewers expect to see them five evenings a week. The station's management hires anchors to lend credibility, convey authority, and serve as the "face" for the station's local presence. The anchors are promoted on billboards and in newspapers and are frequently approached in public on a first-name basis.

Producers must be keenly aware of both the station's financial investment in the anchors and the viewers' emotional investment in them. To make sure the anchors appear on camera and share enough time on-air (often snidely called face time), the line producer should double-check the rundown for anchor balance. If one anchor will present seven readers and the other has only two, then the first anchor will appear on camera much longer than the other. This may happen in an occasional program, but if one anchor is consistently shown on-camera while the other is hidden behind voiceovers, the news director is bound to notice. Even worse, the anchor with less face time will object—and when the line producer is confronted with rundowns that reveal a perceived slant for one anchor over another, the meeting will quickly become unpleasant.

As a side note, newsrooms are filled with anchors who feel they always receive the stories with difficult-to-pronounce foreign names or tongue-twisting medical phrases. Most veteran anchors realize that a pure balance (of either tricky stories or stacks of readers) is difficult to achieve every night. However, the line producer must be fair in balancing the anchors over the course of newscasts.

Still pictures

Many producers tend to avoid still pictures, but when used correctly, especially in a sequence, they can be effective—almost as much as video.

Maps and other graphics also should be used to support copy. If a plane has crashed in some relatively unknown area, it helps the viewer if you show a map and indicate with a star where the plane went down. The map should include at least one town familiar to your audience. Creating the images is easy if the station employs a dedicated graphics artist; simply e-mail over the work request and it can usually be finished before the newscast. Another popular option is downloading still images from the national newsfeed. The most popular feeds, such as CNN's Newsource, offer still images and maps for download. Other services are seen frequently on the air, especially for national and international maps. Google Earth is one example of a map service that can quickly illustrate locations for the viewers.

Live shots

Ever since technology allowed TV stations to go live from the scene on a daily basis, there has been a debate about whether the technique is being overused. If there is a major traffic snarl in New York City because of road construction during the rush hour, does it make any sense to send a reporter

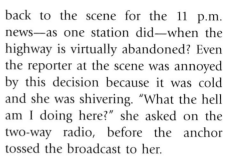

FIGURE 14.7

back to the scene for the 11 p.m. news—as one station did—when the highway is virtually abandoned? Even the reporter at the scene was annoyed by this decision because it was cold and she was shivering. "What the hell am I doing here?" she asked on the two-way radio, before the anchor tossed the broadcast to her.

The need to use the live shot as much as possible seems to have diminished somewhat as the novelty wore off and station managers have complained less to news directors. In the past, the managers often said, "We paid a bunch for this stuff ... make it pay for itself."

Most news managers also say the public tends to believe that a reporter at the scene is more on top of a story than a reporter getting his or her information over the phone. Finally, they say, newsmakers are more likely to talk to a reporter in person than on the phone. "It's easy to say no to a strange voice on the phone," said a producer, "but it's difficult to say no to a reporter while looking him in the eye."

Back timing

One major task for the line producer is to ensure that the newscast gets off the air on time. This is particularly important when computers are in charge of establishing when programs and commercials start and end. We all have witnessed situations when one program is cut off abruptly by a new program. That situation happens because a computer has established the time when the new program or commercial is supposed to start, and start it will, on time.

FIGURE 14.8

The timing is particularly critical when local news is followed by a network program. The network computer will take over regardless. If the local news anchors are still saying goodbye or the station's final commercial or logo is still playing, something is going to get cut off if the newscast timing is not accurate. If your commercial is cut, that revenue goes down the drain.

To defend against such problems, the show producer must track whether the newscast is "running on time." Anchors may stumble on some lines, a tape may be cued to the wrong spot, or the banter between the on-set talent may be too short or long. That's why producing is so difficult; the unexpected often happens. If the newscast is short, something else must be added to fill the time. The opposite is true if the show is running long—something must be cut. As a result, producers use *back timing* to make sure the program ends on time. In most newsrooms, the computer system back times a show for you, but a producer must be able to do the math on his or her own.

The computer tells you automatically where you stand on time at each point in the newscast. A "minus" sign means the show is running long. Figuring the time works like this: Take the total amount of time for the show (i.e., 30 minutes). Subtract time for commercials; the number left is your *news hole*, which is the time you have for news. In most cases, it's between 12 and 15 minutes. Add up the time each story takes, including the anchor introduction, the tape time, and the anchor time, and then see how it works!

The bottom line—whether you use a computer or your own math—is to get off on time. News waits for no one, especially a producer who mistimes a show.

FIGURE 14.9

SUMMARY

The best opportunities for young people entering broadcast news are in producing. The expansion of local news and the spread of all-news channels to more cities have created a need for producers of all kinds. There is a high demand for producers because so many young people want to go on the air because of the perceived "glamour" and higher salaries usually associated with such jobs. The competition for anchor and reporter positions is much greater, even though producer positions may be available.

There also are substantial rewards in producing news programs. Certainly, salaries are going to continue to improve as the demand increases for people to produce news. Although producers work behind the scenes, their jobs are exciting and occasionally also glamorous. The excitement comes in the realization that as a producer you are "in control." What you do in the newsroom determines what goes on the air. You are limited only by your own imagination and creativity. As pointed out earlier, in many newsrooms, the producers are in complete charge of the news.

Along with that power comes a lot of responsibility and risk. You will need good news judgment and other skills in many areas. Good writing is essential. Some experience in reporting is also desirable. You will also need to have an excellent knowledge of production techniques—microwave and satellite feeds, computer technologies, video editing, electronic still storage, and emerging technologies.

Another important consideration is stress. It's a tough, emotionally and physically draining position with long hours. But the potential rewards are great if you have any interest in management. Producers are on the best track to the management offices. You must learn how to do just about everything in the newsroom and how to work with and manage a variety of co-workers. Who could be better qualified for the "boss's" job?

Test Your Knowledge

1. List the various duties of the executive producer.
2. What are the responsibilities of the line producer?
3. Describe what the field producer does.
4. What is a rundown and why is it so important?
5. Explain the "peak-and-valley" theory of producing.
6. What is the meaning of the term *inverted pyramid* in producing?
7. What is a live shot and when should it be used?
8. What's the purpose of the staff meetings?
9. Explain the term *back time*. Why is it so important?

EXERCISES

1. Try to arrange with one of your local TV stations to "hang out" with a producer. Weekends are the best time because the pace is usually slower.
2. Arrange to accompany a field producer on a photo shoot. If there is none in your market, go along with the reporter who, in this case, is the field producer.
3. Take notes as you watch a local newscast and try to determine what kind of a format the producer is using. See if you can spot "peaks and valleys."

IN-CLASS EXERCISE: CREATING A NEWSCAST

As stated earlier, no two producers are likely to decide the exact same order of the stories in a newscast. If you examine the newscasts at different stations in the same market on the same night, you'd see that even the lead stories are often different unless some story completely dominates the news.

For this exercise, assume you are the producer of the 6 p.m. news on a weekday in mid-August. At your 9 a.m. production meeting, you learn of the following stories. Which would you pursue for your A block, B block, and D block? Remember, weather is at the end of B block and sports occupies C block. Also, you will not use all of the stories.

1. From your health reporter: A 1:15 PKG on obesity, the fourth in a five-part series on modern health hazards.
2. From your futures files: The city council will meet at 7 p.m. to discuss school rezoning. You have archival footage and can preview this meeting with a RDR, VO, VOSOT, PKG, or live shot from the location.
3. From the newswire: A Census Bureau report shows your county has gained 9% minority population over the past year—this exceeds the state's 4% gain.
4. From the newswire: Housing starts are down nationwide. Your state and city mirror the national trend.
5. From one of your videographers: Video footage of an early morning house fire in town. The structure was destroyed, but no one was hurt or killed.
6. From one of your videographers: A local Boy Scout troop has built a scale-model home out of toothpicks, which is on display at the mall. The display is to promote awareness of using renewable resources for shelter.
7. From your futures file: The airport authority is meeting at 3 p.m. to discuss a possible runway extension. You can dispatch a crew to cover it or use file footage.
8. From a caller: A local group of approximately 20 activists is alerting all news media of its protest at tonight's city council meeting. They want a local park to be renamed in honor of a local civil rights leader.
9. From the newswire: The summer heat wave shows no signs of abating. High temperatures and humidity are forecast for at least the next week. So far, 11 people have died in your state due to heat stress over the past 6 weeks.
10. From one of your reporters: School will resume next week. A 1:05 PKG on back-to-school preparations is available.
11. From one of your reporters: The local university also begins classes next week. The university reports that student enrollment is down almost 6 percent.
12. From your futures file: The county extension agent will host an open house this weekend to aid farmers with seasonal crops.
13. From the overnight beat checks: An elderly couple was mugged last night while walking near their home. Both of the victims suffered minor injuries. The husband told police he wants revenge and isn't afraid to use his gun.
14. From the newswire: The Centers for Disease Control and Prevention has issued a heat stress advisory for your area due to the ongoing heat wave.
15. From the fax machine: The city public information officer has sent an advisory that residents should restrict watering their lawns to evenings or early morning hours.

CHAPTER 15

Producing the Radio Newscast

KEY WORDS

Actualities	Headlines	Teases
Back Timing	Lead-ins	Voice Track
Futures File	Pad Copy	Wraparound

CONTENTS

INTRODUCTION

It is difficult to generalize about radio news operations and news programs because they are constantly changing. One universal statement that can be made is that newscasts on most local radio stations are getting shorter and less frequent. Changes in ownership often mean a change in programming mentality; thus radio newsrooms are under frequent scrutiny. Due to relaxed Federal Communications Commission (FCC) rules concerning station ownership, more individual stations are being purchased by media conglomerates. The result, sadly, is the loss of local news operations.

On the plus side, the technology for obtaining and delivering radio news has improved greatly. Further, because the career path of many students in collegiate media courses winds through their university radio stations, new talent for radio is constantly being trained.

This chapter provides a brief overview of radio news, discusses how radio newscasts are created and delivered, and also examines the technology that equips radio producers both in the field and behind the microphone in the studio. While there are declining jobs available in radio news, many of the skills learned at radio stations are applicable to those students focusing on television.

THE STATE OF RADIO NEWS

The demise of the significant role that radio had traditionally played in covering the news began with the unfortunate decision by the FCC that radio

245

stations did not have to provide news as a public service. As a result, hundreds of radio stations decided they could save a lot of money by ending their news operations, and they did. Most of those stations now either play music or are in the "talk" business. Talk radio is not the same as news radio, as the talk format is skewed much greater toward opinion and nationally syndicated programs. Radio newsrooms, particularly those that concentrate on local news, are withering at an alarming rate.

The easing of ownership restrictions over the years also played a large role in destroying the close relationship that radio stations traditionally had with their listeners because those landmark stations stressed public service and took pride in serving the community and keeping it well informed. People turned to their radio sets to find out about disasters, such as tornadoes and hurricanes, and routine matters, such as school closings and traffic conditions. But the growth of media giants such as Clear Channel and Infinity Broadcasting has reshaped the operating structure of local radio stations and their newsrooms. Quite frequently, there is no journalist working full-time at the radio stations during the day, which is even more likely to be true at night.

Clear Channel came under fire in January of 2002 following an incident in Minot, North Dakota. Authorities unsuccessfully tried to reach someone at six of the seven radio stations Clear Channel owns in the town to warn residents that a train carrying 10,000 gallons of anhydrous ammonia derailed in the area, causing a toxic cloud. When authorities called the six stations, no one answered the phones. Senator Byron Dorgan of North Dakota used the incident to warn then-FCC Chairman Michael Powell that as large media companies like Clear Channel buy up the last remaining independent media outlets, the public suffers.

As for the impact of all this on local news, in a research survey conducted by the Radio and Television News Directors Association and Ball State University, Professor Bob Papper noted that radio consolidation makes it almost impossible to compare news operations over time. He said more than 95 percent of radio news departments handle the news for more than one station. In fact, he said, the average news department runs news on three stations in the same market. He added that more than 4 in 10 radio news departments say they do news for one or more stations outside their own market.

Papper says there are now four places where you still hear radio news: real all-news stations in major markets; some news/talk stations in some major and large markets; some public stations in a wide variety of market sizes; and, finally, in some small and medium stations where news has remained a key part of their programming. Papper adds that the typical radio newsroom has one person.

FIGURE 15.1

www.clearchannel.com.

As for Clear Channel, its penetration into the national radio market is overwhelming, with 8 stations in Los Angeles, 7 in San Diego, 6 each in Jacksonville and Cincinnati, 5 in Little Rock, and 10 in Poughkeepsie, New York, a city of less than 30,000 people. In Wheeling, West Virginia, another relatively small city of about 30,000 where Clear Channel owns 7 radio stations, it made major cuts in its local news programming and personnel at WWVA, a 50,000-watt station with a strong history of news coverage. It fired the news director and a reporter with the station, Dave Demerest, resigned on the air in disgust because of the cutbacks, which he described as the elimination of seven-and-a-half hours of local programming. Demerest said the changes have left the public with practically no forum for discussion of local interest.

However, as *Washington Post* columnist Marc Fisher pointed out in another article for *American Journalism Review*, in most big cities and in an increasing number of middle-sized markets, the only radio news operations that bother to send reporters out on stories, besides NPR affiliates, are all-news stations. On most music stations, he notes, news is limited to morning drive time and is delivered from a single centralized newsroom belonging to either Metro Networks or Shadow Broadcast Services. Both of these services are owned by Westwood One. Combined, they serve more than 100 radio markets throughout the United States.

YOUR AUDIENCE

One of the continuing debates in both print and broadcast news is whether the news should provide the kind of information that people *need* to know or

FIGURE 15.2

the information they *want* to know. Most journalists agree that the answer lies somewhere in the middle. People must be informed, but it also makes sense to tailor the news for the audience. A station programming easy-listening music probably would not want to provide the same kind of news as a rock station. The rock station would have a relatively young audience, whereas the easy-listening station would have an older audience. If you were the news director at the rock station, you would look for stories that might appeal more to young people. The writing style also would be lighter and less formal than it would be, for example, for the audience of that easy-listening station.

The story selection also would be different for news delivered in urban and rural areas. Stories about the weather would be important in farm country, whereas stories about traffic congestion would be important in the city.

Although you need to consider all these factors, your main concern in putting a news report together is the news itself. A story of overwhelming importance, whether it is local, national, or foreign, always takes precedence over the rest of the news.

ORGANIZING MATERIAL

Radio producers place stories in three broad categories when they stack their newscasts: which story should lead the newscast, which stories should follow, and which stories may be eliminated. Of course, before the stories are shuffled among those three possibilities, you must know what news is available.

A good way to start is to call the police and fire departments to see if anything is going on—these are the beat checks detailed earlier in this text. Then check your news wire service along with the local newspaper. If you've compiled a quick list of Internet shortcuts to Web sites such as the mayor's office or the school board, you should scan those for announcements or meetings. Also, serious newsrooms keep a file marked "futures" that alerts the staff to special events scheduled in the listening area; check this file next.

In a small community there may not be much going on, and if that community is served by an equally small station, any material in the futures file was probably put there by the newsperson who will cover the event. Although the futures file is filled with stories that haven't happened yet, you can always have a newscast tease an upcoming event, such as "The city council meets tonight … ."

After you read the wire copy, the newspaper, and any other sources available, you decide which stories you want to use and in what order. Some producers list all the available stories on a pad and then they figure out a tentative order in which the stories will appear in the script. Others print out the stories from their computer and arrange the stories in the order they wish to use them so that the most important stories are at the top and the less important ones at the bottom. Still others scribble out their rundowns on a dry erase board (much like the television assignment board) to develop their newscasts. There is no right or wrong way to organize copy, so look for the method that is the most comfortable for you.

Writers using computers organize their copy in a variety of ways. Some move the stories they wish to consider for their newscast into a separate computer file. Later, when they are ready to rewrite the stories, they split the screen so that they can look at the wire copy on one side and use the other half, the blank side, to rewrite the copy.

Once that story is written, it is saved, the writer moves on to the next one, and so forth. When all the stories are written, the writer prints them out and puts them in the order in which they will be read on the air.

FIGURE 15.3

WRITING FROM THE BACK

One thing that just about all newswriters agree on is that the first stories they write are those that will not change. Working in this way is called *writing from the back* because the stories that are not likely to change are usually those that are read in the latter part of the newscast.

"Breaking" stories, as their name suggests, will probably change considerably before air time so they should be written last.

FIGURE 15.4

WINS reporter John Montone covering the 1-year anniversary of the World Trade Center attack.

THE LEAD STORY

The method for selecting the first story in the newscast—the lead story—may sound simple: Just pick the most important story. But how do you decide which story is most important? Should a local, national, or international story be the lead? Does the time of day affect the decision? Will any of the stories affect the local audience in some way? The answers to these questions can help you determine which story should lead the newscast.

Most of a station's listeners will be more interested in what is happening in their community than in the rest of the world. There are exceptions, of course, as during the terrorist attacks on the World Trade Center in New York on 9/11 and the tsunami catastrophe in December of 2004, when most Americans turned on their radio and TV sets to get the latest on the disasters. But now, let's examine how we decide what's news to a local audience on a relatively normal news day. News in a town of 5000 is not necessarily news in a city of 50,000. And what is considered news in that medium-sized city may not be too important in a city of a million or more. Here are some story choices on a particular day at a radio station in the hypothetical town of Wheatland, population 10,000.

- The president says he is encouraged by the progress being made in the baseball strike negotiations.

- The Labor Department says unemployment rose another one-half of one percent.

- The governor says he will make major cuts in services and state workers' jobs rather than raise taxes.

- The wife of Wheatland's mayor gives birth to triplets.

The story of most interest in Wheatland, and the story that most listeners would be talking about that day, is the birth of triplets to the mayor's wife. But 100 miles east, in the state capital, the birth would be less important, and the governor's comments on cuts in jobs and services would be the top story. The network newscast would lead with the jump in unemployment because that story holds the most interest for a national audience.

Suppose we add another story to the list: a three-car accident on the freeway near the state capital. While the story may not sound too important, suppose the accident was at 8 a.m. and those three wrecked cars created a gigantic traffic jam. It most certainly would be the lead story on the 8 a.m. news for stations in the capital because that is "drive time," the highest-rated listening period for radio. People listening to their radios on the way to work are more concerned about when they will get to the office than they are about the governor's comments on taxes and jobs. How about the audience in Wheatland? Because the accident took place over 100 miles away, the Wheatland listeners would have no interest in it. The network radio audience would not even know about the accident because it would not be important enough to make the AP wire.

Keep in mind that when you start to prepare your newscast, you should not be overly concerned about which story will lead it. Chances are that what appeared to be the most important story an hour earlier may be overshadowed by a new story that broke before air time. That is the nature of the news business. On some very busy news days—unlikely in Wheatland—a story that was considered the lead at one point may not even get into the newscast. That's why each story should be on a separate sheet of paper to allow for a quick reshuffling of the script.

THE REST OF THE NEWSCAST

You can use the formula you established for choosing the lead story to pick the rest of the stories in the newscast. Once you have selected the lead, determine which of the remaining stories would hold the most interest for your audience, then the next most interest, and so on. The stories would then be broadcast in that order.

There are important exceptions to this formula. Sometimes it makes sense to place stories back to back because they have something in common. During the war in Iraq, for example, it was not unusual for newscasts to carry a report of the fighting and then follow it up with a story from the White House or Congress concerning some political aspect of the military action. Those two stories were often followed by a third

FIGURE 15.5
Reporter Dick Gordon of WBUR radio in Boston finishes a script by candlelight when the generator in his Iraqi office quit one night (courtesy of WBUR radio, Boston, MA).

FIGURE 15.6

Blind disc jockey, Ted McCaw, at radio station WATD, Marshfield, Massachusetts (courtesy of WATD, Marshfield, MA).

that might have been a reaction-type report to the invasion of Iraq from Congress or even a poll of American opinion on the invasion.

Another example would be the linking of weather-related stories. If part of the nation is suffering a drought and another section is in the middle of serious flooding, it would be logical to report those two stories together in the newscast. Without such logical connections, the rule is to report the news in its order of importance.

LOCALIZING THE NEWS

When writing for a local station, always look for some local angle in national and international stories. If a British airliner crashes in Europe, the first thing to check is whether any Americans were on board and, if so, whether any were from the local listening area. If there is overseas military action involving American troops, an interview with service personnel from the region is a solid addition to the newscast. The same rule of thumb holds true for a nationwide drought (find a local farmer), a slump in the housing market (track down a nearby realtor), or a national story on tax cheats (look for an accountant or tax preparer).

Remember, if someone wins a million-dollar lottery, it's a good story. But if the person happens to be from the listening area, it's a *great* story.

STORY LENGTH

The length of a story is determined by the length of the newscast, the importance of the story, and the availability of news at that particular hour. If there is not much news to report, the stories may have to be longer than they would be normally. If there is a lot of news, most stories should be short to allow sufficient time for the major stories.

Before you start to write, you must determine how much time you actually have for news in a newscast. Most newscasters read approximately 15 or 16 lines of copy per minute. So, for a 3-minute newscast, you would need approximately 45 to 48 lines of copy. Again, this can vary greatly due to the speed of the individual.

But is the newscast really 3 minutes long? Probably not. Let's say there are two commercials, each running 30 seconds, in the newscast, which leaves 2 minutes of news. If there is a 20-second weather report, maybe 10 seconds for stocks, and another 5 seconds to sign off, the 2 minutes have been reduced another 35 seconds. What is left is 1 minute and 25 seconds. If that time is converted to lines, you have about 23 lines in which to cover all the news. That is why you must learn to condense your news copy. You may have as little as three lines to tell some of those stories.

ACTUALITIES

The voices of the newsmakers are called *actualities or sound bytes*. They are the heart of radio news. A good writer can tell the story without the actual voice, but he or she faces a greater challenge. Even the best newswriters would tell you that if given a choice, they would rather have the actual sound byte provide the color instead of their paraphrase of what was in the sound byte. Regardless of the writer's and newscaster's talents, it's not possible to capture all of the nuances in a sound byte with a paraphrase and the newscaster's voice. How can anyone better express the remarks of New York City cab drivers than they themselves? And how would the newscaster make up for the missing sounds of the city in the background—the natural sound—without the tape? Good tape is essential.

FIGURE 15.7

Fortunately, recording technology has caught up with the speed required for radio news. Previous generations of radio producers lugged reel-to-reel audio recorders into the field, conducted interviews, and then returned to the studio for editing. This postproduction was accomplished by physically cutting the tape with a razor blade and splicing it back together with tiny strips of tape. It was a laborious, time-consuming process that required accuracy, patience, and a very steady hand; once the tape was sliced, the producer was committed to using that segment for a sound byte.

Today, field recording is digital. The equipment is much lighter, more durable, and tapeless. Once the actualities are recorded, the interview can be uploaded into the computer's audio editing program, such as Adobe Audition, in a matter of seconds. The audio tracks then appear as individual strips that can be edited or mixed as needed. Unlike the previous editing with razors, unwanted audio edits can be undone with a click of the mouse.

Not all actualities require field recording; again, technology has caught up with the industry. Most radio stations' phone lines can be recorded into computer inputs as well, thus allowing the interviewer to simply phone the subject. Of course, this requires a clean phone signal. Far too many phone interviews suffer from poor quality because the interviewee is on a cell phone with a marginal signal.

STUDIO TECHNOLOGY

This same computerized technology is available in the studio. It is common for radio news announcers to *voice track* a number of news breaks in a row. Voice tracking means recording the news break in advance (usually on a computer drive) and then uploading it as an audio file to be played when needed. This is especially popular with news-talk stations, in which a nationally syndicated program, such as Rush Limbaugh, airs for 3 hours every weekday. At the top of the hour, a 5-minute break is left for local stations to add in advertisements, national news feeds, or local news inserts. With dedicated computer software and minimal training, the news announcer records a news break and inserts it into the master playback log. The advantages are that the announcer can do all of the recording in advance and need not wait

in the studio for the next news break. Additionally, the timing of the news breaks can be exact, as the audio recording technology allows for editing, compressing, and expanding the words to fit the exact time required. With this technology, pad copy and back timing (as explained later) are used less often.

WRAPAROUNDS

The combination of sound and words is known as a *wraparound*. This technique, as the name suggests, uses the voice of the newscaster or reporter at the beginning and end of a story or report and the voice of the newsmaker in the middle. You might want to think of a wraparound in terms of a sandwich. There can be more than one thing between the two slices of bread. Wraparounds often have more than one sound byte in the middle. The anchor or reporter may wrap several different pieces of sound with script. Here's an example:

A Conrail freight train today left the tracks near Wheatland, causing some major problems for

FIGURE 15.8

passenger trains that also use the tracks. Railroad officials say the locomotive and eight of the train's 14 cars were derailed. They blamed a broken rail. Remarkably, there were only two injuries—to the engineer and his assistant—and they were not serious. Engineer Brian Potter spoke to us at the hospital.

(sound byte) / 15 sec.

Outcue: "… I was plenty scared."

Potter is in good condition at Wheatland General Hospital. The train was on its way to Southern Kansas with a load of steel and lumber when the accident took place shortly before midnight. Freezing temperatures—dipping into the teens—will make the job of cleaning up a very unpleasant one and will hamper efforts to get service back to normal. But Conrail spokesman Mark Florman is optimistic.

(sound byte) / 20 sec.

Outcue: "… we will know more in a few hours."

Florman also said that Conrail passenger trains will be detoured, causing some delays probably for 48 hours. With your local news, I'm Randy Springfield.

LEAD-INS

Every sound byte, wraparound, and report from the scene included in a news script must be introduced by a line or phrase known as a *lead-in*. Here is one possible lead-in the anchor could have used to introduce the train wreck wraparound if it were done by a reporter at the scene:

Cleanup is ongoing after an afternoon train wreck in Wheatland. Reporter Randy Springfield has the details.

(Take wraparound) TRT 1:10

Outcue "… With your local news, I'm Randy Springfield."

The most important thing to avoid when writing a lead-in is redundancy. One of the worst style errors is a lead-in that says exactly the same thing as the first line of the wraparound or sound byte. The way to avoid this problem is for the writer or anchor in the newsroom and the reporter at the scene to discuss in advance what each is going to say.

TEASES

The short sentences used in a script to hold the audience's attention just before a commercial break are called *teases*. The idea of a tease is to give the audience some reason to keep listening rather than turning the dial. This is best accomplished by giving just a hint of what is to come after the commercial. The cleverer the tease, the greater the chance the audience will put up with the commercial. If the train wreck wraparound were to follow a commercial, this is the way it might be teased:

> Freezing temperatures add to the problems of a Wheatland train wreck. That story after this.
> (Commercial)

If the news is long enough or being written for an all-news station, it's effective to tease two or more stories before going to a commercial. Such a tease gives the writer more opportunities to hook listeners. If they are not interested in the first story that is teased, they might go for the second or third one.

HEADLINES

Headlines are another form of tease. Headlines come at the top of a newscast and should reflect the most interesting and exciting stories to be covered in the upcoming newscast. Often, a headline for an offbeat story is an effective tease. Here is a sample:

- A tornado rips through a small Missouri town, killing six people.
- The cost of living climbs for the third straight month.
- Governor Loudis says he will veto legislation that would restore the death penalty.
- And a pet cheetah scares a lot of people when he decides to take a walk down Campbell Street.
- Those stories and more on the 6 o'clock news.
- Good evening, I'm Tracy Simpson.

Some radio newscasts start with only one headline:

> Six people die in a tornado in Missouri. Good evening, I'm Tracy Simpson with the 6 o'clock news. The tornado ripped through Nixa, Missouri....

Many stations, particularly those that have shortened their newscasts, have eliminated headlines completely on the grounds that they are redundant and take up too much time. On many other radio stations, the only news is the headlines.

PAD COPY

Copy written for protection against mistakes in timing and unexpected changes in the newscast that could affect the timing is called *pad copy*. Most of the time, such copy will not get on the air, so stories that are selected as pad copy should be relatively unimportant.

Because most radio newscasts are relatively short, pad copy normally consists of only a few short pieces totaling perhaps between 30 seconds and 1 minute. More pad copy might be written for longer newscasts.

Note that the chief reason for pad material is to avoid one of the scariest situations in broadcast news: running out of something to say before the program is scheduled to end. With prerecorded newscasts, the need for pad copy has been reduced greatly.

BACK TIMING

Getting off the air on time for a live newscast takes some planning. If a newscast runs over, or is short, it sometimes can create problems for the programs that follow the news. This is particularly true if network programming comes after the newscast.

One way to guarantee that this situation does not happen is called *back timing*. The final segments in the newscast are timed and then deducted from the length of the newscast. Let's look at an example. Suppose the last two items in a newscast are the stocks and weather. Both are timed. It will take 10 seconds to read the stocks and another 20 seconds for the weather. The standard close for the newscast takes another 5 seconds to read. The newscaster will need 35 seconds, then, to read the last three items. So 35 seconds are deducted from the total time of the newscast. The newscaster now knows that he or she must begin reading those three final items at exactly 2:25 into a 3-minute newscast. The three final items should be placed in a separate pile within easy reach on the studio table. The time 2:25 should be written boldly on the top page of this back-timed copy. When the clock reaches the 2:25 mark in the newscast, the reader simply picks up the three pages and begins reading them, regardless of where he or she is in the newscast. Some stories may have to be dropped, and often they are, but that is the only way to guarantee that the newscaster gets off the air on time. In newsrooms that are computerized, timing and back timing are done by the computer itself.

CONVERGENCE AND RADIO NEWS

With the digital technology now available to create and store newscasts, radio newscasts are prime examples of online convergence that can be delivered easily. Once a radio news break has been recorded onto the hard drive, it is a simple matter to move that file onto the station's Web site. From there, listeners can click the newscast and hear the prerecorded stories via popular software such as Windows Media Player or iTunes. The only concern is that someone at the radio station must update those audio clips frequently, lest old news is offered on the Web site.

This delivery solves one of the great difficulties of radio news, which is that a listener cannot go back and "relisten" to a newscast on the air. If a radio station actively posts their radio newscasts, it is another vehicle to attract listeners. In this era of declining local radio news, employees may find that this form of Web delivery is required for them to maintain their listening audience.

FIGURE 15.9

www.wndb.am.

SUMMARY

Working in a radio operation in a small market has always been a good way to break into broadcast news, although many people seem to find the glamour and the pay of TV more appealing. At a small radio station committed to news, you receive a wonderful opportunity to learn how to do everything; you might end up being the writer, reporter, announcer, and technician. In this era of automation, you might be the only "live" person in the building.

As the sole member of the news staff, you would quickly learn how to organize your time and effort because you would have little or no help. Your news judgment would be tested every day. You would get an excellent opportunity to hone your writing and reporting skills. You would also be preparing your-self for the next job in a bigger market.

Even if your main interest is television, radio news provides an important foundation for broadcast journalists. The principles of radio newswriting, reporting, and announcing also apply to television news. You will be required to make some adjustment because of pictures, but if you have absorbed the material in this chapter, you are well prepared to move along.

Finally, while radio does not enjoy the dominance it once enjoyed as a news leader, it still has the ability to offer timely information to listeners. Breaking news, updated traffic reports, and weather updates are vital to an audience that's both at home and driving on the road. Radio news isn't dead; it's evolv-ing in a new direction in this media landscape.

Test Your Knowledge

1. Why is it important when you are writing broadcast news to know about your audience?
2. You are the only newsperson working at your radio station. When you arrive for work, you have 2 hours before you read your first newscast. Explain how you would get prepared.
3. Explain the meaning of the term *writing from the back*.
4. If you were writing news in Wheatland, Missouri, a market of 10,000, which story would you pick for the lead of your newscast? (a) U.S. forces drop emergency relief supplies to flood refugees in Mozambique, (b) 10,000 autoworkers go on strike in Detroit, or (c) Wheatland welcomes home 10 of its servicemen and -women who served in the NATO air attacks on Iran. Explain your choice.
5. If you were writing for a radio station in Ann Arbor, Michigan, which of the stories in question 4 would you lead with? Why?
6. After you have selected the lead of your newscast, how would you determine the order of the rest of the stories?
7. What does localizing news mean? Give examples of how you could localize a story about a fatal fire at a rock concert and a story about the National Basketball Associa-tion draft.
8. If you were writing a 2-minute newscast for radio, approximately how many lines of copy would you need?
9. If you have three commercials in the 2-minute newscast, one of them 30 seconds and the other two 10 seconds each, how many lines of copy would you need to write?

EXERCISES

1. Using the stories reported on the front page of a newspaper, prepare headlines for a radio newscast.
2. Using those same headlines, write teases for two of the stories that will appear later in your radio newscast.
3. Read the front page of the newspaper and decide which of the stories you would lead with in a newscast.
4. What other stories on the front page, and in the rest of the newspaper, would you use in your newscast and in which order?
5. Go to a local radio station that has a news operation and watch how they put a newscast together. Prepare a report on what you saw.

Delivering the News

CONTENTS

INTRODUCTION

Many of you have hopes of anchoring news. How long it takes you to end up at the anchor desk depends mainly on two factors. The first one is talent, which is your ability to deliver the news. The second consideration is the size of the market in which you begin your career.

If you have talent and start working in a relatively small market, you may reach the anchor desk quickly. You will still, however, have to prove you are ready for that job by impressing the news director with your reporting ability. It is extremely rare for a newcomer to start anchoring five nights a week. Instead, the job will typically be advertised for someone to report three days a week and anchor on the weekends. From there, it will take many newscasts to prove your worth behind the anchor desk full-time.

Also, remember that not all reporters become anchors; some good reporters do not have the special talent required to anchor news. Similarly, some anchors make awful reporters.

Regardless of market size, this chapter discusses the qualities you need to anchor or report in front of a camera or microphone. But as a general rule of thumb, if a last-minute anchoring option appears (such as the noon anchor calls in sick), never hesitate to step in as a replacement.

FIGURE 16.1

FIGURE 16.2

David Nussbaum, meteorologist; Sylvia Weatherspoon, co-anchor; and Todd Ross, co-anchor, WBRZ, Baton Rouge, Louisiana (photo by James Terry).

APPEARANCE

In most fields of work, it is illegal to discriminate on the basis of gender, race, or age. While television newsrooms are not exempt from the Equal Employment Opportunity Commission, news directors try to strike a balance among their talent. If there is a job opening for a co-anchor to share the evening newscast with the current anchor (and he happens to be an older white male), expect the news director to subconsciously seek someone from another demographic. A younger male would be acceptable, while a female would be even better. A minority anchor with an African-American or Hispanic background would also "balance" the anchor desk. There are various factors at play in this scenario, but one outcome is clear: the incoming anchor will not be an older white male.

If this seems unfair, bear in mind that newscasters in previous decades were overwhelmingly white men over 40 years of age. CNN's Bernard Shaw was an outstanding news anchor for 21 years who simply happened to be African-American. CBS hired Katie Couric to replace Dan Rather in 2006 as the sole anchor for the *CBS Evening News*. Other broadcast journalists, such as Connie Chung and the late Ed Bradley, reflect the growing diversification of the American public. It should come as no surprise that those appearing on-camera reflect the faces of those who are watching.

CREDIBILITY

Ask news directors what they look for in reporters and anchors and most will tell you *credibility*. They want people who are believable, people who come across as knowledgeable and are comfortable with what they are doing.

Jeff Puffer, a voice coach for one of the nation's major broadcast consulting firms, Frank Magid Associates, says he knows many "reliable anchor–reporters with good potential who just don't seem comfortable in the anchor chair. In person they're spontaneous and charming. But on the air they're wooden, with unnatural speech rhythms and awkward inflection."

FIGURE 16.3

Magid Associates (www.magid.com) is one of the nation's top broadcast consulting firms.

Puffer says that when he's instructing anchors and reporters, he expects them "to show two qualities in their reading: intelligence and genuine sensitivity." He says he looks for "emotion that is appropriate for the story, the person, and the occasion. I want them to demonstrate that they know what they're reading and that they're thoughtfully weighing the facts as they speak. I always want them to say it with feeling, not artificially, but with sensitivity and maturity."

It is not always easy for anchor–reporters to accomplish these goals, and those who coach people in delivery techniques use a variety of methods. Puffer says he doesn't concentrate on speech pathology material such as breathing, diction, and resonance. "We're involved in matters relating to interpretation, making the voice sound spontaneous and conversational, like an ad-lib."

Of course, Puffer admits that his methodology could be called "unconventional or unorthodox," but, he says, "given what we have been finding in neuroscience research, we know that the whole of human intelligence is not just the left side of the brain, the intellectual side. It's also intuition, artistry, abstractions, pattern recognition, and the like."

ONE-WAY COMMUNICATION

According to Puffer, the difficulty in broadcast training is the *noninteractive environment*. He points out that there is "no give and take, it's largely one way. The result of that strained environment is that the communicators do not automatically use all their self-expression when looking into a camera or speaking on mike as they would in a face-to-face dialogue." Puffer adds: "What we try to do is restore that quality and feeling in the delivery. We try to trigger that part of the brain that is responsible for artistry, abstraction, etc."

Another rookie mistake is evident when a broadcaster tries to mimic someone else on the air. Puffer notes that he's not trying to make a person's voice sound like someone else's. "We all have developed and cultivated a wealth of knowledge regarding what is appropriate interpersonal communication over the years," he says. "We all know the tools; we know how loud to speak; how to emphasize and articulate our words; how to use our face and eyes with accompanying gestures; no one has to tell us how to do these things. The idea," Puffer adds, "is to tap into those resources and help bring them into the environment that is not interactive, like the broadcast studio."

Puffer says he typically begins a talent coaching session by indicating (in these exact words), "I am not going to teach you today anything you don't already know." I believe, he says, "to the core of my being that for a young adult to have achieved success in relationships with others throughout his or her life, that person has developed considerably useful instincts regarding the ways to use volume, pitch, pacing, inflections, emphasis, eye contact, etc. to gain attention, hold interest, and create an atmosphere of goodwill and trust." Puffer goes on, "The difficulty occurs when that same person moves into the sequestered environment of a studio to anchor or into an edit suite to record the voice track for a package." He says without the benefit of direct contact with the receiver, the speaker automatically faces a disadvantage.

He says any number of unintended peculiarities can begin to creep into the delivery, making that person's speech sound stilted. Puffer adds that this is where talent coaches like him come in—they help anchors and reporters "translate to the broadcast not only the behaviors and mannerisms consistent with conversation but also the attitudes and frames of mind that invite lively, expressive conversation with your best friend or your mom." But Puffer says it's not as easy as telling the student to pretend that you're talking to your friend or mom. He says there is an intermediate step that sets the exchange of conversation between two people in motion, and it's understanding those subtleties involved in getting started that proves to be the most effective in getting the authentic self to come forward.

Puffer also discusses what he describes as the "single, most common delivery trap that broadcasters fall into—the pattern characterized by lifting or raising the inflections at the end of sentences, which is referred to as "comma splicing" or "circumflex."

To illustrate the problem, Puffer offered this exercise: Read the following sentence the same way you would if you were to say, "I dunno," as you finish the sentence.

> "The state board of regents voted not to increase tuitions at their final budget meetings yesterday."

Puffer says the inflection pattern not only is inconsistent with the way a person speaks in an actual explanation, but it also risks hurting one's credibility in either of two ways. First, he said, it can register in the ears and minds of the audience as being dismissive. He says the rising intonation is the same that occurs most typically when someone says (shrugging), "You can listen if you want, but you don't have to." Or Puffer adds, alternatively, the intonation can suggest ambivalence—uncertainty. He says it's the same sound you hear when you or someone else says, "May-BE." Puffer concludes, "Learn not to speak this way so as not to compromise your credibility through indifference or ambivalence."

GETTING HELP WITH YOUR DELIVERY

If you are having problems with your voice, diction, and delivery, it's a good idea to deal with the problems while you are in college. Speech and debating courses sometimes help, but if you have serious problems, you may need a voice coach. Voice coach Carol Dearing Rommel advises students who are intent on being in front of a microphone or camera to "do all they can to prepare themselves before they leave college." She says that without professional help, some students "fall into habit patterns that will work against them."

FIGURE 16.4

DIALECTS

Traditionally, station managers and news directors look for people who speak "standard American speech" when they hire on-air personnel. That's another way of saying they like Midwestern voices, which are considered "neutral."

Don't count yourself out if you were not born and reared in South Dakota. Some dialects can be eliminated with good coaching. If they cannot be corrected, it's still possible to work in an area where your dialect is the primary one. "If you have a Southern dialect you can work in the South," says coach Rommel, "but you are not likely to get on the air in Chicago." She said that same rule applies to people who were born and reared in Chicago. "If they have a strong big-city dialect they are not likely to make it in Dallas."

Mary Berger, a speech pathologist and author in Chicago who works with young people, says it's important to let students know, if they have a dialect that reflects a minority racial or ethnic background, that there is "nothing wrong with them. Many have been told that they are stupid because of the way they speak. Once you tell them that you do not intend to change the dialect but develop a new 'style' for use in the workplace, they relax." Berger explains her methods in her book *Speak Standard, TOO*.

Like Jeff Puffer, Berger says many of her colleagues may consider her approach to speech problems "unorthodox." She recalls that she was asked by Columbia College, in Chicago, to design a course after the college got feedback from graduates indicating that they were having trouble finding work because of voice problems.

"What we find in our classes," she notes, "are a lot of students with high-pitched, nasal-sounding, unpleasant voices not acceptable for air. We don't try to correct those problems in the traditional way, working on pitch and inflection, etc. What we do is give them an 'indirect hint' that says, 'Your voice is different but you can change it without too much help from us.'"

Berger says the first thing she has the students do is record their voices and then listen to them. "They detect immediately the high pitches and other things that they would like to change. Then we say, 'OK, now pretend that you are someone else, like newscaster Bill Curtis or a general giving orders to troops.' Amazingly, their voices suddenly get deeper."

Berger stresses that there are times when students obviously cannot change their readings. "When their voices are straining, for example, when they try to change their pitch, we direct them to people who deal with such problems."

Voice coach Rommel says that pitch is one of the most troubling problems for young people. "Young ladies," she says, "usually have too high a pitch. When they read their copy, it sounds as if they are much younger and less credible than they really are." But Rommel warns young women that trying to change the pitch of their voice dramatically without professional help can be dangerous.

Rommel, an adjunct at Southern Methodist University, says another common problem is articulation. She says many people going into broadcasting have a minor lisp. But Dearing says this problem is easily correctable and should not prevent anyone from moving forward as a reporter or an anchor.

LISTENING TO YOURSELF

In the chapters on style, you learned that it is always a good idea to read your copy aloud because your ear catches mistakes and detects poorly constructed copy that your eye misses. Similarly, reading aloud alerts you to any problems you have with pronunciation, articulation, and awkward speech patterns.

Most students talk faster and in a higher pitch than they acknowledge. The simple solution is to simply slow down and relax, but the first step is to record your voice and then listen with a critical ear. If you don't listen to the shortcomings of your news delivery, it is impossible to correct them.

CORRECT PRONUNCIATION

A number of newscasters avoid using words that are difficult to pronounce. The mind understands the meaning of many words, but sometimes it has trouble relaying the pronunciation to the tongue, which causes newscasters to stumble over their copy. Tricky words and phrases invite trouble.

Sometimes writers and anchors have no choice. Proper names, for example, cannot be changed. Spelling them correctly does not guarantee that they will be pronounced correctly. The writer of a newscast must identify the correct pronunciation of any difficult names in a script. Reporters should ask the people whom they are interviewing for the proper pronunciation of their names. Names of towns also should be checked if there is any doubt. For example,

> Biloxi in Mississippi is pronounced Bi-lok'-si. Acadian in Louisiana is pronounced E-kay'-di-en. Kankakee in Illinois is pronounced Kang'-ka-ke. Cairo in Illinois is pronounced Ka'-ro.

If a job takes you to a new part of the country, it is a good idea to seek out someone who has lived in the area for some time. Colleagues who have been working at the station will be able to help, and someone at the local library or historical society will probably be happy to answer questions about the pronunciation of nearby towns or local family names.

K
Ahmed Tejan Kabbah—AH'-mehd TEH'-jahn KAH'-bah
Kabul—kah-BOOL' (though the pronunciation KAH'-bool is also common)
Farouk Kaddoumi—fah-ROOK' kah-DOO'-mee
Akhmad Kadyrov—kuh-DEE'-ruhv
Thomas Kaenzig—KEN'-zig
Kalai-Zal—kah-LAY'-zahl
Peter Kalikow—KAL'-ih-koh
Elaine Kamarck—KAY'-mahrk
Melina Kanakaredes—kah-nah-kah-REE'-deez
Kanawha—kah-NAH'
Kandahar—kan'-duh-HAHR' (slight stress on first syllable; stronger
    stress on third syllable)
Karachi—kuh-RAH'-chee
Radovan Karadzic—RA'-doh-van KA'-ra-jich
Karbala—KAHR'-bah-lah
Islam Karimov—EES'-lahm kah-REE'-mahv
Mohamed Abdirahman Kariye—ahb-deer-uh-HAHM' ky-EED'-eh
Mel Karmazin—KAHR'-muh-zin
Raed Karmi—RAH'-ed KAHR'-mee
Karnei Shomron—kahr-NAY' shahm-ROHN'
Hamid Karzai—HAH'-mihd KAHR'-zeye
Qayum Karzai—ky-OOM' KAHR'-zeye
Kaspiisk—kahs-PEESK'
Mikhail Kasyanov—kah-see-AH'-nahf
Moshe Katsav—KAHT'-sahv
Jorma Kaukonen—YOR'-mah KOW'-kah-nen
Yoriko Kawaguchi—yoh-ree-koh kah-wah-goo-chee
Kazimiya Shrine—KAH'-zi-mee-yah
Thomas Kean—kayn
Bernard Kerik—KEHR'-ihk
Teresa Heinz Kerry—teh-RAY'-zah
Khaldiyah—KAHL'-dee-yah
Zalmay Khalilzad—ZAHL'-may kah-LEEL'-zahd
Ali Khamenei—hah-meh-neh-EE'
Abdul Qadeer Khan—ahb-DOOL' kah-DEER' khahn
Khaneqin—hah-nah-KEEN'
Mohammad Khatami—HAHT'-ah-mee
Essid Sami Ben Khemais—EH'-seed ... keh-MEES'
Khobar—KOH'-bahr
Mikhail Khodorkovsky—mih-hah-EEL' khoh-dohr-KAHV'-skee
Ayatollah Khomeini—ah-yah-TOH'-lah hoh-MAY'-nee
Khost—hohst (heavy stress on first "h")
Mwai Kibaki—mwy kih-BAH'-kee
Kim Jong Il—kihm jawng eel
Kiowa, Kansas—KY'-oh-wah
Kiribati—keer-ih-BAH'-tee
Kirkuk—keer-KOOK' or keer-KUK'
Heidi Klum—kloom
Junichiro Koizumi—joon-ee-chee-roh koh-ee-zoo-mee

FIGURE 16.5

Sample of an AP pronunciation guide.

Valery Korzun—val-uh-ree kohr-ZOON'
Vojislav Kostunica—voh-YEE'-slahv kosh-too-NEET'-zuh
Frank, Martha (Stewart) Kostyra—kah-STY'-rah
George Kouloheras—koo-loh-HEHR'-us
Dennis Kozlowski—kahz-LOW'-skee
Ray Kubilus—koo-BIL'-uhs
Robert Krughoff—KROO'-gahf
Ryszard Krystosik—RIH'-shahrd krih-STAW'-sehk
Kok Ksor—kahk kuh-SOHR'
Dennis Kucinich—koo-SIN'-ich
Andre Kuipers—KEYE'-purz
Kunar—ku-NAHR' (the vowel sound in "ku" is similar to the double-o
    sound in "took")
Kunduz—KUHN'-dooz
Kushiro—koo-shee-roh
Kut—koot
Aleksander Kwasniewski—kvahsh-NYEV'-skee

L
Hemant Lakhani—HEH'-muhnt luh-KAH'-nee
Landstuhl—LAHND'-shtool
Anthony LaPaglia—luh-PAH'-lee-uh
Amel Larrieux—lahr-RYOO'
LaSalle County, Illinois—luh-SEL'
Lashkar-e-Tayyaba—LAHSH'-kar ay TEYE'-buh
Jorge Lazareff—HOR'-hay
Lee Hoi-chang—lee hweh-chayng
LaSalle Leffall—leh-FAWL'
Leganes—leh-GAN'-ehs
John Lehman—LAY'-man
Leipzig, Germany—LYP'-sihg
Camp Lejeune—lih-ZHOON'
David Lereah—lur-RAY'
Mark LeTexier—lah-TEKS'-eer
Katrina Leung—lee-YUNG'
Daniel Libeskind—LEE'-behs-kihnd
Lien Chan—LEE'-ehn jan
Likud—lee-KOOD'
Lindsay Lohan—LOH'-han
Jose Lopez Portillo—hoh-say loh-pehz pohr-TEE'-yoh
Los Olivos—lohs oh-LEE'-vohs
Kim Louagie—LOO'-wah-jay
Loya jirga—LOY'-uh JEER'-guh
Richard Lugar—LOO'-gur
Constantine Lyketsos—ly-KEHT'-sohs

M
Dan Macagni—muh-KAHN'-yuh
Macclenny, Florida—MAK'-klen-ee
Madhya Pradesh—MUH'-dyuh PRUH'-desh
Imam Mahdi—EE'-mahm MAH'-dee

FIGURE 16.5   *Continued*

The wire services send out pronunciation guides to their customers, which are particularly useful when covering national and international stories. If your news operation is computerized, these guides should be stored for future use.

In cities large enough to have a wire service bureau, the staff will help its clients find the proper pronunciation of a name or place in the city or state. The wires also have a phonetics desk that helps with hard-to-pronounce names in national and international news stories.

For many international stories, it is not always necessary to use the names of foreign dignitaries. If you do use them, it is a good idea to refer to the dignitaries by their titles during the rest of the story, particularly if the names are unusually difficult to pronounce. When using difficult names, write them phonetically in the copy to help the person who will be reading the script. This phonetic spelling can be given after the word or written above the word. Writers working on a newscast should ask the anchors which style they prefer. Here are examples of the two methods: Cayuga (Ka-yoo'-ga) Indians still live on the land. (Ka-yoo'-ga) Cayuga Indians still live on the land.

Dictionaries, which give the proper pronunciation of words, as well as their meanings, are invaluable tools. On the Internet, the Web site www.dictionary .com provides instant pronunciation guides. Several dictionaries of pronunciation are also available for purchase, and most newsrooms keep copies on hand. If you are unsure about the pronunciation of a word, look it up.

PACING

What else can you do to improve your delivery? *CBS News* correspondent Charles Osgood says pacing is important. Osgood advises using a pause to get attention when you want something you just said "to sink in…. A pause can be very telling, provided you know something." He says the "most remarkable pacer in our business is ABC newscaster Paul Harvey. You can drive a truck between 'Paul Harvey' and 'good day.' He's doing that for a reason."

Osgood recalls times when he's been traveling with a news crew and everyone is talking among themselves until Harvey begins broadcasting. "When Paul Harvey comes on the radio," Osgood says, "everybody stops [talking] and listens to Paul Harvey. You cannot not listen to that man."

For his own writing, Osgood says that he uses a lot of ellipses (series of three dots). "I want to remind myself that that is supposed to be a pause. I will also capitalize certain words … because I want to hit that particular word for it to work."

The *CBS News* correspondent also says it's important to remember when you are on the air that "you're talking to somebody, which means that you have to be conscious at all times that there's somebody there." Osgood notes that you can't assume people are listening; you "have to get their attention, you don't automatically have it."

MARKING COPY

Most newscasters mark copy to help them remember when to pause or to emphasize certain words. They mark the copy as they read it aloud, which also helps them control their breathing. Because long sentences require extra breath, newscasters must either pause more often or rewrite the sentence. Otherwise, they sound as though they are running out of breath. Often, inexperienced newscasters try to speed up their delivery when they realize that they might have trouble getting through a complicated sentence, but that's a poor solution. If you find yourself leaning toward this solution, rewrite your copy until you can read it at a normal pace.

Bruce Kirk, a former anchor at KPNX–TV in Phoenix, uses slash marks to indicate pauses and underlines words that he wishes to emphasize. Some anchors use a double underline for words that require extraordinary emphasis. Other anchors use all caps for words they wish to stress. Some anchors use ellipses to indicate pauses, and still others use dashes. Some anchors like their scripts typed in all caps, whereas others prefer upper- and lowercase (which, according to studies, is easier to read).

Christine Devine, an anchor for KTTV in Los Angeles, says she doesn't always have time to mark her script, but when she does "it results in a better show." Devine uses a bracket to let herself know she's starting to read a new paragraph and a new thought, and after a sound byte so she doesn't lose her place. She uses an ellipsis to signify the end of a phrase, but not the end of a thought.

Devine underlines key words for emphasis, which seems to be standard practice among anchors. She also routinely underlines "not." In addition, Devine says she underlines for contrast when, for example, contrasting Republicans and Democrats.

CHARACTERISTICS OF SUCCESSFUL ANCHORS

Jim Boyer, the former news director of WWL–TV in New Orleans, says

FIGURE 16.6
An anchor reviews copy.

that "people watch people. They don't watch helicopters or satellites and they prefer to watch anchors they like and are comfortable with." Boyer recalled the work of one of his anchors, the late Bill Elder, who worked for WWL for 20 years. Boyer said Elder was like an old friend telling them what's going on and it's very easy for them to watch. Speaking about his career a few years ago, Elder stressed that it is also important for anchors to be involved in the production of the show. He liked to boast that he would write a third of the news, even on days when he was working on special projects.

A number of anchors we spoke with also stressed how important it is to keep up with things, even if they are not part of their own culture, like the rock band scene and other things that appeal to younger people.

News directors we spoke with say it is important for anchors to understand that there is more to the job than looking and sounding good on the air. They also say anchors should be involved in the community through personal appearances or charity work. They also stress that it's important for anchors to be working journalists, who should be able to handle a school board meeting or a foreign story with equal ease.

Most news directors use the same language when they speak about successful anchors, and words such as *credibility*, *honesty*, and *genuine* keep cropping up, along with concern and caring about what's going on in the community. Another common denominator is that successful, top-rated anchors are all genial people who are well liked by their co-workers and their viewers.

Diane Doctor, the news director of WCBS–TV in New York, says it's difficult to define why some anchors are more successful than others, but she also used the words credibility, on-camera presence, and a comfort level that good anchors share with the audience. Obviously, she said they have to be intelligent to begin with and the audience has to believe that what the anchors are telling them is true. Doctor, who worked in a number of local markets and for NBC and WNBC in New York in both management positions and as a reporter and producer before joining the CBS organization, agreed that it's also important for anchors to be active in the community so that viewers tend to think of them not so much as performers but as part of the family.

COSMETICS

It has always been true that anchor people, in addition to having good voices, also must be attractive on camera. Fortunately, the problem of "looks" is not quite as bad as it once was when it was virtually impossible to get on camera unless you were beautiful or handsome. News managers still want people with pleasing faces, regardless of race or gender, but we do see anchors wearing glasses and wrinkles are not outlawed as they once were. But those who select their on-camera talent often want to change their looks and delivery, even though they liked them well enough to hire them.

Among the absurdities that anchors must sometimes put up with from their bosses is this particularly amusing one related by *ABC News* correspondent Judy Muller when she was still at CBS. According to Judy, her boss called her into his office to complain about the way she was saying the traditional cutaway phrase before a commercial break—"Now this." At the time, Muller didn't think the criticism was very funny. She said it is memorable to her because it "took aim at possibly the only thing I was secure about at the time: my on-air delivery."

Muller was puzzled because she asked herself: How many ways can you say "Now this"? But she said she dutifully practiced different inflections: with authority, drawn out in a provocative manner, queried in an inquisitive manner, "every way until I had it just right, which is basically the way I was saying it before, but with a touch of suspense."

This encounter with a boss over such a petty issue is described by Muller as a lesson in understanding that, just when you think you've got a thing wired, something comes along to short-circuit that notion, to pull you up short and remind you that now, of all things, you "must deal with this. It may be something petty, or improbable, or unpredictable, but you cannot proceed without dealing with it."

Muller obviously did not forget the lesson. Many years later when she wrote her memoirs she called the book: *Now This* (Putnam Publishing Group, 2000). In her book, Muller also recalls an incident when she moved into TV reporting for the first time and was given some advice on how to improve her appearance.

A consultant hired by *ABC News* to help new correspondents took Muller into a screening room where they looked at some of the correspondent's stories. After viewing a few of them, the consultant told Muller that she obviously did not need any help with her writing or delivery. Muller then asked about her looks. "Well," the consultant replied, "I really only have one word for you." Muller asked: "And what would that word be?" The consultant leaned close to Muller and whispered in her ear: "*Scarves.* I think they will help soften your angular face." Muller said that during her radio career she didn't have to worry about her angular face. She said that she never realized that she *had* an angular face.

Muller said she began to understand that the "face" thing is important to the people who hired you, like the day she arrived at the Los Angeles Bureau with a new, very short haircut and the person on the news desk said with a shocked expression: "Did you talk to New York before doing that?" Muller replied: "No, I didn't know I had to." As for the consultant, Muller said despite the advice she never managed to get into scarves, much less figure out how to tie them.

She says despite all the attention given to cosmetics by TV producers and managers, she still believes that, scarves or no scarves: "A reporter's best accessory is the string of words that, like so many pearls, can make for a beautiful story."

Muller added that good camera presence has always been an asset for television reporters, but more and more, at least at magazine shows, correspondents are increasingly valued more for that attribute than their writing skills.

In her memoir *Reporting Live* (Simon & Schuster, 1999), Lesley Stahl, a long-time *60 Minutes* correspondent, recalls that when she was hired for the job by executive producer Don Hewitt, he told Stahl that there was just one thing that he wanted her to change. Sensitive to what he was about to tell Stahl, he prepared her: "I have to do something that I'm afraid is going to make you angry," he went on. "You're going to be really upset with me. I hate to say this." Stahl replied: "What already?" Hewitt blurted out: "I hate your hair, you have to change it, it's too stiff."

Stahl writes that if she had been younger, "I would have chafed at the insult—how dare he." But she wasn't offended. She told Hewitt that because she couldn't be futzing with her hair in the middle of covering the White House, with everything that was going on, she teased her hair and sprayed it and forgot about it. But she told Hewitt: "If you want me to change it, no problem, I'll change it." Stahl said that she spent as much time as she could spare on her appearance. She got her hair done twice a week and bought enough makeup "to open my own boutique."

Stahl recalled another occasion when she and a group of correspondents were meeting with the former president of *CBS News*, Eric Ober, and he complained that there seemed to be a reluctance at the network to discuss cosmetics. He noted that one of CBS's finest correspondents, Bob Simon, needed voice lessons. Stahl yelled out: "Guess it's time for my facelift!" "No!" said Ober. "Older is more authoritative. People want their news from older-looking people." "Thanks," replied Stahl.

Stahl also admitted that there were many times when she was anxiety-ridden on the air when she was co-anchor of *CBS Morning News.* "I never froze," she said, "but I tightened up when the camera light went on. I did this strange thing," she continued, "that showed some teeth that was supposedly my smile, but I couldn't look into that camera and be me." She added: "That's the most important thing for anybody on television. The audience can sense when you're not relaxed, and they don't like it." Stahl said her mother called her to say that she had found a teacher for her—to teach her how to smile. Stahl said she had a lesson and "had to find 'me' in there, and that took a long time."

Asked if working as an anchor made her respect the work that network anchors do, she replied that she had always respected their work—not because they read well but because of the way they perform in a crisis: "A space shuttle disaster, the President's been shot—when they're thrown on the air and don't know the complete story and are flying by the seat of their pants. This is when they earn their money," she added. "The anchors remain calm and set the tone for the public so they don't panic."

Jill Geisler, a former anchor and news director who now heads the Leadership and Management program at the Poynter Institute, says that because anchors are "the face of the news, the voice they carry forward needs to be an informed one." Geisler adds that the informed voice is best achieved when anchors are active leaders rather than passive participants in the editorial process. "To be a successful leader," she says, "anchors must develop the ability to influence those around them." She says the three key elements to having real influence on others are competence, integrity, and empathy. Geisler notes that the best anchors get involved in the editorial process early in their day, usually with the editorial meeting. "The process works well," she says, "when reporters in the field will talk to the anchors as well as the producers and managers as they develop their stories."

Geisler points out that this approach creates a connection between the on- and-off air staffs that results in better stories and, ultimately, a better news-cast. Writing in the RTNDA magazine, *The Communicator*, Geisler quotes an anchor at KPRC in Houston, Khambrel Marshall. "It sets a better tone in the newsroom," he says, "when the anchor is willing to roll up his sleeves and work on the programs." But, he adds, it's also important to work as an equal with the production team. Marshall cautions, "You have to be careful to strike a balance so that you don't irri-tate the producers and the others who work hard on the news." He adds, "The goal is to contribute, not to 'big foot' the process."

FIGURE 16.7
Matt Lauer and Katie Couric interview New York City Mayor Michael Bloomberg on NBC's Today Show *(courtesy of Max Franklin, Getty Images).*

In a roundtable discussion that Geisler conducted with a group of network and local anchors, there was agreement that anchors, to be successful, must be leaders in the newsroom. Anchor Karen Foss of KSDK in St. Louis told her colleagues that "the sleight of hand that makes an anchor's job look easy masks the effort it takes to put together a confident, coherent broadcast." She

FIGURE 16.8

added, "As an anchor you are the lead journalist in your newsroom and your standards influence … the tone of many in the newsroom."

Barbara Cochran, president of RTNDA, listed some common qualities among some of the stand-out anchors she has known, including Bob Schieffer, Tom Brokaw, Dan Rather, and Peter Jennings. She noted that "they all consider themselves reporters, not anchors … they're curious and really put a lot of emphasis on their own writing, and on good writing, appearing in their newscasts."

SUMMARY

If you wish to report or anchor for radio and television, you must analyze your voice as soon as you can. One of your instructors may be able to tell you if you need help and where you can get it. If speech courses are not offered in your journalism program, seek out the speech department. Consider the help of a coach if you have some special problems with your voice or diction.

Remember that a regional or cultural dialect will not necessarily eliminate you from contention as a reporter or anchor. Many of those problems, if they can't be eliminated, can at least be modified sufficiently for you to work in the area where you were born and reared.

If you have a good voice, learn to use it properly. Get accustomed to reading your copy aloud before you go in front of a microphone. In addition to alerting you to grammatical errors or awkward phrases you may have missed, reading your copy aloud will help you discover that certain words and names in the copy are hard to pronounce. If so, add the phonetic spellings next to or above the difficult names and places. Finally, reading your copy aloud gives you the opportunity to determine what words you want to emphasize and how you can use pacing effectively.

Test Your Knowledge

1. Name some of the talents you must develop if you wish to become a radio reporter.
2. What additional talents will you need if you wish to report or anchor for television?

3. If you are having troubles of any kind with your voice, how soon should you get an evaluation?

4. If you have problems with diction, breathing, or dialect, what kind of help can you get?

5. What are some of the approaches to solving voice problems?

6. Two of the voice coaches quoted in this chapter say some of their techniques might be considered unorthodox. Discuss.

7. The wire services offer some pronunciation assistance to their clients. What kind of help?

8. Why is Paul Harvey so effective in getting and holding an audience's attention?

9. Why do anchors mark their copy? What are some of the symbols they use?

EXERCISES

1. Read a few newspaper stories silently and then read them into a tape recorder. Make a note of the things you discovered were a problem in the copy only after reading it aloud. After making appropriate changes in the copy, read it into the tape recorder a second time and note any improvements.

2. Write a 1-minute radio script based on information from a newspaper or newspaper wire. Then read the script into a tape recorder. Listen to the recording and make notes on anything that you did not like about your reading, such as inflection, breathing, pitch, or pace.

3. Do a second reading, but this time mark your copy before doing so. After reading, note whether there was an improvement in your delivery.

4. Go through a newspaper or newspaper wire copy and find words that are unfamiliar to you. Look up the words in a dictionary for meaning and pronunciation and in a pronunciation guide if one is available. Write the words phonetically along with the rest of the sentences and read them into a tape recorder. Then replay the tape for other members of your class and note whether they understood the meaning of the words.

5. After you have noted the words that fellow students did not understand, find synonyms for them and rerecord the sentences with the new words. See if the students understand the copy this time.

Network and Global News

CONTENTS

INTRODUCTION

For many in broadcast journalism, a career begins and ends with network news affiliates. This is typical for graduating college students, who see local news on a daily basis and are familiar with the format, delivery style, and work expectations of their neighborhood affiliate. Applying for a job at the news station in one's hometown is generally seen as the path to a career in broadcast journalism; starting at a small, local affiliate and then working within progressively larger news markets has long been the traditional employment arc.

Viewers of local affiliates also have a sense of community with their local news personalities. Local news reporters and anchors develop a kinship with an audience that is more familiar than that between an audience and a national news anchor, especially if the on-air talent is frequently seen about town at charity events or covering stories.

Yet there are a number of journalism outlets that go unnoticed because they are not the news stations down the block. These companies still deal in news, but are not as familiar as those newsrooms in the local markets. Even though these outlets have Web sites that stream video, offer news reports, and provide news outside of the local community, they are often ignored. How many U.S. college students check the Deutsche Welle (DW) news Web site as frequently as their Facebook page?

This chapter examines news outlets that are beyond the typical network affiliate. These outlets include network news hubs, wire services, and international

279

news operations. While each of these works under the same umbrella of broadcast journalism, there are differences in their daily operations and organizational structure. Additionally, we'll take a look at the development of online news portals, the relationships among U.S. broadcasters and other global newsrooms, and how freedom of the press varies greatly around the world.

To begin, we first define how the current network and affiliate relationship functions in this country. This provides a thorough grounding of the traditional news delivery structure before we examine other broadcast journalism entities.

NETWORKS AND AFFILIATES

ABC, CBS, Fox, and NBC are the four dominant networks in the United States. Each of these networks feeds their programming into different cities via affiliated stations, or affiliates. These affiliates maintain business arrangements to air the networks' programs at scheduled times.

Each affiliate serves a *market,* which is a simple way of saying *Designated Market Area (DMA).* These markets are geographic regions that typically center around an urban area. New York City is the largest market in the country due to the number of viewers who live there. Los Angeles, Chicago, Philadelphia, and Dallas–Fort Worth are the other top five markets.

Not all markets are so well known. There are 210 DMAs across the country with the smallest markets broadcasting in remote areas. Alaska, some small communities in the West, and rural stretches in the Upper Midwest all host stations with comparatively tiny viewing audiences. The smallest is in Glendive, Montana, with a mere 3800 households.

Obviously, four competing television stations cannot make enough money in advertising to survive in Glendive, Montana; there simply aren't enough people living there. In fact, many of the smaller cities have only one or two local affiliates. However, this network/affiliate relationship works for the vast majority of television stations in this country. It is this degree of familiarity that lends many in broadcast journalism to view their hometown news stations as the primary source of news.

NETWORK NEWS STRUCTURE

The 24-hour news cycle forces differences in the basic operation of their newsrooms. The typical local affiliate offers a number of newscasts throughout the day, each headed by a different producer targeting somewhat different audiences. The noon newscast is more consumer-oriented, while the 5 p.m. contains a few more features and "lighter" news. The 6 p.m. is a hard-hitting local newscast, whereas the 10 p.m. (or 11 p.m., depending on the time zone) contains both local news and a bit of breaking national news. Additionally, the affiliate may offer local cut-ins at 7:25 and 8:25 a.m. These cut-ins are quick, 5-minute updates with brief local headlines and a regional weather forecast inserted during a network's morning program, such as the *Today Show* or *Good Morning, America.*

As discussed in the chapters on gathering news and producing the newscast, broadcast journalists are keenly aware of the time limitations placed upon them. As the usual 30-minute newscast only has 22 minutes of news (remember, weather, sports, and teases are still in that tally), producers constantly jockey numerous stories into a finite amount of time.

The situation is similar at network news operations, such as the *CBS Evening News* or the *NBC Nightly News.* Again, there is a very limited amount of time to cover all of the day's events. For the networks, there is also the added pressure of maintaining beats that aren't necessary at the local level. In addition to a White House correspondent, there are one or two stationed on Capitol Hill, another at the Pentagon, plus a few others who cover Washington politics as needed. There are financial reporters who cover Wall Street and finance in New York, perhaps an entertainment guru in Los Angeles, and international bureaus scattered around the globe.

There are striking differences between network and local newscasts. At the network level, producers have free reign to ignore weather and sports blocks, thus gaining valuable minutes for news. The reporters can also create longer packages. The 90-second package can be expanded for more in-depth storytelling, giving way to a 3-minute analysis of a financial crisis. Conversely, readers are often truncated to a mere sentence or two.

The structure of the network news does not lend itself to easy coverage of live, breaking events. An ongoing car chase on a California freeway, which may be played out for an hour on a cable news channel, will not fit on network news. However, stories with reporters who are live in the field blend in quite well.

The networks also pride themselves on reporters who have a strong affiliation to a specific news beat and set up their beats accordingly; this allows for stronger coverage of stories than relegating assignments based on geographic region. In this way, the science reporter will cover a NASA shuttle launch from Florida as well as a biotechnical discovery in Utah. There are war correspondents, political reporters, consumer affairs journalists, and a number of other specialized beats that can be better sustained at the national level. From the viewpoint of someone pursuing broadcast journalism as a career, they often find that the "general news reporter" label fades once the network level is achieved.

Finally, the caliber of interview subjects between networks and the local media can vary greatly. A one-on-one interview with a cabinet member or even the president is old hat for the networks. Unless the local affiliate is a powerhouse in the top 10 market, such high-level appearances with affiliates will be limited to an open press conference.

The greatest similarity between network and local newsrooms is that each has a short amount of time to relay a great amount of news. Competitive pressure is also paramount for all news producers, as earning ratings, breaking stories, and being regarded as a news leader are all critical elements of the job, no matter what size the audience.

NEWS ON PUBLIC TELEVISION

Later in this chapter we discuss several international broadcasters that receive government subsidies to fund their operations. Two of these, the British Broadcasting Corporation (BBC) and Germany's Deutsche Welle, have a long history of reporting stories objectively, including those that may not necessarily show their respective governments in a favorable light. Another international broadcaster, Al Jazeera, is a relatively young network that is already garnering a reputation for tackling tough issues.

In the United States, the federal government helps fund the Corporation for Public Broadcasting (CPB). This entity oversees two major broadcasters, the Public Broadcasting Service (PBS) and National Public Radio (NPR). These originated as a result of the Public Broadcasting Act of 1967, which was signed into law by President Lyndon B. Johnson.

As a 24-hour broadcaster, PBS offers a wide range of programs, including children's cartoons and documentaries. It airs on 356 member stations, reaching more than 65 million viewers. Its primary news program is *The NewsHour with Jim Lehrer*, which anchors its evening programming lineup. Polls commissioned by PBS have consistently placed the service as America's most trusted national institution.

CPB's radio organization, NPR, serves nearly 800 radio stations across the United States. Its flagship programs are two drive-time newscasts: *Morning Edition* (which airs when most listeners are driving to work) and the afternoon's *All Things Considered*.

The production facilities are not extensive for either of CPB's broadcasters. NPR has major production facilities in Washington, DC, and Culver City, California. PBS has a similar structure with its east coast headquarters in Arlington, Virginia, and west coast operations in Burbank, California. The member stations that relay NPR and PBS are scattered throughout the country and vary in the number of news staff and programming facilities, although there are some baseline criteria. NPR affiliates, for example, must operate at least 18 hours per day and have at least five full-time employees.

DOMESTIC NETWORKS, GLOBAL REACH

A handful of U.S.-based news organizations produce broadcasts that have international impact. The largest two, CNN and Fox News, operate news head-quarters that boast round-the-clock news channels, offer content on a number of different platforms, and have relationships with news agencies around the globe. While many U.S. viewers are aware of CNN and CNN Headline News (HLN), these two channels are just a slice of the news operations within that conglomerate. Others include:

CNN.com
CNN Airport Network
CNN en Espanol
CNN International
CNN Mobile
CNN Newsource
CNN Radio
HLN in Asia Pacific
HLN in Latin America

This list does not include joint ventures, such as CNN+, CNNj, CNNMoney .com, CNN Turk, CNN-IBN, CNN.de (German), and CNN.co.jp (Japanese).

The advantage of such globalization is obvious to those charged with produc-ing a newscast. These affiliations cast a much broader net of producers and reporters to find news; they also allow for local, specialized news teams to uncover stories that may be unnoticed by those from afar.

Critics of such news operations point to several problems with this type of news-sharing arrangement. First, larger networks can command more adver-tising dollars, thus pushing out smaller news operations in a competitive market. Second, from an audience perspective, the same story can appear on multiple channels, which saturates the news reports to the detriment of other stories. Finally, the spirit of different viewpoints partaking in the media is severely constrained as a dominant media form shapes the news market.

ONLINE NEWS PORTALS

Joining the fray of news outlets are those media companies that exist either only online or primarily online with a limited broadcast presence that serve as gateways into other news companies. These *portals* are Web sites that gather news from multiple sources, choose which ones are most important, and then provide links to the stories from their Web site. Because these portals link directly to the other news sources (and do not cut and paste stories), they avoid copyright infringement.

For example, the Drudge Report is a news portal that offers news stories and opinion columns that have been gathered from other Web sites. In late 2009, the Drudge Report noted that it was receiving more viewers on the Web than the Web site operated by *The New York Times* newspaper.

The main criticism directed at such portals it that they essentially serve as news gatekeepers, taking in news from multiple sources before filtering it down for their own purposes. Additionally, these portals sell advertising space on their Web sites while generating little (if any) original content. Despite these contentions, such portals are growing in popularity in both their number and their number of Web site hits.

NEWS WIRE SERVICES

Previous chapters discussed how newsrooms use the wire services within their newscasts. The individual station subscribes to the wire services, such as the Associated Press (AP) or CNN's Newsource, and then uses downloaded text, audio, and video in their broadcasts. The stations obtain this data through *downlinking*; this refers to a station using its satellite dish to receive the information from an orbiting satellite's signal, thus bringing the story "down" from the overhead signal.

Using satellites is costly, however, so many stories are now sent from the wire services to the affiliates via the Internet. The more contemporary term *downloading* is used for this delivery method. Regardless of terminology, the pattern of getting the news from the wire services to the affiliates remains the same. The wire services collect stories and post them on a continually updated menu, the local affiliates search the menu for stories of interest, and then they are retrieved for the nightly newscast.

Stories on this news menu are generated by the local news stations that subscribe to the wire service. It is important to note that these arrangements are reciprocal. If a plane crashes in an Indiana wheat field, the local news station will send out a news team. As this story is produced for the local newscast, it is also sent to their wire service. This is called *uplinking*, which is the reverse principle of downlinking. Here, the individual news station sends the news story "up" to the wire services. This allows stations in distant markets to share their video through a central agent.

The Associated Press is a cooperative news agency owned by its members, which are newspapers, radio, and television stations in the United States. This cooperative agreement allows members to readily give and receive stories among themselves. Outside of the U.S. borders, many stations sign on as subscribers, giving them the opportunity to use AP news without contributing content.

The AP's reach on the news audience around the globe is stunning. According to the AP's own research, more than half of the world's population sees its news on any given day. It does this by serving 1700 newspapers and 5000 radio and television outlets in the United States, plus it has many more international subscribers.

THE INTERNET'S DELIVERY OF GLOBAL NEWS

The following chapter provides an overview of how media convergence and the Internet are altering the practice of broadcast journalism. Not only are reporters able to find more stories quickly with database searches and Internet links, they are also being called upon to write blogs, post stories online, and interface with the public more often in the digital realm.

At the same time, global journalism has become much more accessible. International Web sites readily offer an inside glimpse into overseas news practices, provide a fresh perspective of global stories, and give a wealth of story ideas that can be localized for a news affiliate.

This section looks at several exemplary news organizations that originate in foreign countries. Even though some of them are based in non-English-speaking lands, they each offer English-version Web sites for the Internet user.

Deutsche Welle has been broadcasting for more than 50 years from its headquarters in Germany. It is largely funded by the German federal government from tax revenues collected in that country. DW offers news on a variety of platforms, including television, radio, and even shortwave. The operation employs 1500 employees in 60 countries worldwide. In addition to broadcasting in 30 different languages, DW also offers instructional courses for those who wish to learn the German language. This innovative concept allows news consumers to simultaneously catch up on the day's event as they strengthen their skills in another language.

Also based in Europe, the British Broadcasting Corporation is funded by an annual allowance from the British government. The BBC was the world's first broadcasting company, founded in 1922 as a radio network. It later expanded into television and other digital delivery platforms. Currently, the BBC consists of a number of channels, including BBC World News, BBC America, BBC Arabic, BBC Canada, BBC Knowledge, and BBC Lifestyle.

Statistically, the reach of the BBC's World News channel is impressive. It broadcasts in English in more than 200 countries and territories across the globe, reaching into more than 276 million homes. Additionally, it also appears in 1.5 million hotel rooms, 57 cruise ships, and even on 42 different airlines. The BBC's global reach is evident with its news and analysis in 32 languages, ranging from Albanian to Vietnamese. Its home page also links to English instructional courses for those who wish to learn the language.

Headquartered in Doha, Qatar, Al Jazeera has emerged as a leading news network when covering stories from the Middle East. This relatively young news operation (it went on-air in 1996) is available worldwide on various satellite and cable systems. It launched an English-language edition of its online content in 2003, broadening its reach to a greater number of potential customers. Interestingly, the Arabic and English sections of Al Jazeera's Web site are editorially distinct. This allows each section to select its own news and editorial opinions.

Like the BBC and DW, Al Jazeera also manages a number of other media outlets. In addition to its Arabic and English news channels, it also offers a children's channel, a documentary channel, and four different sports channels. Of course, other countries have news markets and network-affiliate relationships similar to the United States. Due to economic pressures, many of the smaller news markets around the globe are facing the same challenges to make their news operation more cost-effective while expanding their reach across multiple delivery platforms.

PRESS FREEDOM

As we discuss news from foreign countries, it is vital to note that freedom of the press as guaranteed under the U.S. Constitution's First Amendment is not a universal right. A number of countries have a great deal of press freedom (a handful of western European countries arguably enjoy more than the United States). Other governments are much more repressive, clamping down on journalists and newsrooms in a variety of ways.

These techniques can range from merely distorting information to actual violence against the reporters. Worldwide, there are numerous examples of governments shutting down television stations, restricting reporter access, levying heavy tax burdens on newsprint, and coercing reporters into acting as mere spokespeople for the approved "official" viewpoint.

The Freedom House tracks media independence in an annual report. This global survey of journalism freedom rates nearly 200 countries as "free," "partly free," or "not free." To derive these rankings, the organization examines three broad categories: the legal environment, the political environment, and the economic environment. Specifically, the Freedom House breaks down criteria as follows.

The *legal environment* encompasses an examination of both laws and regulations that could influence media content and the government's inclination to use these laws and legal institutions in order to restrict the media's ability to operate. We assess the positive impact of legal and constitutional guarantees for freedom of expression; the potentially negative aspects of security legislation, the penal code, and other criminal statutes; penalties for libel and defamation; the existence of and ability to use freedom of information legislation; the independence of the judiciary and of official media regulatory bodies; registration requirements for both media outlets and journalists; and the ability of journalists' groups to operate freely.

Under the category of *political environment*, we evaluate the degree of political control over the content of the news media. Issues examined in this category included the editorial independence of both state-owned and privately owned media; access to information and sources; official censorship and self-censorship; the vibrancy of the media; the ability of both foreign and local reporters to cover the news freely and without harassment; and the intimidation of journalists by the state or other actors, including arbitrary detention and imprisonment, violent assaults, and other threats.

Our third category examines the *economic environment* for the media. This includes the structure of media ownership; transparency and concentration of ownership; the costs of establishing media as well as of production and distribution; the selective withholding of advertising or subsidies by the state or other actors; the impact of corruption and bribery on content; and the extent to which the economic situation in a country impacts the development of the media.

SUMMARY

Broadcast journalism does not begin and end with local news affiliates. Instead, the local television newsroom is merely the most visible component of news gathering. Cities have competing local newscasts, anchors and reporters are well known in their markets, and a number of college graduates target their job searches at the newsrooms located down the street.

However, this perspective artificially constricts the true nature of how broadcast journalism operates. Local stations are affiliates of broader networks, submitting and retrieving stories from one another on an ongoing basis. The network home offices also dispatch teams of reporters and producers, while the separate wire services also have a full complement of journalists that generate news content.

Beyond the United States, other nations' residents also share a passion for wanting to know the daily events. Media conglomerates such as CNN readily offer international feeds for these viewers; these global relationships also allow news to flow back into this country. In addition, each country obviously has its own news stations, many of which are network members and wire service subscribers. Some of these stations, such as the British Broadcasting Corporation, Deutsche Welle, and Al Jazeera, offer international news via Web sites and satellite delivery for viewers around the world.

Finally, the globalization of news also reveals that there is no level playing field for international reporters. The freedom of press accorded to reporters under the First Amendment is not a universal right. Those reporters who travel around the planet, as well as those viewers who monitor news from abroad, should be aware of the restrictions that may be placed on those reports.

Test Your Knowledge

1. What is the difference between downlinking and uplinking?
2. What is a network?
3. What is the difference between an affiliate and an independent station?
4. How many affiliates are in the United States?
5. What is an example of a U.S. media outlet that broadcasts in other countries?
6. What are the three environments that the Freedom House monitors to evaluate freedom of the press around the world?
7. What are some of the opportunities that exist for broadcast journalists who do not want to work at a local news affiliate?
8. Why are so many of the foreign news Web sites accessible to U.S. audiences?

EXERCISES

1. Watch a local television newscast and identify which stories were downlinked from a wire service. How much of the newscast's time was filled by these stories?
2. Search the Internet for jobs at international news stations. Is there a foreign language requirement or other special skills needed for these positions? Are the jobs similar to those you would find at a local news affiliate?
3. Briefly explain the relationship between a network and an affiliate. Then identify the television stations in your area and the networks to which they belong.
4. There are a handful of independent stations remaining in this country that do not have any network affiliation. If you identify one of these in your market, ask for an interview with the general manager or owner to determine how such a station still survives without network support and if it has considered joining a network for programming purposes.
5. Read a local newspaper. Stories from the Associated Press will be noted as either contributions from the Associated Press or simply AP. How many of these stories can be found in the news and sports sections? Are these reports from around the state, national in scope, or recapping international events?
6. Identify a story that may be of international interest, such as a major financial treaty or a war. Look at three different news Web sites that originate in various countries, such as Deutsche Welle, BBC, and Al Jazeera. Compare the coverage among the three Web sites. Do they offer different viewpoints? Are the stories placed more prominently in some Web sites than others? Is the tone of the articles similar or different?

CHAPTER 18

Convergence and the Media
(with Sherlyn Freeman)

CONTENTS

INTRODUCTION

Contrary to popular belief, *convergence* is not a new word; the term has actually been around for a number of years. When it comes to mass media, convergence means the intersecting of broadcast journalism, print journalism, and technology. What does that mean for someone entering the field? Simply put, the more you know, the easier it will be for you to have a career. There are a few things you need to know in order to be able to find long-term employment.

This chapter reviews how convergence and the Internet have reshaped the duties of broadcast journalists. The days of merely filing a story for a newscast are over. Now, blogs must be written, podcasts must be updated, and Web site offerings need constant tending. While some large market newsrooms may have a convergence specialist available to help out, the work of rewriting, uploading, and updating typically falls to the reporter.

CONVERGENCE MODELS

Reporters in previous eras only needed to know their area of specialization: Print journalists only concerned themselves with newspapers, television reporters focused on that visual medium, and so forth. But as the modes of delivering the news evolved with digital technology, reporters across the media are increasingly faced with the growing expectation of knowing about

289

convergent media. As the business of news changed from the big three broadcast channels to include cable news, the natural progression was to have an Internet presence. Some media companies have done it successfully; others have not.

The following is an actual job posting. Note that the skill set required is far beyond merely finding and writing the news:

> An award-winning newspaper that covers politics and state government in Phoenix seeks a talented multimedia expert to join its growing operation and take its Web site to the next level. We're searching for a Web editor who can generate content, create video, slide shows and podcasts, blog, and lead our social media efforts. If you are a self-starter with excellent news judgment, and if you have at least 1-2 years of web experience, then we want to talk to you. Ideal candidates will have a degree in journalism or a related field, experience with Word Press, basic HTML, FinalCutExpress and Photoshop.

With convergence, reporters cover a story for one medium, do the same story for other media owned by the same company, or may simply share information. As with the "one-man band," convergence is also dictated by economics. One person does the job that used to be handled by two or three. In addition to saving money, advocates maintain that convergence results in a better product.

Here's how it works: A television reporter's company also owns other media in the same market, such as a radio station or the local newspaper. The reporter writes his story for television and then does radio and newspaper versions of the same story. Alternatively, the newspaper reporter could start the ball rolling, and the process can involve other media, such as a cable channel. Additionally, updates to the Internet are expected, as reporters rework their stories into a Web site–friendly format.

Just as the one-man-band concept is not new, neither is a marriage between different media. While these constructs have been around for years, they're developing at a "much more rapid pace than ever," according to Barbara Cochran, president of the Radio and Television News Director's Association (RTNDA). She noted a number of such cooperative efforts:

FIGURE 18.1

News has evolved with developments in digital technology.

- In Tampa: WFLA–TV, the *Tampa Tribune*, and Tampa Bay On Line (TBO. com). This was the first truly converged newsroom in the country.

- In Chicago: WGN radio, WGN–TV, and the *Chicago Tribune*

- In Cedar Rapids, Iowa: KCRG radio, KCRG–TV, and the *Cedar Rapids Gazette*

- In Orlando: the *Orlando Sentinel* shares content with the Florida Cable News Channel

FIGURE 18.2
The first truly converged newsroom—Tampa Bay On Line (www.tbo.com).

Not only are different media owned by the same company converging, but media owned by different companies are also forming partnerships, although limited ones, in which they tap into each other's expertise. Some examples are NBC and the *Washington Post* and their Internet resources; CBS and *The New York Times*; and WBZ–TV and the *Boston Globe*.

How serious is the endeavor? In Tampa, a television station, newspaper, and Web site are working side by side in a Media General $40 million complex devoted to convergence, reports the *RTNDA Communicator*. "They share news tips, resources, and reporters in a convergence effort far more ambitious than anyone else has ever tried."

Editors from the various media sit next to each other on the assignment desk, which is the "nerve center" of the converged operation. A camera is set up near the *Tribune* newsroom. It enables newspaper reporters to tell about stories they covered during the television newscasts. The company, Media General Inc., has built a $40 million, four-level, state-of-the-art news complex devoted to convergence, called the News Center.

FIGURE 18.3

The Gazette Company of Cedar Rapids, Iowa, also converged some of its operations, but not all. It originally intended to construct a new building to house all its news operations but instead settled for two newsrooms, one to house both radio and TV and the other for print and online operations. Chuck Peters, the company's chief operating officer, said the Gazette Company converged six different subsidiaries into the two operations just mentioned. But he said that while the print and broadcast people are committed to sharing information, the news director and newspaper editor exercise independent judgment but cooperate where they can.

Rick Ragola, president of WFLA, told the *Communicator* that convergence combines the immediacy of the Internet, the urgency and emotion of television, and the depth of print media. How is the concept working in actual practice? Some worry that quality suffers when reporters spend so much time shifting gears as they prepare stories for the various media. Another criticism is that a reporter who serves more than one medium can't cover as many stories as a reporter who serves just one medium. *Tampa Tribune* reporter Lisa Greene told the *Communicator* that presenting her story on more than one platform gives her greater reach, but she fears it takes time away from reporting on other topics.

There are other problems with convergence. Reporting for print, radio, and TV requires different skills. Print reporters must learn how to integrate pictures and sound into a television story and how to perform in front of a camera. Broadcast journalists have to learn to write for the print media. And still photographers must learn how to tell a story with motion pictures and sound. That's no easy task. It's much easier for videographers to take still pictures than for still photographers to handle a motion picture camera.

One newspaper reporter said convergence has improved his writing, forcing him to be more concise when writing for television. A television reporter says she can write concisely for television and use more depth in the newspaper version of the story and still greater depth—or at least length—in the Internet story.

The Internet version often includes not only the complete stories used on the air and in print but also facts edited out of the broadcast and print versions of the story, or *outtakes* as they are referred to in broadcast parlance. With convergence comes greater impact, or exposure. Stories that might normally appear only on television, for example, with convergence might also appear in the newspaper, on the radio, and on the Internet. Convergence enables the viewer or reader to go to the Internet for more details on the same story.

So, if you are planning to go into broadcast news, here's a word to the wise: In addition to broadcast journalism courses, take courses in print reporting and even the Internet, as you may have to work in all three media. A print reporting course not only helps you master a different medium, but because you're required to do more reporting and writing in print than in broadcast reporting courses, it also adds greatly to your reporting and writing skills.

Shortly after America Online (AOL) absorbed CNN–Time Warner in 2001, CNN announced a layoff and redefined the role of its reporters. Both actions were designed to cut costs. Reporters were ordered to learn how to use light-weight digital cameras and editing equipment. In addition, they would also be expected to file their stories on the Internet at AOL and on CNN radio. So the question was asked, were convergence and the one-man band hitting the big time? Convergence seemed to be in, as was at least a modified form of the one-man band.

Top CNN executive Eason Jordan was quoted as saying, "Correspondents whose expertise is TV reporting must know how to write for interactive and provide tracks for radio and deliver them as needed." The *Wall Street Journal* quoted another executive as saying that the merger provides "significant cross-promotional opportunities" because AOL reaches 27 million homes. Jordan said deploying compact digital cameras and editing equipment "will allow us to deploy smaller reporting teams of one or two people, at times when it makes sense." He added that "larger teams will be with us for some time to come."

Reporters were less than excited about doing camera and editing work. Legal correspondent Greta Van Susteren was flabbergasted, the *Wall Street Journal* said. "I would certainly like to learn to do it, but I'd like to learn to speak French," she added. "For this reason, they don't ask me to do makeup in the makeup room. I don't think they'll ask me to do this."

BROADCAST JOURNALISM AND PRINT JOURNALISM

Ten years ago, broadcast journalists were very different from those in print journalism. As more newspapers dissolve and more television news stations embrace digital technology, the types of newsroom jobs available will change.

Until newspapers figure out what their final outcome will be, knowing how to write both styles of journalism helps you in the long run. Regardless of style, remember that the content is what people will read or the package you create for the Web site. Your content can easily appear on television and be streamed online.

The difficulty can best be illustrated by examining style books from the Associated Press. As shown in Chapter 7, *News Writing Style*, AP print style and AP broadcast style differ in areas ranging from identifying newsmakers to writing down numerals. Since newsroom's Web sites are neither print nor video (but a hybrid delivery platform), journalists across all media will need to adapt their writing styles to the Internet's emerging presence.

HYPER TEXT MEDIA LANGUAGE (HTML), XHTML, AND CASCADING STYLE SHEETS (CSS)

The reason both styles of Internet pages are acknowledged is that, in order to understand one, you need to understand the other. Basic HTML or XHTML gives you the foundation you will need to work for any media organization that has a Web site. Although you will not be building the page, you will be updating it. If there is a problem on the page that you were hired to fix, the out-of-the-box software is not going to assist you. Knowing what should be happening on the page by reading the source in HTML will be better in the long run. Additionally, most companies have proprietary software that only is used by them; they may use the basic out-of-the-box software but the Web page only works with their version.

More and more companies are using cascading style sheets (CSS), which still have their basis in either HTML or XHTML. Whatever changes are made on CSS are changed automatically on any Web pages that point to it. In other words, when a broadcast journalist makes a change to page A, pages B, C, and D will have the same changes because there is an HTML/XHTML code that points to it.

To see how this works in practice, view the page source of your favorite news Web site, where you will find codes such as "li," "img src," "a href=," and "ul." To decipher these codes, *li* means list, *img src* (image source) is usually a picture, *a href=* is an external Web site or internal Web page, and *ul* means underline.

DIGITAL VIDEO

The quality of Internet video has improved greatly and, as consumers move further into high definition, digital video will improve as well. One advantage for digital video in newsrooms is that it replicates at exceptional quality, and thus degrading dubs that occurred through copying tapes are a thing of the past. It also means that the same footage shot in the field (and recorded onto a portable hard drive) can be encoded into a nonlinear editor and then fed to the newsroom's main server for playback during the actual newscast.

Apple's Final Cut, Microsoft's Premiere, and Avid are the main digital editing software used in newsrooms; knowing one or all three makes aspiring broadcast journalists more marketable. While no reporter will be called upon to know the nuances of all three postproduction platforms, the best suggestion is to learn one well while having some familiarity with the other two. Because reporters don't always know where they will work throughout their career, a broad knowledge is needed to move from one newsroom to another.

FIGURE 18.4

Avid (www.avid.com) is on one of the main types of digital editing software used in newsrooms.

Other important knowledge comes through learning about streaming video, file compression and decompression (codecs), file sizes, and "Flash" video. While numerous Web sites and industry magazines are available, it is important that broadcast journalists work hands-on with the software as often as possible.

DIGITAL PHOTOGRAPHY

Just as you need to know how to set up a shot in video, the same rules apply for photography. Photoshop is regarded as the industry standard, although a number of other variations are used throughout newsrooms; as always, it's best to find out what platform is favored by your potential employer. Knowing Photoshop will help you use any other.

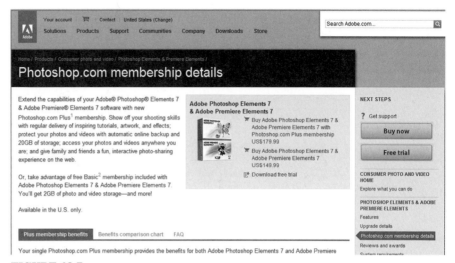

FIGURE 18.5

Photoshop (http://adobe.com/products/psprelements/membership/) is an industry standard.

There is a difference in creating photos for your personal use and what should be used on the Web. Remember, the longer it takes the picture to download, the fewer the number of people who will wait until it is fully displayed. Not everyone has an up-to-date computer, so millions of colors may not always work. Also, because .gif files are easier to read on more basic computers, they may be used for visual photos instead of .jpg files. Functionally, they operate in a similar fashion.

DIGITAL AUDIO

Although digital audio and digital video are very similar, they differ greatly due to their sizes. Digital video is much larger and needs some compression (that's what some codecs do for you). Audio doesn't need as much, as the computer is only dealing with one type of media.

For field recording, digital audio doesn't require much equipment to achieve quality sound. Audio can stand alone (typically at radio station Web sites) or accompany an article or photomontage. The audio codecs most in use today are MPEG-3 and MPEG-4. Even as digital video evolves, audio file delivery changes as well; thus broadcast journalists must keep abreast of the ever-changing technology.

Previous generations of radio journalists relied on reel-to-reel recorders, which needed to be edited with a razor blade and splicing tape. Today, digital audio recorders make obtaining audio as simple as pressing a button, while editing and mixing are accomplished via computer. Due to their relatively small size, audio files can be transferred around a radio station easily via a dedicated server, as well as offered on radio station Web sites if desired.

PODCASTING

Many news organizations have a presence on Apple's iTunes as well as their own Web sites. There are literally thousands of podcasts that range from scientific to totally off the beaten path. Because podcasts are inexpensive and extremely user-friendly, the learning curve for a news reporter to create a podcast is minimal.

While much of the current podcasting is still based in audio, new technology is incorporating video as well. These advances are coming from both increased speed and compression (from the sender) and more advanced storage and playback capabilities (with the receiver). As mobile communication and the public desire for on-demand information increase, journalists will be expected to incorporate delivery platforms like podcasting as part of their working day.

FIGURE 18.6

SOCIAL NETWORK PAGES

News organizations large and small are creating fan pages on social networking sites such as Facebook, MySpace, and LinkedIn. These personalized Web pages allow more interactivity with anchors and reporters. Given the popularity of these Web sites with younger adults (a much coveted marketing demographic), many newsrooms actively encourage their employees to develop such sites, update them frequently, and obtain as many "friends" as possible.

Another relatively new communication tool is Twitter, which debuted in 2006. This social networking site uses microblogs (text-based posts that can be no longer than 140 characters). Field reporters can use this device to quickly update their followers on news stories. The advantages are that it is quick to use, very simple in design, and allows the audience to feel a greater connection to the reporter. On the downside, only about 40 percent of Twitter's users are retained.

BLOGS, E-MAILS, AND MOBILE DEVICES

Technology is no longer constrained by traditional Internet Web sites offering news stories and Web links. The opportunities for reporter interaction have increased dramatically in recent years as portable technology, viewer

FIGURE 18.7

Reporters are encouraged to create blogs.

FIGURE 18.8

feedback, and a heightened sense of immediacy have altered broadcast journalism.

For example, a growing number of news organizations encourage their reporters to create *blogs*. Blogs are online diaries that are open to anyone to read and comment upon. In the beginning, news organizations didn't want their employees blogging. Now, they are embracing blogging as a way for build interaction between the journalist and the viewing audience.

E-mail updates are another way that newsrooms maintain viewer loyalty. The technique is simple: viewers sign up on the newsroom's Web site, opting it to the e-mail update server. The newsroom then sends e-mails (typically twice a day) to the users' e-mail accounts, providing them with current news and a glimpse of what will be featured on the evening's newscasts.

While blogs and e-mail updates are based in the newsroom, technology is also shifting broadcast journalism in the field. Cell phones were a boon to newsrooms in the 1980s, as reporters could suddenly communicate to the newsroom from virtually anywhere. The newer generation of cell phones has evolved into true mobile data devices that are Web enabled and complete with rudimentary video recording; these allow field reporters even greater ability to grab footage and send it in. The quality of the footage is still primitive, but the possibility of more immediate field reports is a powerful argument that can sway news producers to use cutting-edge mobile devices.

SUMMARY

Each of the areas just listed, such as digital video, digital audio, and digital photography, appear on news Web sites with increasing frequency. The technology is not overly difficult to master; any reporter with a working knowledge of basic cut-and-paste word processing can make the mental transition to cutting and pasting audio and video clips with few problems.

Additionally, an increasing number of reporters now make their individual presence known via social networking pages and blogs. This familiarity with new technology makes them more employable, especially as the Bureau of Labor Statistics (BLS) advises that the job outlook for news reporters is tepid at best. Only those with computer skills (the BLS lists those with pure newsroom/computer jobs as "computer specialists") are expected to have job security in the coming years.

FIGURE 18.9

Test Your Knowledge

1. What are the three standard video editing platforms used for digital video?
2. What are the differences among a blog, a social networking site, and a Twitter account?
3. Why is it easier to process digital audio than to process digital video?
4. Why are cascading style sheets so popular for broadcast Web sites?
5. What platform is the industry standard when using digital photography?

EXERCISES

1. Identify the Web sites of your local television stations. How many of them use streaming video, audio clips, and reporters' blogs?
2. Find the Web site for your local newspaper. If they do not have video or audio clips available, can you determine what types of convergent technologies they feature on their Web site?
3. If you subscribe to a social networking site such as Facebook, see if any local reporters maintain a presence there.
4. Examine a local news Web site under the "Page View" function. Try to identify as much code, such as "ul" and "img src," as you can.
5. Determine how many of your local newsrooms deliver news content through podcasting.
6. Discuss what skill sets are required among reporters today that were not expected 10 years ago. Once done, predict what skills may be needed to be a competitive reporter 10 years from now.

Glossary

Abbreviations Shortened words in a news script. Abbreviations should be avoided in news copy, as they can confuse news anchors.

Accuracy Verifying a story's truth by consulting multiple sources.

Active voice Writing style that focuses on the action rather than the receiver of the action.

Actuality Voices of people involved in a news story. Also called a sound byte.

Ad-libbing Ability to improvise an impromptu speech without preparation.

Advancing stories Finding new angles to update ongoing stories.

Affiliates Radio and TV stations serviced by networks.

Al Jazeera Qatar-based news operation that primarily covers stories in the Middle East.

Ambush interview Forcing someone to speak with you on camera against his or her will.

Anchor Someone who reads news on the TV set.

AP Associated Press, one of the major wire services.

Assignment board Dry erase board that lists stories, reporters, and details on individual news assignments.

Assignment desk Newsroom's central hub that coordinates news coverage.

Assignment editor Newsperson who assigns stories to reporters and camera crews.

Associate producer Assistant to the line producer in creating the entire newscast or an individual news story.

Attribution Source of a news story.

Audio Sound used in a radio or TV newscast.

B-roll Film term still often used to describe the use of video to cover an interview or narration. Sometimes referred to as *cover footage*.

Back timing Timing of the final part of a broadcast to assist the newscaster or producer to get off the air on time.

Background briefings Government meetings in which reporters agree to keep the officials and agencies anonymous.

Balancing the anchors Ensuring that co-anchors roughly split the amount of time they have on-camera.

Batteries Portable energy sources used to power cameras, microphones, and some portable lights.

Beat Assignment given to a reporter on a continuing basis.

Beat checks Phone calls made to local law enforcement agencies.

Black Control track on a videotape. Also, a complete fade from a picture.

Blind lead-in General lead-in to a report from the field, used when you do not know what the reporter will say at the top of the report.

Block Segment of the newscast bordered by commercial breaks.

Blog Online diary created by a reporter for the news station's Web site.

Box Used on rundowns to indicate that a picture, freeze-frame video, or graphic will appear in a box next to the anchor's head.

Bridge Words that connect one piece of narration or sound byte to another.

British Broadcasting Corporation The world's first broadcast company that now airs news in more than 200 countries and territories around the world.

Bulletin Important late-breaking news item.

Bump Short, generic headline delivered by anchors before commercials in a TV newscast to hold the audience's attention.

Byte See *sound byte.*

Camera body Component of the video camera system that physically holds the videotape and records the inputs from the lens and microphones.

Capital numbers Symbols on a computer keyboard created when the SHIFT key and a number key are pressed simultaneously.

Cascading style sheets (CSS) HTML extension that allows styles to be specified within a document.

Character generator Electronic device used to produce supers (fonts).

Chroma-key Electronic placement of pictures behind the newscaster.

Close Ending of a reporter's news story.

Cluster Combination of related stories placed together in a newscast.

Cold open Beginning a news package with a sound byte instead of reporter's narration.

Communication chain Video and audio information passed back and forth between a newsroom and a field reporter.

Confidentiality Promise made by a reporter to keep a source's name anonymous.

Conflict of interest When a journalist accepts gifts or favors from a news source.

Conjunctions Words that link sentences, parts of sentences, and even related news stories to one another.

Contractions Words that are shortened by omitting or combining letters.

Convergence Intersection of various forms of news delivery across media, such as via the Internet and broadcast outlets.

Conversational style Writing for the ear in short, declarative sentences.

Copy Material written for broadcast. Also, wire copy distributed by wire services.

Cosmetics Make-up used by on-set anchors and reporters.

Cover footage Video shot at the scene of a news story; used to replace the newsmaker and/or reporter while their voices are heard. Sometimes referred to as *B-roll*.

Crash Colloquialism for serious problems in a newscast.

Credibility Believability of a newscaster.

CU Close-up camera shot.

Cue words Words at the start and end of audiotape or videotape to identify how a sound byte begins and ends.

Cutaway Video shot used to avoid a jump cut.

Cutoff time Time when a reporter must leave the scene of a story in order to make broadcast.

Database Collection of information accessible to journalists.

Delayed lead Keeping the most important information in a story until the middle or end to create suspense.

Delivery How a reporter or anchor presents the news with their individual speech patterns and physical gestures.

Descriptors Physical characteristics, such as age or race, that describe a person.

Deutsche Welle German news operation that broadcasts in 60 nations worldwide.

Digital audio Audio signals recorded, stored, or transmitted digitally.

Digital photography Computer images recorded, stored, or transmitted digitally.

Digital video Video signals recorded, stored, or transmitted digitally.

Dining table solution Telling the story in conversational sense as if you were speaking to your family around the dining table.

Direct competition Other news outlets of the same medium in the same market.

Directories Published lists of contact information, such as a phone book.

Dissolve Special video effect that slowly replaces one image on the screen with another.

DMA Designated Market Area, which defines media markets based on geographic areas.

Double-sourcing Confirming a story through two sources before airing on the news.

Downlinking Newsroom practice of receiving network or wire stories via satellite or Internet download.

Drive time Indicates the time of day when people are going to or coming from work. Usually the highest rated time periods for radio stations.

Earphones Small devices that transmit audible sound to the ears.

Enterprised stories News stories created by reporters outside of spontaneous or planned stories.

Establishing shot Wide shot of a scene, usually used at the beginning of a news story.

Evergreen Story, usually a feature, that can be used anytime.

Executive producer Person responsible for the long-term look of the newscasts.

Fade Dissolve from a picture to black.

Fair comment Defense that may be offered in a libel suit when a comment is made that is unflattering to a public figure.

False light Juxtaposing audio and video to create a false impression of someone.

Feature event Event that can provide a *kicker* to a newscast.

Feeds Material distributed by networks and others to affiliates and other stations for use on local newscasts. Also known as syndication feeds.

Field producer Person responsible for the content of an individual news package.

Fill copy Also called *pad copy*. Relatively unimportant news copy for use near the end of the newscast if needed to fill time.

Filter Camera's internal electronic or physical apparatus that corrects color temperature in a given shooting location.

Five Ws and H rule Journalism tradition that required the who, what, where, when, why, and how of a story to appear in or near the lead.

Flash Headline used by wire services to describe news of an extreme nature, such as the death of a president.

Font See *Super.*

Frame Segment of a videotape that lasts for 1/30th of a second.

Freedom of Information Act (FOIA) Passed by Congress to permit access to all but the most sensitive government documents. Similar acts, called "sunshine laws," have been established in all 50 states.

Freeze frame Still video image seen next to or behind the anchor while he or she is reading copy. Mostly used in a box next to the anchor's head.

Futures file Folder or computer file used by the assignment desk to keep track of stories that may be covered in the future.

Gatekeeper Person who allows or denies a story to get on the air.

Grand opening Planned event featuring a new business or organization.

Graphics Graphs, photos, maps, and other visuals used in a TV news story or newscast.

Gratuities Gifts offered to journalists to sway their reporting on an issue.

Handheld microphone Audio capturing device that can be held by a reporter or affixed to a mount.

Hard lead Lead that places the most important information in the first sentence.

Headlines Series of one-line sentences describing news events. Used at the top of a newscast.

Hold for release Wire service story or press release that cannot be used until the time specified.

HTML Hyper Text Markup Language, the universal language used for designing Internet Web sites.

Identifiers Title or position that identifies a person in a news story.

Immediacy Ability of electronic media to disseminate breaking news instantly.

Incident report Police report on a specific crime or incident.

Indirect competition Other news outlets of different media in the same market.

Information overload Putting too much information in a lead sentence or paragraph.

Interrupted feedback Return audio signal that allows the field reporter to hear questions from the news studio.

Interviewing Conversation between a reporter and someone from whom he or she seeks information.

Investigative reporting Developing news reports in depth, usually about something that someone is trying to hide.

Jump cut Erratic movement of a head that occurs when video is edited to eliminate some of a speaker's words.

Kicker Light story used at the end of a newscast.

Lavaliere microphone Audio capturing device attached to clothing with a small clip.

Lead Opening line of a news story. Also refers to the first story in a newscast.

Lead-in Sentence that is read by the anchor that introduces a reporter's news package.

Leading question Asking a question during an interview that tries to elicit information the reporter wants to hear.

Leaks Information from unidentified sources within the government, political, or corporate world.

Lens Part of the video camera system responsible for making sure the image is in focus, in frame, and composed correctly.

Libel Publishing defamatory or inaccurate statements.

Licenses Government-issued permits for an individual or company to conduct business.

Line producer Person responsible for the content of an individual newscast.

Lineup Arrangement of stories in a newscast. Also called the rundown.

Listening Paying attention to the person being interviewed during a news story.

Live shot Reporting from the scene of a story as it is happening.

Local angle Details of a news story that are of special interest to the audience in your community.

Local news Stories dealing with your community.

Localization Developing distant news ideas into stories with local impact.

Long shot (LS) Wide view of the scene. See *Establishing shot*.

Man-on-the-street interviews Interviews with random persons in a public setting.

Market Geographic region served by broadcast affiliates.

Marking copy Revising a news script so it is easier for anchors to read on-air.

Medium shot (MS) Between a close-up and long shot.

Meeting Assembly of people that may provide information for a news story.

Microwave Beaming a TV signal between two points using microwave antennas.

Minicam Lightweight video camera.

Mixed light Setting in which lights of different color temperatures are present.

Motor vehicle accident report Police report on a vehicle accident.

Natural sound Ambient noise of a location. Also called nat sound or room tone.

Negative lead Lead sentence that contains the word "not." To be avoided.

Network Central news and programming business that provides content for its affiliate stations.

News director Person in charge of the news operation at a radio or TV station.

News hole Amount of time remaining in a newscast after commercials, bumps, teases, sports, weather, and other nonnews elements have been removed.

News judgment Ability to recognize the relative importance of news.

Noninteractive environment State of communicating one way without an immediate audience response.

Nonnews lead Beginning of a news story that conveys no information.

Numbers Quantifiable units often simplified or rounded for newscasts.

O/C Abbreviation for on camera.

Objectivity Neutrality about an issue.

Off the record Information that is given with the understanding that the reporter will not broadcast it on the air.

Outcue Last words in a sound byte.

Pacing Speed of a newscaster's delivery.

Pack reporting Mindset where all reporters interview the same spokespersons.

Package Story put together by a reporter that includes interviews, narration, and cover footage.

Pad copy See *Fill copy.*

Pass Recording over a given segment of videotape. Repeated recording over the same segment results in multiple passes.

Passive voice Writing style that focuses on the receiver of the action rather than the action.

Peaks and valleys TV production technique that spreads important stories throughout a newscast, not only at the top.

Phone interviews Interviews conducted over the phone, usually by a radio station.

Phrasing Delivering a question to elicit a usable sound byte from the interviewee.

Planned stories News events and meetings scheduled in advance.

Podcasting New delivery method that allows the news audience to listen or watch the news content at their convenience.

Political campaign Series of events that lead up to an election.

Portal Web site that links to news stories that originated at other Web sites.

Press conference Information-sharing session within a political, corporate, or civic context.

Primary sound Dominant sound of a news story, such as the reporter's narration or an interview sound byte.

Prime time Time when radio and TV have their largest audiences.

Privacy Act Law designed to prevent unwarranted invasion of a person's privacy.

Privilege Legal area in which a news report relays what was said in a legislative or judicial action. In these cases, the reporter has a defense against a libel action.

Producer Newsperson who decides which material will go into a newscast and in which order. Also, in larger markets, someone who helps reporters put together packages.

Pronunciation How sounds and words are articulated by newscasters.

Public information officer (PIO) Spokesperson for a governmental or law enforcement agency.

Punctuation marks Standard symbols used in written English.

Question lead Lead sentence that asks a question directly to the viewer.

Quotes Direct repeat of what a subject said by a news anchor. Rarely used in broadcast copy.

Reader Story without video read by an anchor on camera. Also a radio story that contains no sound bytes.

Records Official government or legal documents that may be used for news stories.

Reenactment To stage or perform an action if it was not obtained on video when it originally occurred.

Reporter's notebook Slim notebook designed for portability.

Reuters British news agency.

Reversal Shot of the reporter looking at the person being interviewed; an editing device.

Reverse question Shot of the reporter repeating questions asked during the interview; an editing technique considered by some newspeople as somewhat unethical.

Rip and read Broadcasting of radio wire copy without any rewrite.

Room tone Ambient noise of a location. Also called natural (or nat) sound.

RTNDA Radio and Television News Directors' Association.

Rundown Spreadsheet that outlines the elements of the newscast, including stories, anchors, and running time.

Running story News story in which there are new developments, usually for more than one day.

Sequence Collection of individual video shots recorded in one location and then edited into a segment of a news story.

Shotgun lead News story lead that includes information about more than one related story.

SIL Abbreviation for silent; used on the video side of a split page to indicate use of videotape that has no sound.

Slug Word or two written in the upper left corner of a script to identify the story.

Social network Interactive Web sites in which users offer personal information and viewpoints to others.

Soft lead Lead in which the most important fact is not given immediately.

SOT Abbreviation for sound on tape; used on the video side of a split page to indicate the tape has sound.

Sound byte Portion of statement or interview that is in a news broadcast or package. Also known as a byte.

Sound under Keeping the natural sound low when used under the voice of a reporter or newscaster.

Source Someone who provides information used in a news story.

Split page Standard TV news script. The left side of the page is used for video directions, and the right side is for the script and audio cues.

Spontaneous stories News stories that occur without prior knowledge.

Sports Dedicated block in the newscast devoted to sports information.

Spot news Spontaneous, unscheduled events that warrant coverage in a newscast.

Stacking Placing stories in a newscast in the order they will be delivered.

Stand-up Report on camera at the scene. Can be an *open* (start of the story), *bridge* (middle of story), or *close* (end of story).

Subjectivity Advocating one side of an issue over another.

Sunshine laws Laws requiring that governmental meetings are announced in advance and are open to the press.

Super Also called a *font*. Short for superimposing lettering, graphics, or videotape. Used mostly for the names, addresses, and titles of people being identified in a news package or newscast.

Suspense lead Lead that keeps the most important part of the story until the very end.

Syndication Sale and distribution of news material to stations by independent companies and the networks.

Tag Sentence or two used by a reporter or anchor at the end of a story or newscast. Sometimes referred to as an on-camera tag.

Talking head Colloquial for person being interviewed on camera.

Tease Short headline that describes a story to follow a commercial. In TV, usually accompanied by a few seconds of the upcoming video story. More specific than a generic *bump*.

Teleprompter Electronic device that projects news scripts on monitors so they can be read by anchors. Also known as a prompter.

Time coding Recording of the time of day on the edge of videotape as it is being shot.

Timing Reading a story for time duration to make sure it fits into the newscast.

Toss Unscripted banter among news anchors to move the viewer's focus to another speaker, such as the sportscaster.

Touch and go Writing technique that allows the reporter to reference the first shots of video before moving into other information.

Tough questions Questions that may put the interviewee on the defensive.

Trial balloon Government news tip designed to gauge public reaction.

Tricycle principle Limiting reporter involvement in stories if such involvement takes away from the newscast.

Triple-sourcing Confirming a story through three sources before airing on the news.

Tripod Three-legged camera mount.

Trivia lead Lead sentence that uses a bit of obscure information to interest the viewer.

Truth Verified or indisputable fact.

Two-shot Camera shot of two people.

Upcut Loss of words at the beginning of audio- or videotape.

Update New details in a news story that require a rewrite.

UPI United Press International, one of the major wire services.

Uplinking Newsroom practice of sending stories to a network or wire service via satellite or Internet upload.

Urgent Wire service term indicating an important story, but not as important as a bulletin or flash story.

Videophone Device that allows reporters in the field to send sound and video to a receiving station without technical support.

Videotape Physical medium used to record video and audio signals.

Viewfinder Part of the video camera system that allows the camera operator to see the image while recording.

Voice track To prerecord a number of news breaks in a row, allowing them to be inserted into the program as desired.

Voiceover (V/O) Used on the left-hand side of a split page to indicate that the anchor is speaking over video. Also indicates a reporter narrating over cover footage.

Voiceover sound-on-tape (VOSOT) News story that incorporates cover footage and a sound byte but not the reporter's narration.

VTR Videotape recording.

Warming up Bantering with the interviewee before the actual interview begins.

Weather Dedicated block in the newscast devoted to weather information. Often abbreviated as WX in newsrooms.

White balance Adjusting a camera's circuitry to read white (and thus all other colors) correctly.

Wire News services provided by AP, CNN, Reuters, and other organizations.

Wrap To complete work on a story. Also short for "wraparound," in which a reporter's voice is heard at the beginning and end of a sound byte.

Writing from the back Used primarily in radio, this occurs when journalists write the last stories in the newscast first, as later stories will not require updating before the newscast airs.

WS Wide camera shot.

Index